GUIDE TO incoterms 1990

by

Jan Ramberg

Professor of Private Law,
University of Stockholm

ICC PUBLISHING SA

Published in May 1991
by ICC PUBLISHING S.A.
International Chamber of Commerce
38, Cours Albert 1er
75008 - PARIS, France
Tel.: (1) 49 53 28 28
Telex: 650770
Telefax: (1) 42 25 36 21

Designed and composed by Arcotec - France
Proof-editor Eleanor Levieux
Printed by Van Boekhoven Bosch - Netherlands

ICC Publication N° 461/90
ISBN 92-842-1088-7

FOREWORD

The new *Guide to Incoterms* is the first to appear since the 1981 edition ten years ago. In the intervening years, the 1981 *Guide* had become recognised as the authoritative companion work to Incoterms. We expect nothing less of this 1991 edition, a new service rendered to business by the ICC.

Incoterms 1990, which came into force on July 1st 1990, has a number of changes of critical importance to users: All terms were arranged in four major groups; two terms, "FOB Airport" and "FOR/FOT," were dropped; the term "Free Carrier" was expanded to take care of all modes of transport; and the possibility of EDI (electronic data interchange) usage was incorporated into several of the terms.

These changes reflect the ICC practice of making Incoterms flexible enough to adapt to changes in trade practice. They also created the need for a new *ICC Guide to Incoterms* which would explain the changes clearly and effectively.

Since 1936, Incoterms have been recognised as practical, cost-saving tools, used worldwide to smooth the international trading process. When both parties to a transaction specify the delivery as being according to Incoterms, there need be no dispute arising from that aspect of the transaction.

The new *Guide* has been drafted by Professor Jan Ramberg of the University of Stockholm. Author of the highly-acclaimed 1981 *Guide,* Professor Ramberg is a widely respected writer and lecturer on Incoterms. Assisting Professor Ramberg has been a talented team. Ray Battersby, Director-Procedures at SITPRO in the United Kingdom, served as a senior editorial adviser and gave a close and critical reading to the text. As chief editor, Ron Katz, special consultant to the ICC, was responsible for clarifying and sharpening the language. Other invaluable editorial contributions were made by Lynn Murray of SITPRO; Gray Sinclair, consultant to ICC UK; and David Green of the United Kingdom's Freight Transport Association.

The result of this fruitful collaboration is a reference book designed with the user in mind. Its lucid commentary explains how each of the 13 Incoterms applies in a multiplicity of situations. Whether you are a trader, carrier, forwarder, insurer, banker, lawyer or researcher, the *Guide to Incoterms 1990* will be a trusted companion in your work.

Jean-Charles Rouher
Secretary General of the ICC

TABLE OF CONTENTS

PART I
UNDERSTANDING INCOTERMS

I / INTRODUCTION

II / INCOTERMS AND THE CONTRACT OF SALE

III / THE FOUR GROUPS OF INCOTERMS: MAIN COMPONENTS

TABLE OF CONTENTS

PART II
GOING THROUGH THE 13 INCOTERMS:
A SECTION-BY-SECTION ANALYSIS

ANNEXES

PART I

UNDERSTANDING INCOTERMS

I. INTRODUCTION

Why are trade terms important?

Trade terms are key elements of international contracts of sale, since they tell the parties what to do with respect to

- carriage of the goods from seller to buyer and
- export and import clearance.

They also explain the division of costs and risks between the parties.

Short expressions need clarification!

Merchants tend to use short expressions, such as FOB and CIF, to clarify the distribution of functions, costs and risks related to the transfer of the goods from seller to buyer. But unfortunately misunderstandings frequently arise with respect to the proper interpretation of these expressions.

In the 1920s, the International Chamber of Commerce conducted a study on the interpretation of the more important trade terms. This study demonstrated that the terms were understood differently in different countries. Therefore, the outcome of a dispute between seller and buyer often depended on the place where the dispute would be resolved and the applicable law. This, of course, involved juridical risks for the seller or the buyer which could create serious disputes and adversely affect future business between them.

For this reason, it was considered important to develop rules for the interpretation of the trade terms which the parties to the contract of sale could agree to apply. Incoterms - for international commercial terms - constitute these rules of interpretation. These rules were first published in 1936, and their official title is "International Rules for the Interpretation of Trade Terms".

The trend towards delivered terms

While the first edition of Incoterms focused on trade terms used for the carriage of goods by sea, later revisions have reflected the increasing use of other modes of transport in international trade. They have also reflected the increasing trend to sell goods on delivered terms.

A thorough revision of Incoterms was completed in 1953, delivered terms were added in 1967 and a term for goods carried by air was added in 1976.

In 1980, trading requirements connected with changed transportation techniques and documentary practices resulted in the addition of two important new trade terms, namely "Free carrier ... named point" (FRC, now FCA), and "Freight, carriage and insurance paid to" (CIP). One important reason for the 1990 revision was to take into account the increasing trend towards paperless trading, when communicating partners use electronic messages (so-called EDI for electronic data interchange) instead of documents.

The use of electronic data interchange

■ Equivalent electronic messages instead of documents

In international trade there is a growing trend to replace documents by electronic messages or, as it is now usually called, electronic data interchange (EDI).

Since Incoterms 1980 were based on the exchange of documents, it became necessary to make Incoterms 1990 compatible with EDI practice. In Incoterms 1990, therefore, all A8 and B8 provisions contain the words "or equivalent electronic message". These are intended to be used when the seller and the buyer agree to communicate electronically.

■ EDI practice and code of conduct

Incoterms do not go further than the above paragraph in explaining how the electronic communication should be implemented. This will be governed by the practices which the parties develop between them.

Since electronic data interchange requires a computer-to-computer language, where the messages must appear as structured data, it is vital to follow closely the international systems developed under the auspices of the United Nations for this purpose, called EDIFACT (Electronic Data Interchange for Administration, Commerce and Transport) and UNCID (the Uniform Rules of Conduct for Interchange of Trade Data by Teletrans-mission).

■ Delivery with an EDI message

All terms - except EXW which has no obligation to provide proof of delivery - contain the stipulation when the parties have agreed to communicate electronically. The documents referred to in A8 may be replaced by an equivalent "electronic data interchange (EDI) message".

Some particular problems can arise when a replacement of the bill of lading is intended, either by the issuance of sea waybills or by electronic messages. Such problems are caused because the bill of lading is required to obtain goods from the carrier at destination or to sell them in transit. Uniform Rules for Sea Waybills and so-called Electronic Bills of Lading were adopted by Comité Maritime International (CMI) at its 1990 World Conference. The CMI Rules provide a mechanism to enable those who wish to communicate electronically to do so while keeping the existing contractual obligation of the carrier intact.

Changes in transportation techniques: The container revolution

The revision of Incoterms 1980 was heavily influenced by changes in transportation techniques and documentary practices as a result of the so-called container revolution. There is a fundamental difference between the traditional method of lifting on and lifting off cargo over the ship's side for loading and discharge and the method whereby cargo is stowed in containers and subsequently shipped and delivered directly to the consignee or removed from the containers at the port of destination or at an inland depot. In the container method, it is inappropriate to divide functions, costs and risks over the ship's side.

It should be stressed that such transportation techniques are by no means limited to maritime container traffic, since similar changes also occur when the goods are placed in various transportation units to be loaded later on the ship (so-called cargo unitization). This occurs in roll on-roll off traffic when the goods are loaded in lorries or railway wagons in combined road/sea or rail/sea traffic, or loaded on pallets before the arrival of the ship at the port of loading.

New trade terms: FCA and CIP

In Incoterms l980, the terms FCA and CIP were added. Under these two trade terms the seller does not effect delivery at the ship's rail as under FOB and CIF. Delivery occurs when the goods are received into the transportation system.

When several modes of transport are used for the carriage of the goods, the new trade terms are particularly suitable when the seller - as is normally the case - wishes to avoid bearing the risk of loss of or damage to the goods up to some intermediate point in a multimodal transport operation. Therefore, under FCA the point designated is when the goods are handed over to the multimodal transport operator rather than the point where the goods are handed over at a later stage for carriage by sea.

Likewise, under CPT and CIP the point is fixed in the same manner, e.g. delivery to the first carrier and not to subsequent carriers, if any.

The elimination of FOR/FOT and FOB Airport

While in the 1980 revision of Incoterms the terms FOR/FOT and FOB Airport were unchanged, they are omitted in the 1990 revision. This is because they were based on exactly the same principle as the FCA term in fixing the point for handing over the goods for carriage to a particular place rather than to a means of conveyance.

Consequently, in the 1990 revision the FCA term has become fully adaptable; it can be used regardless of the mode of transport. Indeed, if a seller still feels it is better to divide functions, costs and risks precisely at the ship's side rather than at some other point, FCA can still be used, naming the ship's side as the relevant point.

Wrong term creates unnecessary risks

The FOB seller may be unpleasantly surprised if something happens to the goods after the point when they have been duly delivered for carriage but before they have passed the ship's rail. This will be the case particularly if he has not taken out insurance to protect the goods all the way to the "FOB point".

Though the buyer may have taken out insurance which covers loss of or damage to the goods before the FOB point has been reached (so-called warehouse-to-warehouse insurance), the insurer may still refuse payment, since the FOB buyer has no "insurable interest" before the goods have arrived at the FOB point. Moreover, the insurer may not be inclined to pay someone who is not the insured party under the insurance policy.

In this respect, the CIF seller is better placed, since the insurance is to his benefit before the FOB point (i.e. the ship's rail) and to the benefit of the buyer thereafter. However, the seller is exposed to claims from the buyer for his failure to reach the ship's rail in time. This may involve a liability for breach of contract and an obligation to provide substitute goods, unless the seller has adequate protection through other clauses in the contract of sale.

It follows that the seller should avoid trade terms such as FOB and CIF when handing over to the carrier does not take place at the ship's side but rather at some other point. There is almost always another point in multimodal transport operations or in cases when the goods are unitised in lorries, railway wagons, containers, igloos (containers for air transport) or on pallets (so-called cargo unitisation).

Delivery to carrier at the ship's side

use: FAS, FOB, CFR, CIF

The maritime Incoterms - FAS, FOB, CFR and CIF - are appropriate when goods are handed over to the carrier at the ship's side.

No delivery to carrier at the ship's side

use: FCA, CPT, CIP

The Incoterms FCA, CPT and CIP are suitable for universal use, and are especially suitable in multimodal transport or whenever goods are unitised or handed over to the carrier at some point other than the ship's side.

The "mirror method" of presenting the terms

Until the 1990 revision, Incoterms did not present the terms in a similar and systematic manner. While it was possible to read each term on its own without relation to other terms, the previous method of presentation made the choice between various alternatives more difficult. Also, the separate responsibilities dealt with in the various terms had not been consistently arranged.

In the 1990 revision Incoterms are presented in a logical sequence, grouping the matters dealt with in each term under the same headings having the same numbering throughout. Using this technique the obligations of the parties are mirrored across the pages; this method clearly indicates how an obligation for one of the parties relieves the other party of that same obligation.

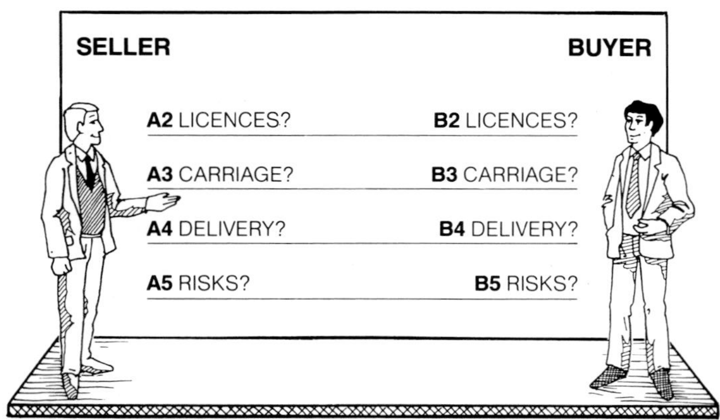

The new "mirror" presentation of Incoterms enables the buyer and seller to easily check their rights and obligations against the corresponding rights and obligations of their trading partner.

Grouping of obligations under 10 headings

The obligations of the parties for each term are grouped under the same main headings "THE SELLER MUST" and "THE BUYER MUST". There are 10 obligations which may fall upon the parties; these are numbered with headings as follows:

THE SELLER MUST	THE BUYER MUST
A1 Provision of goods in conformity with the contract	**B1** Payment of the price
A2 Licences, authorisations and formalities	**B2** Licences, authorisations and formalities
A3 Contract of carriage and insurance	**B3** Contract of carriage
A4 Delivery	**B4** Taking delivery
A5 Transfer of risks	**B5** Transfer of risks
A6 Division of costs	**B6** Division of costs
A7 Notice to the buyer	**B7** Notice to the seller
A8 Proof of delivery, transport document or equivalent electronic message	**B8** Proof of delivery, transport document or equivalent electronic message
A9 Checking-packaging-marking	**B9** Inspection of goods
A10 Other obligations	**B10** Other obligations

Since not every one of these obligations is applicable to every Incoterm, one may find the words "no obligation" under a particular heading. Nevertheless, it was considered helpful to retain all of the 10 headings. This is both for the sake of consistency and to make it easier for the reader to determine whether a party has an obligation to the other party with respect to the fundamental point involved, e.g. contract of carriage, export or import formalities, proof of delivery and insurance.

Matters not covered by Incoterms

The trade terms only deal with the question of whether a party has an obligation to the other party according to a particular term. They do not deal with whether it is common or prudent for a party to take certain measures on his own behalf even though he has no obligation under the Incoterm to do so in relation to the other party.

An obvious example of the latter is a FOB or CFR buyer who has no obligation to the seller to take out insurance. But since the buyer has to bear the risk of loss of or damage to the goods from the moment they have been loaded onboard the ship, it would be normal commercial practice for him to insure against such risks.

Neither do Incoterms deal with how the goods should reach the agreed point of delivery. Nor do they convey what a buyer might wish to do after taking delivery. For example, there is no explanation in Incoterms that an EXW buyer should arrange carriage; it is up to him whether he lets the goods remain at the place where the seller is domiciled or takes them to a destination in the same or another country. Likewise, under the D-terms there is no obligation mentioned for the buyer to carry the goods farther after delivery in the country of destination. Consequently, the words "no obligation" will be found under the B3 headings in these trade terms.

Similarly, it is the seller's problem how he reaches the delivery point, and the trade terms cannot be expected to explain how he should do it.

There are some exceptions to this general principle, however, with respect to export and import formalities: The seller who has sold the goods on D-terms has to obtain the import licence and the export licence under DEQ and DDP. This has been noted under the A2 headings, though the seller is of course not thereby prevented from fulfilling his contract with goods from the country of destination.

II. INCOTERMS AND THE CONTRACT OF SALE

What do trade terms tell you?

Trade terms constitute only a part of the contract of sale. While the contract of sale determines the quantity and quality of the goods - as well as the price which should be paid for them - trade terms deal with questions relating to the **delivery** of the goods.

It is not sufficient that the contract of sale merely refer to the trade term as such - e.g. FOB or CIF - since these trade terms only indicate that the goods should be delivered in a certain traditional manner and that certain basic costs should be paid by either the seller or the buyer. The parties to the contract of sale need to know much more than that, e.g.

- who should clear the goods for export or import;
- who should pay the costs of loading and discharging the goods;
- how should the risk of loss of or damage to the goods be divided between them; and consequently
- who should take out insurance as a protection against these risks.

An answer to any of these questions requires a more detailed interpretation of the trade term, either by specific provisions in the contract of sale or by the applicable law or custom of the trade.

The need for specific contract terms or rules of interpretation

In practice, contracting parties do not usually provide for a specific elaboration of the points mentioned above unless the sale concerns commodities to be carried in ships engaged on charter party terms. In such cases, it is essential to match the terms with the terms of the contract of sale. For this reason, rules of interpretation for the trade terms are of the utmost importance in international trade.

Traditionally, the rules of interpretation - explaining the meaning of at least some of the more common trade terms - have been contained in national Sale of Goods Acts. However, in recent years trade terms have had to be updated separately to make them compatible with contemporary commercial practice, since statutory provisions cannot very well be updated at intervals for this purpose.

As a result, national and international legislators have left the task of developing rules of interpretation to other organisations, such as the International Chamber of Commerce. Thus, in the 1980 United Nations Convention on Contracts for the International Sale of Goods (CISG) no specific provisions appear explaining the meaning of various trade terms; in the preparatory works to that Convention a reference is made instead to Incoterms.

How are Incoterms incorporated into the contract?

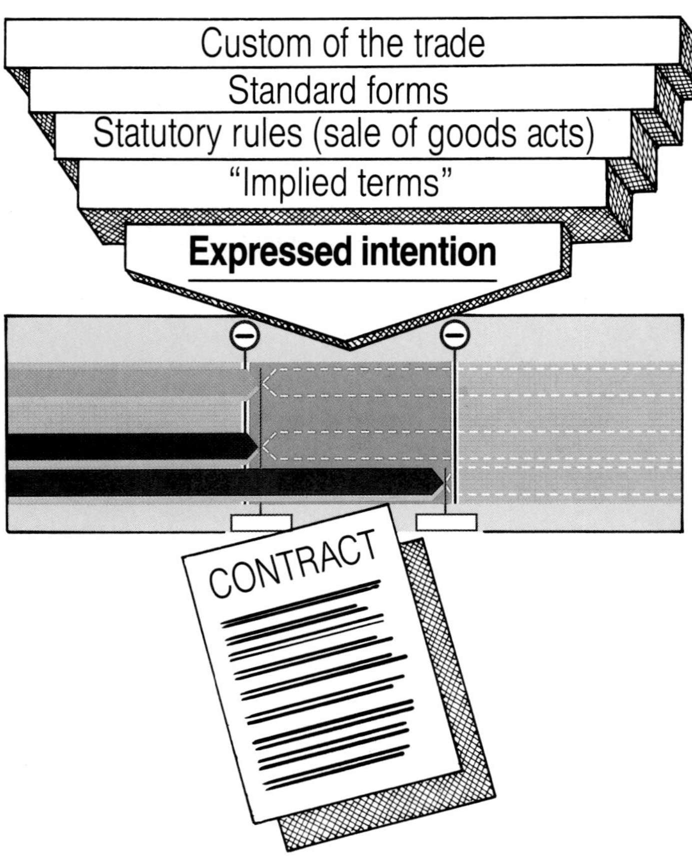

When do Incoterms apply?

Incoterms do not enter into the contract of sale automatically in the same way as an applicable national law or international convention, although in some cases they may be incorporated into the contract of sale

- by reference to a standard contract elaborated by an international organisation (e.g. ECE 188);
- as an international custom of the trade; or
- by assuming that the parties have intended to apply them (so-called implication).

In contracts of sale between parties from different regions of the world - e.g. between a buyer in Europe and a seller in the United States - it is strongly recommended that a reference to Incoterms be specifically made in the contract of sale, since the Uniform Commercial Code of the United States refers to the 1941 American Foreign Trade Definitions.

Even if the parties are both European, courts may hesitate to regard Incoterms as an international custom of the trade which can be accepted in the absence of a specific reference to them in the contract of sale. The parties in these instances should use a phrase such as "Incoterms 1990" in direct conjunction with the trade term chosen.

It follows that the parties have two options: (1) to deal with all of the important aspects relating to the trade term by specific provisions in the contract of sale, or (2) perhaps the more practical option, to add "Incoterms 1990" in conjunction with the trade term.

The question of property rights

While Incoterms specifically deal with questions of division of risk of loss of or damage to the goods between seller and buyer, they do not deal with property rights; in other words, they do not involve questions relating to the transfer of property or transfer of title to the goods. Indeed, it was not even possible to agree on uniform rules on these questions in the 1980 UN Convention on Contracts for the International Sale of Goods (CISG).

Therefore, the parties to a contract of sale should provide for these matters themselves in the contract of sale and closely observe what the applicable law requires for the transfer of ownership to the goods and other property rights.

Delivery and breach of contract

Moreover, Incoterms do not themselves deal with breach of contract and consequences following from it. Again, such matters should be resolved either by specific provisions in the contract of sale or by the applicable law. There is an interrelation between the trade term and the rules relating to breach of contract, since the trade term determines the basic fact of when the goods shall be considered to have been delivered from the seller to the buyer.

According to the CISG and national Sale of Goods Acts, the point of delivery also constitutes the effective point where the question of whether the seller has duly performed his obligation to deliver the goods in time and in contractual condition is normally resolved. Only when the seller has failed to do so can he be held responsible for non-fulfilment of those obligations.

III. THE FOUR GROUPS OF INCOTERMS: MAIN COMPONENTS

Introduction: Important differences between shipment and arrival contracts

There is an important distinction between the delivered-terms ("D-terms") and the other trade terms with respect to determining the critical point when the seller has performed his delivery obligation. Only with the D-terms (DAF, DES, DEQ, DDU and DDP) is the seller's delivery obligation extended to the country of destination. Under the other trade terms he fulfils the delivery obligation in his own country, either by making the goods available to the buyer at his (the seller's) premises (EXW), or by delivering the goods to the carrier for shipment (FCA, FAS, FOB, CFR, CIF, CPT and CIP).

To make the important distinction between this fundamentally different nature of the "groups" of trade terms, contracts of sale are often classified accordingly, as, for example, when the D-terms would turn the contract of sale into arrival contracts. Contracts using F-terms or C-terms would fall into the category of shipment contracts.

It is important to note that the seller's obligation to arrange and pay for the carriage does not in itself extend his delivery obligation up to the point of destination. On the contrary, the risk of loss of or damage to the goods will pass at the point of delivery, and the insurance which the seller has to take out under the trade terms CIF and CIP will be for the benefit of the buyer, who has to assume the risk after the delivery point.

The C-terms, by extending the seller's obligation with respect to costs of carriage and insurance respectively to the destination, make it necessary to consider not one but two critical points: One for the division of risks and another for the division of costs. Because this dual split is not always evident, the C-terms are frequently misunderstood by merchants, who believe them to be more or less equivalent to D-terms. This, of course, is completely incorrect.

A seller having sold his goods on C-terms is considered to have fulfilled his delivery obligation even if something happens to the goods after the point of shipment, while a seller having sold the goods on D-terms has not fulfilled his obligation in similar circumstances.

Consequently, if the goods are lost or accidentally become damaged after shipment but before the goods have arrived at the agreed destination point, a seller having sold the goods upon D-terms has not fulfilled his contract and can therefore be held liable for breach of contract. He will normally have to provide substitute goods in place of those lost or damaged, or make other agreed restitution.

In this respect, the interrelation between the trade term and the other terms of the contract of sale is vital, since the risk falling upon the seller may be eliminated, or at least modified, by various so-called relief clauses or *force majeure* clauses in the contract of sale.

It follows that the parties must always observe the fundamental difference between the C-terms and the D-terms and that a seller having sold the goods under D-terms should carefully consider the need to protect himself against breach of contract and non-fulfilment risks by adequate force majeure or other relief clauses in the contract of sale.

Note the difference between C- and D-terms!

The basic distinction between C - and D-terms becomes crucial when goods are damaged in transit. With C-terms, the seller has already fulfilled his delivery obligations, while with D-terms the seller may be liable for breach of contract.

The abbreviations: E-, F-, C- and D- terms

The different nature of the trade terms can be evidenced by the new grouping of the terms in four categories, using the first letter as an indication of the group to which the term belongs. The first group has only one trade term, namely EXW. But in the other three groups there are three F-terms (FCA, FAS and FOB), four C-terms (CFR, CIF, CPT and CIP) and five D-terms (DAF, DES, DEQ, DDU and DDP).

- The letter F signifies that the seller must hand over the goods to a nominated carrier Free of risk and expense to the buyer.
- The letter C signifies that the seller must bear certain Costs even after the critical point for the division of the risk of loss of or damage to the goods has been reached.
- The letter D signifies that the goods must arrive at a stated Destination.

This grouping and identification of the various trade terms should enable merchants to understand the different fundamental meanings of the terms and guide them to the most suitable option.

INCOTERMS 1990		
Group E Departure	**EXW**	Ex Works
Group F Main carriage unpaid	**FCA**	Free Carrier
	FAS	Free Alongside Ship
	FOB	Free On Board
Group C Main carriage paid	**CFR**	Cost and Freight
	CIF	Cost, Insurance and Freight
	CPT	Carriage Paid To
	CIP	Carriage and Insurance Paid To
Group D Arrival	**DAF**	Delivered At Frontier
	DES	Delivered Ex Ship
	DEQ	Delivered Ex Quay
	DDU	Delivered Duty Unpaid
	DDP	Delivered Duty Paid

1. The term EXW: Making the goods available at the seller's premises

EXW represents the seller's minimum obligation, since he only has to make the goods available at his premises. Although it may appear from the contract itself or from the surrounding circumstances that the buyer intends to export the goods, it is entirely up to him whether he wishes to do so. According to the trade term, there is no obligation for either party to do anything with respect to export.

Nevertheless, it follows from B2 that the buyer must carry out all tasks of export and import clearance, and, as stipulated in A2, the seller merely has to render his assistance in connection with these tasks. The buyer has to reimburse the seller for all costs and charges incurred in rendering this assistance (B6).

Neither of the parties has any obligation to the other with respect to contracts of carriage and insurance. However, if the buyer wishes to have the goods carried from the seller's place he should, for his own benefit, arrange for carriage and cargo insurance.

2. F-terms and C-terms: The carriage-related terms

F-terms: Main carriage not paid by seller

■ F-terms and pre-carriage

While under the F-terms the seller has to arrange any necessary pre-carriage to reach the agreed point for handing over the goods to the carrier, it is the buyer's function to arrange and pay for the main carriage. A3 of the F-terms does not mention anything with respect to pre-carriage, since there is no need to explain how the seller is able to reach the point for the handing over of the goods to the carrier.

■ FCA and handing over goods for carriage

As noted, FCA is the main F-term which can be used irrespective of the mode of transport and should be used whenever handing over to the carrier is not completed alongside a ship or over a ship's rail. In the two latter cases, the terms FAS and FOB should be used instead of FCA.

The circumstances defining the handing over the goods to the carrier differ according to the mode of transport and the nature of the goods. Practices also vary from place to place. Since the buyer has to arrange for the transport, it is vital that he instruct the seller precisely regarding how the goods should be handed over for carriage. He should also ensure that the precise point where this will occur is mentioned in the contract of sale; but this is not always possible to do at the time of making the contract, since the exact point may be decided subsequently.

In this event, it is important that the seller, when quoting his price, consider the various options available to the buyer so as to subsequently give precise instructions for handing over the goods for carriage. The seller should, of course, know how the goods should be packed, if they are to be containerised, and whether they should be delivered to a terminal in his vicinity or otherwise.

■ Full loads and less than full loads

The quantity of the goods will determine whether they are suitable to constitute so-called full loads (railway wagon loads or container loads) or whether they must be delivered to the carrier as break bulk cargo to be stowed by him, usually at his terminal. In the container trade, the important distinction is made between full loads and less than full loads (FCL for full container load and LCL for less than full container load).

Although it may not be necessary from a legal viewpoint to specify the obligations with respect to the handing over of the goods for carriage under FCA, the usual procedures for the different modes of transport have been briefly indicated in A4 to draw the attention of the parties to the several alternatives.

■ In practice, the seller often contracts for carriage

Although all of the F-terms clearly place the obligation to contract for carriage on the buyer, the seller frequently performs it in practice when the choice is more or less immaterial to the buyer. This is particularly common when there is only one option available, taking into account the place and the nature of the goods, or when the freight would be the same even though there are several options for carriage.

For carriage by air and by rail, Incoterms 1980 indicated - under the terms FOB Airport and FOR/FOT (now deleted) - that the seller might contract for carriage. But it was underlined that he had no duty to do so and that whatever he did, carriage would be for the account of the buyer and at the buyer's risk and expense.

When there is a so-called "liner service" from the seller's country, the seller frequently contracts for carriage under FOB. This practice is called "FOB additional service". In many cases the practice with respect to road transport is less firm; indeed, it may vary from forwarder to forwarder and from carrier to carrier. Nevertheless, the seller frequently contracts for the road carriage, though it is intended that the buyer should pay for it. In Incoterms 1980, no trade term dealt specifically with road carriage, though, of course, the previous FCA, then called FRC, could be used for this purpose.

Current commercial practice makes it difficult to set down in a legal text what the parties are obliged to do. But though from a strictly legal point of view the seller is not concerned with the main contract of carriage, his duties according to commercial practice are reflected under the heading A3. If there is such a practice, the seller may contract for carriage on usual terms at the buyer's risk and expense.

■ When the seller declines or the buyer wants to contract for carriage

But the seller may decline to contract for carriage and may notify the buyer accordingly. The buyer may also specifically ask the seller to assist him or tell the seller that he intends to contract for carriage himself.

It is important for the buyer to notify the seller of his intentions if, for instance, he has a special relationship with a carrier making it important for him to exercise his right according to B3 to arrange the contract of carriage.

■ **Buyer's risk if transport is unavailable**
Even though the seller is requested or intends to perform the contracting for carriage according to commercial practice, the buyer always will bear the risk if transport facilities fail to be available as contemplated because of unforeseen circumstances.

■ **Division of loading costs under FOB**
When the cargo is delivered containerised or in less than full loads to the carrier's terminal, the division of loading costs seldom presents any particular problems. However, the situation is quite different when under FOB the cargo is to be delivered in the traditional manner over the ship's rail.

If the ship's rail is used for the division of loading costs, one has to count the costs of labour, hiring of cranes, etc. by counting man hours and time used before and after the passing of the ship's rail. This, however, is not done in practice.

Instead, the custom of the port will decide the extent to which loading costs under FOB should be distributed between seller and buyer. If this is known to both parties no difficulties should arise. But frequently the buyer may not know the custom of the port in the seller's country and indeed may find out later that the custom works to his disadvantage.

For this reason, it is important that the FOB buyer consider this problem when negotiating the contract of sale and the price for the goods.

■ **Export clearance under FAS different from under FOB**
It should be stressed that not all F-terms require the seller to clear the goods for export. Traditionally under FAS Incoterm - presumably because of the traditional importance of the ship's rail as dividing line between the seller's and the buyer's functions - the FAS-seller does not have the obligation to clear the goods for export. In this respect there is a most important difference between A2/B2 of FAS and A2/B2 of FOB.

In a sense, the ship's rail also serves as an imaginary border between "the seller's and the buyer's country". This distinction between FAS and FOB may not always be observed by merchants, but it was nevertheless decided to retain the previous distinction in Incoterms 1990. In most cases, no practical problems arise, since export clearance formalities are usually straightforward. But circumstances can easily change when political conditions are unsettled, and the FAS buyer is therefore advised to exercise care, since any export prohibition would be at his and not at the seller's risk.

Note the difference between FAS and FOB

In FAS contracts, the buyer has the primary responsibility for clearing goods for export. Under FOB, the seller must clear for export.

C-terms: Main carriage paid by seller

■ C-terms are not equivalent to D-terms!

As noted, the C-terms may present some difficulties, since only the point of destination is mentioned after the respective term, e.g. in a contract of sale concluded between a buyer in New York and a seller in London, only New York would be mentioned after the C-term; nothing is usually said about shipment from London. Obviously, in the above example this can give rise to the false impression that the goods are to be delivered in New York and that the seller has not fulfilled his obligation until this has happened.

Consequently, it is not uncommon that the contract provides, for example, "Delivery New York not later than..." (with a particular date being given). But this would demonstrate that the contracting parties have failed to understand the fundamental nature of the C-term, since under such a term the seller fulfils his obligation by shipping the goods from his country.

This confusion arises because the seller undertakes to arrange and pay for the main carriage up to destination. This payment obligation, however, is only **in addition to** the fundamental obligation to ship the goods from the seller's place.

■ Two "critical points" under C-terms

Since the C-term must show the extent to which the seller undertakes to arrange and pay for the main contract of carriage - with the addition of insurance under CIF and CIP - the indication of the point of destination is inevitable. The C-term also establishes that the seller fulfils his delivery obligation by handing over the goods for shipment in his country, and that this has to be accepted as delivery by the buyer (A4 and B4 respectively).

Thus under the C-terms there will not only be one relevant point as under the F-terms - the point of shipment - but two critical points, one coinciding with the point of shipment under the F-terms, the other indicating the point up to which the seller would have to pay for carriage and insurance. It would be easier for traders to understand the fundamental nature of the C-terms if both of these critical points were mentioned as normal practice. However, this is usually not done, since the seller at the time of entering into the contract of sale may prefer to retain a certain liberty on the exact point or port of shipment. A seller in Stockholm, for example, having sold the goods under CFR or CIF to a buyer in New York, may wish to delay deciding whether he wishes to ship the goods directly from Stockholm, or to have them carried by road to Gothenburg or perhaps even to Rotterdam for carriage by sea to New York.

■ Do not stipulate date of arrival under C-terms!

If the contract of sale refers to a C-term, but also indicates arrival at destination on a particular date, the contract becomes ambiguous. One would then not know if it is the intention of the contracting parties that the seller has breached the contract if the goods do not actually arrive at destination on the agreed date, or whether the fundamental nature of the C-term should supersede this interpretation.

In the latter case, the seller's obligation is limited to shipping the goods so that they could arrive at the destination on the agreed date, unless something happens after shipment, which, according to the C-term, would be at the risk of the buyer.

■ Two groups of C-terms

There are two groups of C-terms. One is exclusively intended to be used when the goods are carried by sea - CFR (also frequently referred to as C&F) and CIF. The other (CPT and CIP) can be used for any mode of transport, including sea transport and multimodal transport.

■ Do not use CFR or CIF for other than sea transport!

Sometimes the parties fail to observe the important distinction in the previous paragraph, and they use CFR and CIF for modes of transport **other** than carriage by sea. The seller then puts himself in the unfortunate position of being unable to fulfil his fundamental obligation to present a bill of lading, or to present a sea waybill or similar document as required under CFR or CIF A8.

But when the buyer, for example, intends to sell the goods in transit, he may lose this option if he receives the incorrect transport document. In such a case, he would be able to cancel the contract because of the seller's breach in not providing the correct document. Also, when the market for the goods falls after the contract of sale has been entered into, a buyer could, in certain circumstances, use the seller's breach as a means of avoiding the market loss by cancelling the contract of sale.

■ Seller's insurance obligation under CIF and CIP

In Incoterms the C-term exists in two forms: CFR and CPT when there is no insurance obligation for the seller, and CIF and CIP, when, according to A3b, the seller must obtain and pay for the insurance.

Otherwise, CFR and CPT are identical to CIF and CIP respectively.

■ Cost of insurance depends on intended transport

Under CFR and CPT, where the seller has no insurance obligation, the buyer should be aware of the relation between the cost of insurance and the intended carriage of the goods. If the goods are deemed to be exposed to greater risks during the transport (for example, during the shipment of goods on deck or in older ships), the insurance premium will become more expensive if insurance is available at all.

■ Use of CFR and CPT requires particular caution

Statistical evidence indicates that fraud occurs more frequently under the CFR and CPT terms than under other terms, largely because the buyer does not normally have sufficient control over the particular method and the type of transport involved. Therefore, the CFR or CPT buyer is advised to consider specific stipulations in the contract of sale restricting the seller's option to arrange for carriage as he pleases (e.g. the buyer can mention a particular shipping line or identify the carrier).

■ How to obtain payment prior to delivery of the goods

Sellers uncertain about the buyer's ability or willingness to pay the price can take measures to prevent delivery of the goods before payment has been made. There are two ways to do this: (I) Instructions to prevent the buyer from obtaining the goods before payment can be given to a carrier, a freight forwarder or a bank; and (2) instructions to require cash from the buyer on delivery (COD instructions) can be given to the carrier or a freight forwarder, and the bank can be instructed not to release the original(s) of the bill of lading until payment has been made. This would probably best be achieved by means of a documentary collection arranged through the international banking system.

■ The irrevocable documentary credit

Payment can also be arranged by requiring the buyer to open an irrevocable documentary credit (also called a letter of credit, L/C) with the seller as beneficiary. This alternative gives the seller the additional advantage of receiving payment earlier, when the goods are shipped from his own country. He would then avoid having to transport the goods to destination before payment, when he could run the risk of the buyer failing to collect the goods.

As beneficiary under a documentary credit the seller will be paid, provided he presents the stipulated documents to the bank completely in order with the requirements of the letter of credit and within the period allowed. The bank which is to pay under the documentary credit can also be requested to add its confirmation to the irrevocable undertaking of the bank which opened the credit (the so-called opening or issuing bank). In this case the seller obtains a promise to receive payment, not only from the issuing bank, but separately from the confirming bank as well (See the "Uniform Customs and Practice for Documentary Credits", ICC Publication No. 400. See also "Guide to Documentary Credit Operations", ICC Publication No. 415).

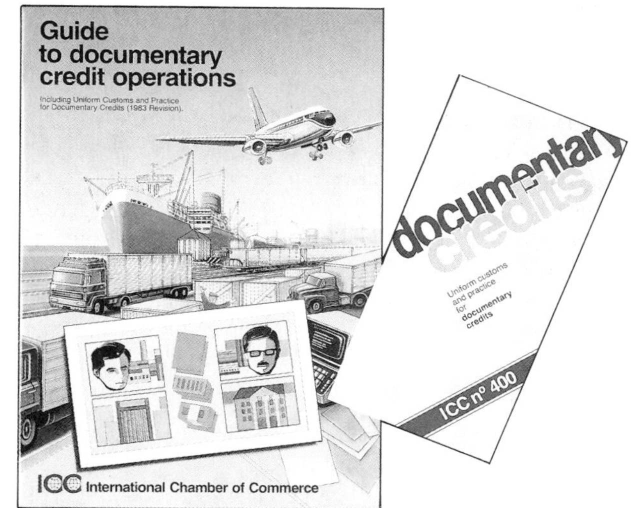

Documentary credits are often used with C-terms, and in these cases they are fully consistent with the basic nature of the terms. This is because the seller fulfils his shipment obligation with shipment in his own country and has to provide evidence with the documents stipulated in the documentary credit which satisfy the paying bank and the buyer that he has fulfilled that obligation.

Nevertheless, buyers should be aware that banks
- are not concerned with the contract of sale or the contract of carriage;
- limit their service to the contract of finance as such;
- do not undertake to check whether the goods in fact correspond to the contract description;
- only check that the documents "on their face" appear to be in order, and
- do not assume any responsibility for the solvency or standing of parties having issued the documents.

Thus, the buyer does not receive comprehensive protection merely by using the documentary credit service.

■ The "minimum cover" principle of CIF and CIP

The obligation of the seller to obtain and pay for cargo insurance under CIF and CIP A3b is based on the principle of "minimum cover" as set out in the Institute Cargo Clauses drafted by the Institute of London Underwriters. But such minimum cover could also follow any other similar set of clauses.

In practice, however, so-called "all risk-insurance" (Institute Clause A) is preferred to less extended cover (Institute Clauses B or C), since the minimum cover is only appropriate when the risk of loss of or damage to the goods in transit is more or less confined to casualties affecting both the means of conveyance and the cargo, such as those resulting from collisions, strandings and fire. In such cases, even the minimum cover would protect the buyer against the risk of having to pay compensation to a shipowner for his expenses in salvaging the ship and cargo, according to the rules relating to general average (the York/Antwerp Rules of 1974).

■ Unsuitability of minimum cover for manufactured goods

Minimum cover is not suitable for manufactured goods (particularly not for goods of high value) because of the risk of theft, pilferage or improper handling or custody of the goods. Therefore, extended insurance cover is usually taken out as protection against such risks (Institute Clause A is then advisable). A buyer of manufactured goods should stipulate in the contract of sale that the insurance according to CIF or CIP should be extended as indicated. If he does not, the seller can fulfil his insurance obligation by providing only minimum cover (Institute Clause C).

The buyer may also wish to obtain additional cover not included in Institute Clause A, e.g. insurance against war, riots, civil commotions, strikes or other labour disturbances. This would normally be done by specific instructions to the seller.

The question of whether it is correct to follow the principle of minimum insurance cover has been much debated. One proposal during the drafting of Incoterms 1990 was to take the extended cover (Institute Clause A) as a "point of departure". The contracting parties, it was said, could then deduct from this extent of the cover when the contract of sale concerned rough cargoes only exposed to major casualties. After much discussion, this was discarded.

Moreover, the option of allowing the seller's insurance obligation to differ according to the nature of the goods and the intended transport was not chosen, because of the uncertainty which would arise about the seller's insurance obligation. (Compare the earlier and now discarded version of the seller's insurance obligation in CIP Incoterms 1980.) But the fact remains that the principle of minimum insurance cover can be a serious trap for the unwary buyer.

It follows that CFR and CIF should never be used when carriage other than carriage by sea is intended. The buyer should always consider the need to restrict the seller's options with respect to arranging the carriage and should require additional insurance cover from the seller. Under no circumstances should a stipulation as to time for delivery be mentioned in connection with arrival at destination; it should be mentioned only in connection with the shipment of the goods. If buyers wish to ensure that the goods actually arrive at destination at a particular time, D-terms should be used instead of C-terms.

3. D-terms
Delivered terms

■ The trend towards choice of delivered terms
As noted in the Introduction, there is a growing demand from buyers to be quoted for delivered terms. A seller of manufactured goods, whose products have to compete in the country of destination and who has to extend his obligation to the buyer by contract guarantees, would find it strange to limit his obligation under the contract of sale by fulfilling the contract at some earlier point, e.g. before the goods are dispatched or before they have reached destination. As one car manufacturer said: "Although I may be relieved of the risk of damage to my cars sold under a FOB contract, I am not pleased to see how they are being damaged when hopeless efforts are made to squeeze them into a cargo hold of a wholly inappropriate ship."

■ The seller's need to plan and control cargo movements
Practical problems with respect to arranging the carriage often make terms whereby the seller fulfils his obligation by handing over the goods to a carrier inappropriate and less economical. An exporter of goods with a constant flow of cargo in various directions often finds that transport economy (so-called logistics planning) requires him totally to control carriage as well as the delivery at destination.

In addition, the seller is often in a better position to obtain competitive freight rates than his buyers.

■ Factors determining use of different D-terms
When choosing among the different D-terms three factors have to be taken into consideration:
- the mode of transport;
- the distribution of costs and risks connected with discharging the goods at destination;
- the distribution of functions in connection with the clearance of the goods for import.

■ DES and DEQ for sea transport
The terms DES and DEQ are traditional for carriage of goods by sea. The former means that the buyer must take the cargo out of the ship, the latter places the burden on the seller to ensure that the goods are discharged on to the quay. When the goods are to be carried on liner terms, discharging expenses are usually included in the freight, in which case the term DES is out of place. If, on the other hand, the goods are commodities carried in ships to be chartered by the seller, the distinction between DES and DEQ is particularly important.

■ DES and "free out" stipulation in charter parties
If the contract of sale is concluded on DES, the seller charters the ship on terms relieving the shipowner from the discharging operation. Thus, the charter party will be concluded between the seller and the shipowner on terms "Free out", when the word "Free" means that discharging operations are not included in the charter party hire. In such cases, the charter party may make clear that the loading operation is also "free" to the shipowner. If so, the loading expenses have to be borne by the seller, since loading and carrying the goods to the agreed destination under delivered terms would fall upon him. The charter party term in such a case would read "Free in and out" (FIO).

■ FIO stipulations in charter parties and contracts of sale
There are also variants of FIO used when further distinctions are made, e.g. "Free in and out stowed and trimmed" (FIOST) and similar expressions in the charter party. These and similar terms can also appear in the contract of sale. But a contract of sale on delivered terms only has to deal with discharging functions and expenses, since it is unnecessary to deal with expenses which inevitably must fall upon the seller before the goods arrive at the agreed destination.

However, the term FIOST is sometimes used in FOB contracts of sale when the seller's obligation is limited to placing the goods on board the ship in the port of shipment. But such a charter party term is out of place in the contract of sale, since the FOB seller is not concerned with discharging operations in the port of destination. Here the correct term in the contract of sale to specify what the seller has to do in connection with the loading of the ship would read: "FOB stowed and trimmed".

■ Buyer needs to know time of arrival

Under the terms DES and DEQ it is vital that the buyer know the time of the ship's arrival so that the ship is not detained in the port of discharge waiting for the cargo to be removed. It is also important that the goods, when they have been discharged, be removed from the quay as quickly as possible. It is common practice for the seller in the contract of sale to give the buyer notice of the estimated time of the arrival of the ship (ETA) and also for the contract to require the buyer to discharge the ship and remove the cargo from the quay within an agreed time.

■ Demurrage and dispatch money

If the buyer fails to discharge the ship and remove the cargo from the quay, he may have to reimburse the seller for expenses incurred because the charter party conditions have not been realised. (These expenses are called "demurrage".) Alternatively, the buyer may have to pay port authorities or stevedoring companies for additional storage expenses. To induce the buyer to discharge the cargo, the seller may be prepared to give him an extra bonus for saving time. Corresponding stipulations may also be found in charter parties to the benefit of the seller in his capacity as charterer (so-called dispatch money).

Outside of charter party operations demurrage can also be charged by the owners or lessors of containers, when the containers have not been unloaded within an agreed period and are unavailable for re-use.

■ Consistency required between charter party and contract of sale

It is important to make the terms of the charter party and the contract of sale compatible on questions of demurrage and dispatch money. Terms relating to the time the vessel is available for loading and discharge (so-called laytime) and terms relating to demurrage and dispatch are usually complicated, since some events (e.g. circumstances which could be attributed to the carrier or events beyond the control of either party, such as labour disturbances, government directions or adverse weather conditions) can extend the time available. For these reasons as well, it is necessary that the provisions of the charter party and the contract of sale be consistent.

■ DAF, DDU and DDP - for all modes of transport

The other D-terms (DAF, DDU and DDP) can be used regardless of the mode of transport. In practice, however, DAF is primarily used for through rail transport, where it signifies that the seller's obligations extend up to the border of the country mentioned after the term. This is usually the border of the buyer's country, but it could also be some third country through which the goods are to be carried in transit.

■ Avoid "free border" or "franco border"!

Terms such as "free border" or "franco border" are even more common than DAF in practice. Nevertheless, these terms are **not to be used,** since misunderstandings frequently arise with respect to the extent of the seller's obligations. It is clear that the seller has to bear the costs up to the agreed point, but it is not clear whether that point should only have the function of a so-called "tariff point" or whether a real "delivery point" is intended. If the latter is the case, the seller is also responsible for what may happen to the goods from the time of dispatch until the agreed point is reached.

As noted in the explanation of C-terms, the mere fact that the seller undertakes to pay costs does not necessarily mean that he also has to assume the risks connected with the carriage. For this reason, terms using only the words "free" or "franco" are to be avoided. The term "delivered" should be used instead, if it is intended that the seller bear the risks as well as the costs for loss of or damage to the cargo or for failure to reach the delivery point. If this is not intended, one of the C-terms, e.g. CPT or CIP, should be used instead of DAF.

■ The through railway consignment note under DAF

In railway traffic a physical delivery of the goods to the buyer seldom takes place precisely at the border of the buyer's country. The seller often obtains a through consignment note from the railway, covering the whole transit up to the final destination, and also assists the buyer to do whatever is necessary to clear customs and pass the goods through third countries before they reach the destination. But the seller in these cases can perform these "additional" services at the risk and expense of the buyer in the same way as he would under FCA and FOB terms (see the discussion of FCA and FOB above).

Then if something goes wrong after the goods have reached the agreed point mentioned after DAF, this would be at the risk and expense of the buyer. Conversely, if something happens which delays the cargo or prevents it from reaching that point, it would be at the seller's risk and expense.

■ Railway cargo consolidation by freight forwarders

Break bulk cargo is usually handed over to freight forwarders for railway cargo consolidation. In these cases, the freight forwarder unitises the cargo in full wagon loads and enters into contractual arrangements with the railways on terms which differ from the terms which the seller or buyer could have negotiated with the railway for each individual parcel.

Freight forwarders have their own tariffs and they debit sellers and buyers accordingly.

■ DAF - a risk division point as well as a tariff point

The point mentioned after DAF, as discussed two paragraphs earlier, would then serve as the "tariff point", so that the costs relating to the carriage before the point will be debited to the seller and the costs thereafter to the buyer. In most cases, the cargo is not discharged from one railway wagon and re-loaded on another at the point mentioned after DAF. Nevertheless, if something happens to the cargo or the traffic is interrupted, the point mentioned after DAF would also serve as a point for the division of the risks between seller and buyer.

Presumably, sellers and buyers contracting on the term DAF will not consider more than the division of costs. It was therefore debated whether DAF should be retained at all in Incoterms 1990. As noted, the terms CPT and CIP are quite sufficient if only a division of costs between the parties is intended. But since DAF is still used in some areas, it was decided to retain the term.

■ EXW, DDU and DDP do not specify loading and discharging

When cargo is to be collected or delivered at the seller's or buyer's premises respectively, difficulties arise in determining exactly what should be done by the seller and the buyer and how the costs should be distributed between them for loading and discharging. For instance, should the buyer under the term EXW have to pay costs for moving the cargo from the interior of the seller's warehouse? Or should a seller, having contracted on the trade terms DDU or DDP, have to pay all costs until the goods have been placed in the interior of the buyer's warehouse?

It is true that under EXW the seller only has to make the goods available to the buyer at the seller's place. But the term does not explain how this should be done. In the same manner, DDU and DDP do not explain how the goods should be delivered to the agreed destination point.

■ Clarity required in determining when delivery occurs

Is it sufficient that the goods arrive on the vehicle provided by the seller? Or do they have to be removed from that vehicle at the risk and expense of the seller? If so, can the buyer debit the seller for the work performed by his own personnel in receiving the goods at a ramp in his warehouse? Answers to these questions normally follow from commercial practice or from previous dealings between the same contracting parties.

Such matters, which frequently give rise to disputes, may not normally involve a great deal of money but can cause irritation. However, if something should happen to the cargo in connection with the loading on the vehicle under EXW or the discharging from the vehicle under DDU or DDP, the dispute can sometimes involve the whole value of the cargo.

The parties are therefore advised to seek further precision in the contract of sale to ensure that no such disputes will arise, e.g. by clarifying that the cargo should be deemed delivered as soon as the vehicle with the cargo loaded upon it has arrived at the agreed point (e.g. by stipulating DDU or DDP upon arrival of the vehicle). Alternatively, delivery could be deemed to occur when the goods have been discharged from the vehicle (e.g. DDU or DDP discharged from arriving vehicle) at the agreed point.

If the seller under DDP has to place the goods in the buyer's warehouse after discharge from the carrying vehicle, he has fulfilled the **maximum** obligation under Incoterms. The seller's **minimum** obligation under EXW is met if the seller simply has to make the goods available to the buyer in his warehouse before they have been loaded on to the vehicle provided by the buyer.

■ Import clearance under D-terms

With respect to customs formalities the D-terms can be divided into two groups: First, DES, DAF and DDU, which do not require the seller to arrange import clearance and pay import duties, VAT and other official charges in connection with importation; second, the group consisting of DEQ and DDP which require the seller to do so.

■ Seller should avoid DEQ and DDP if difficulties expected

If any difficulties seem likely to arise in relation to the importation of the goods into the buyer's country, the seller should try to avoid the terms DEQ and DDP.

Even if no difficulties are expected, each party is usually better suited to assess the possible risks in his own country. Therefore, it is normally better that the seller take upon himself the task of clearing the goods for export, while the buyer procures the import formalities and bears any extra costs and risks incurred in that connection.

Also, it may be that the applicable statutory provisions relating to duties, VAT and similar charges require payment from a party domiciled in the country concerned. A party from abroad, having undertaken to pay these charges, then cannot benefit from advantages accorded to parties domiciled in the country of exportation or importation. Moreover, if the costs are paid by a non-resident, difficulties may arise in deducting the expenditure in the VAT forms submitted to the authorities.

■ The ship's rail as imaginary customs border under DES

In practice, DEQ is often to be preferred to DES to ensure that all discharging expenses are borne by the seller. But the parties may forget that - as is the case with the distinction between FAS and FOB - the ship's rail would then serve as an imaginary customs border which distinguishes these two D-terms. While the DEQ seller would have to clear the goods for import into the foreign country of the buyer, the DES seller would not.

If the parties still wish to use DEQ, in order to place all costs of discharge on the seller, they should add the words "duty unpaid", or better yet, "duty unpaid not cleared for import", if they want to avoid the costs of duty and import clearance also falling upon the seller.

Note the difference between DES and DEQ

Under DES, the buyer must clear goods for import. Under DEQ, it is the seller who must clear the goods.

■ The new term DDU

The term DDU is new in Incoterms 1990. While it may be desirable for a seller to use DDP to become competitive in the buyer's country, it normally does not matter if the costs of duty, VAT and other charges fall upon the buyer. Such costs are usually known beforehand and can easily be considered when the seller quotes his price.

Also, the risk of these costs increasing is usually foreseeable well in advance and, in any event, more easily foreseeable by the buyer than by the seller. Moreover, the function of clearing the goods for import can easily be performed by the buyer or his freight forwarder, and these costs too are easy to assess beforehand.

■ Choice of DDP with exclusion of duty and/or other charges

The seller or his freight forwarder may be prepared to clear the goods for import, but without paying duty, VAT and other official charges connected with the import clearance. If so, DDP may still be used but with the addition of the phrase "exclusive of duty, VAT and other importation charges".

DDP with such an exclusion is not equivalent to DDU, since the obligation to clear the goods for import still falls upon the DDP seller. If the seller wishes to avoid the latter obligation as well, he would have to use the term DDU. It is also possible to use DDU, then to add that some costs connected with importation should be borne by the seller.

■ DDU and difficulties of reaching the final destination

Serious difficulties could arise in using the term DDU when the goods have to pass through customs at an earlier point than the agreed point of destination. If so, the goods may be prevented from reaching the destination point as contemplated if they are held up at the customs station, either because of the failure of the buyer to do whatever is required by the authorities or for other reasons.

Since under DDU it is the buyer's task to clear the goods for import, all of the above events are at his risk and expense. This may be cold comfort for a seller who has his transport arrangements interrupted at the customs station but with the remaining obligation to deliver the goods at the agreed final point of destination. Consequently, sellers are advised to be cautious and to avoid the term DDU when difficulties of this kind cannot be excluded.

By adding the term "cleared for import", it is possible to use DDU and still place the obligation to clear the goods for import on the seller. This means that the seller's obligation is limited to the clearance as such and that the duty, as well as other official charges levied upon importation, will be unpaid and have to be paid by the buyer.

IV. SELLER'S AND BUYER'S OBLIGATIONS: AN OVERVIEW

The basic nature of the various trade terms having already been briefly explained, the following section-by-section examination will make it easier for the user of this Guide to determine the risks and responsibilities of the parties.

Sections A1, B1: The obligation to exchange goods for money

The essence of any contract of sale is the exchange of goods for money. Incoterms, in sections A1 and B1 respectively, simply contain a reminder of this. Needless to say, the contract of sale must specify which goods the seller has to provide and what the buyer must pay for them. In A1 there is also a reminder that the seller should provide the "commercial invoice" and any "evidence of conformity" the contract may stipulate.

Section A9: The seller's packaging obligations

Any particular requirement with respect to checking and marking which the buyer desires solely for his own purposes must be stipulated in the contract of sale. Section A9 makes clear that the costs required solely to place the goods at the buyer's disposal are for the seller's account. In this respect, government agencies in some countries may request that the goods be checked before they are admitted for import or export. Some goods may have to be marked, measured, weighed or counted as a condition for the carrier's acceptance of the goods for carriage. When the contract of sale does not contain detailed provisions on packaging of the goods, or when this cannot be ascertained from previous dealings between the parties, the seller may be uncertain as to what he should do. Under normal circumstances, the seller has to provide some packaging.

However, how the goods should be packed and prepared for the intended voyage may be unclear. A long sea voyage could require strong packaging and special preparations to protect against rusting caused by condensation and humidity. This same degree of protection is unlikely to be required for air carriage of the same cargo.

The seller must pack the goods as required for the mode of transport, but only to the extent that the circumstances of the transport are known to him before the contract of sale is concluded. If these are known, he can take them into consideration when he quotes his price. Therefore, it is important that the buyer duly inform the seller of his intentions, particularly when the contract has been concluded on EXW or under F-terms, when the seller may not otherwise know the buyer's intentions with respect to the carriage.

Section B9: Pre-shipment inspection

Pre-shipment inspection (PSI) may apply when the buyer requires a licence or permit from the authorities to ensure that the goods conform with the contract. In these circumstances, the authorities order an inspection and generally engage an independent inspection agency to perform it. Legislation in the country of importation will determine whether and to which extent the authorities can require reimbursement of costs paid by them for the inspection; but if reimbursement is required from one of the parties, the buyer will normally bear the cost.

Contractual stipulations relating to inspection usually require the buyer to pay for it. However, there are other variants which require the seller to pay, wholly or partly, for the inspection; in others, the seller has to pay for it to the extent that the inspection shows that the goods were not in condition to satisfy the contract.

PSI should be distinguished from an inspection required by the buyer himself without the involvement of his authorities. Such an inspection may be important for the buyer if he has any reason to doubt that the seller will hand over goods for shipment in conformity with the contract. Using such an inspection can ascertain whether a commodity - such as oil, ore, foodstuffs, or timber - meets this test, for example.

An inspection can also be arranged when the contract of sale is concluded between parties who are not familiar with one another from previous dealings and who may not intend to establish future commercial relations (as in so-called "one off" contracts on the spot market).

Finally, an inspection can be a means of avoiding maritime fraud. In some notorious cases it has been possible for a fraudulent seller to obtain payment under a documentary credit by presenting documents relating to a cargo and a ship even though neither the cargo nor the ship existed. If an inspection had been performed in these cases, the outcome could have been quite different. Since the inspection is normally performed in the buyer's interest, section B9 of Incoterms requires the buyer to pay the costs unless otherwise agreed. There is an exception to this principle when the inspection has been mandated by the authorities of the country of exportation.

Sections A2, B2:
The obligation to clear the goods for export and import

A reference to Incoterms 1990 may sometimes be made in domestic contracts of sale, although this is not usually necessary or appropriate. The overwhelming usage concerns international contracts of sale when the cargo must be carried from country to country. There it is necessary to decide what the seller and the buyer are required to do to clear the goods for export and import, and in Incoterms this is dealt with under the heading "Licences, authorisations and formalities" (A2, B2).

The division of functions with respect to export and import clearance is important in several ways. First, the parties must know who is responsible for doing what is necessary to obtain any required licences or official authorisations and to submit official forms and requests in the country concerned. Second, the obligation to clear the goods - particularly for import - frequently results in the obligation to pay duty, VAT and other official charges. Third, the parties must resolve who bears the risk if it is not possible to clear the goods within the agreed time or at all (for example, if there are export or import prohibitions).

■ Take precautions against the risk of export and import prohibitions!

A seller who has undertaken to clear the goods for export - and particularly for import - is well advised to negotiate with his buyer an extension of the time for delivery or the right to terminate the contract in case of unforeseen restrictions or prohibitions relating to export or import.

More than this, it is important that the seller not undertake any activity that he or his agent either cannot do or are expressly forbidden to do by the receiving country.

■ Obtaining assistance to clear customs

A party having undertaken to clear the goods for export or import or to move them through a third country may often need the assistance of the other party to obtain various documents, e.g. documents showing the origin or ultimate destination of the goods. Therefore, sections A2 or B2 set out the extent to which the seller or the buyer, as the case may be, has to render this assistance to the other party.

Sections A10 and B10 stipulate that the seller and the buyer respectively have to reimburse any costs incurred by the other party for rendering the requested assistance, which is always provided at the risk and expense of the other party.

Sections A3, B3, A4:

The obligation to contract for carriage and the seller's obligation to hand over the goods for carriage

■ Why divide functions, costs and risks between the parties?

While it may often be more practical for either the buyer or the seller to be responsible for the whole transport from point of origin to the agreed destination - as is the case under EXW or D-terms - the majority of international sales still use terms under which the obligations of carriage are divided between the parties. Under the F-terms pre-carriage is arranged by the seller; under the C-terms the seller only undertakes to arrange for the carriage and pay the costs, but the risk is transferred from him to the buyer when the goods are shipped. Presumably, this commercial practice is based to a large extent on the tradition in commodity trading which frequently requires the chartering of ships. In this case, the F- and C-terms are still appropriate.

■ For economy of transport, do not divide functions

A large number of sales transactions now using F- or C-terms involve manufactured goods. In these cases, the optimal transport economy may depend on either the buyer or the seller arranging and paying for the whole of the carriage. This is particularly true when the transport facilities available make it possible for the buyer or the seller to integrate the whole of the transport in one contract of carriage with the operator, even if this involves a contract using more than one mode of transport (so-called multimodal transport).

In such circumstances, the use of F- and C- terms may well diminish. However, in practice the term FCA can come very close to EXW, particularly if the words "cleared for export" are added after EXW. This is because under both FCA and EXW the buyer may be required to let the carrier pick up the goods at the seller's premises. The buyer would then be in the same position under both EXW and FCA, since he would be responsible for arranging and paying for the whole transport. But under EXW the seller is only obliged to make the goods available at his premises. The loading on the carrier's vehicle is at the risk and expense of the buyer unless otherwise agreed.

■ Additional service to the buyer under F-terms

Although there is a fundamental difference between F-terms (FCA, FAS, FOB) and C-terms (CFR, CIF, CPT and CIP), this distinction is blurred in practice because sellers using F-terms still, as an additional service to the buyer, normally arrange the carriage (but at the buyer's risk and expense).

From a strictly legal viewpoint, parties using the F-terms should not find it necessary to specify how the seller should hand over the goods for carriage, since he simply has to follow what the contract of sale specifically provides or the buyer's instructions. But the seller - though he has no duty under an F-term to do so - would frequently take care of the interests of the "absent" buyer. This explains why the FCA term sets forth in some detail how the goods should be handed over to the carrier.

■ Handing over to the carrier under A4 of FCA

Section A4 of FCA - the longest rule of interpretation in all of Incoterms - explains how delivery to the carrier is completed in seven different situations, namely:

1. Rail transport
2. Road transport
3. Transport by inland waterway
4. Sea transport
5. Air transport
6. Unnamed transport (i.e. a transport which could use any mode or combination of modes and when the parties do not know the mode or combination of modes beforehand), and
7. Multimodal transport (i.e. a combination of at least two different modes of transport).

■ FAS and FOB only for carriage by sea

While FCA can be used regardless of the mode of transport, FAS and FOB can only be used when the goods are carried by sea or inland waterway transport. The term FOB Airport was introduced in Incoterms 1976 but was omitted from the 1990 revision. It was rarely used in practice and the expression "FOB" (for Free On Board) was not considered appropriate for air carriage, particularly since reference in the term was made not to the aircraft itself but to the airport. In fact, "FOB" in such cases really means "Free" as in "Free Carrier".

The distinction between FAS and FOB is well established on the question of handing over the goods for carriage. FAS means that the goods should be placed alongside the ship and FOB that they should be placed on board. Nevertheless, difficulties have always been connected with the use of FOB, since the ship's rail as a point for the division of functions, costs and risks between seller and buyer is seldom practicable.

The reference to the ship's rail may have been appropriate in earlier times when the cargo was lifted parcel-by-parcel (i.e. break bulk) on board the ship by the ship's own crew and equipment. Then "land costs" would fall upon the seller, "ship's costs" upon the buyer.

■ The custom of the port

These days stevedoring companies usually perform the whole of the loading operation, using either their own cranes or those belonging to the port authorities. Problems then arise as how to divide the bill for their services between the seller and the buyer, since the reference in FOB to the ship's rail does not give sufficient guidance. Instead, it is necessary to follow the custom of the port, which unfortunately may vary considerably from one port to another and which can range from

- the buyer having to pay for the whole of the loading operation (as if FOB in this respect were equivalent to FAS);
- splitting the costs according to various customs and methods; or
- having the seller pay all costs of the loading.

■ Caution when using FOB if custom of port not known

A buyer who does not know the custom of the port in the seller's country should be cautious when using FOB and should require a precise stipulation concerning the loading costs. Short expressions are sometimes used for this purpose (e.g. "FOB stowed", "FOB stowed and trimmed").

While it may be clear that the seller's obligation to pay the loading <u>costs</u> is extended by these additions, it is <u>not</u> immediately clear to what extent the seller must also bear the <u>risk</u> of loss of or damage to the cargo which could occur subsequent to the passing of the ship's rail. The parties are therefore advised to clarify their intentions in this respect (e.g. by adding a phrase such as "FOB stowed, costs and risks in connection with loading on the seller").

■ Handing over to the carrier under C-terms

When under the C-terms the seller has to arrange and pay for the carriage, handing over of the goods for carriage should not present any particular problem for seller or buyer. This is because the seller has to perform his duties according to the contract of carriage, which he has himself concluded with the carrier.

■ Dividing the costs of discharge at destination

Problems could arise at the other end of the transport when the goods have to be discharged from the ship or from another means of conveyance. While delivery from a road, rail or air carrier should not normally present any difficulties, considerable problems may arise when the goods are carried by sea. Liner shipping companies usually include costs of loading and discharge in their freight rates, but in charter party operations there may be provisions stipulating that the discharging operations should be wholly or partly "free" to the carrier ("free out" stipulations). In these cases the buyer must know the ship's time of arrival and the time available for the discharging operations (the so-called "laytime"). He must also ascertain the extent to which he is exposed to the risk of having to pay compensation (demurrage) to the seller if the laytime is exceeded.

Because of these variations, the rules of interpretation in Incoterms cannot specify how discharging costs should be divided between seller and buyer under the different C-terms. The parties are therefore advised to deal specifically with the relevant points in the contract of sale.

Failing such specific arrangements, guidance must be sought from any custom which the parties have developed between them in previous dealings, or from the custom of the port.

Section A8:
The seller's duty to provide proof of delivery and the transport document

All terms except EXW require the seller to submit to the buyer a formal proof that he has fulfilled his delivery obligation (A8). (The difference in EXW, of course, is that the buyer picks up the goods at the seller's premises.)

Under the C-terms, when the seller has to arrange and pay for the carriage, the transport document becomes very important, since it must show, not only that the goods have been handed over to the carrier by the date agreed, but also that the buyer has an independent right to claim the goods from the carrier at destination.

■ CFR, CIF and on board documents

A further problem occurs with CFR or CIF, both of which require the seller to provide more than just a bill of lading. Specifically, he must provide an on board bill of lading, since the document must evidence shipment on board. Not surprisingly, container lines prefer to issue the transport document as a receipt for the goods when they are received for carriage, not at some later stage when the container with the cargo is lifted on board the ship.

Although it is common for the container line, upon the request of the shipper, to convert the "received-for-shipment" bill of lading with an "on board notation", this causes further paperwork and frequently delay for sellers when payment is to be collected under documentary credits requiring an on board bill of lading rather than a received-for-shipment bill of lading to be presented within a prescribed period after the date on which the ship takes the goods on board.

Here again, it would be better to avoid the trade terms CFR and CIF and use instead CPT and CIP when reference is not made to a bill of lading but rather to the "usual transport document", which may or may not be a bill of lading. But this is only appropriate when the buyer really has no need for a bill of lading, for the sale of the goods in transit before they have been collected by him at destination.

■ Surrender of original bill of lading essential

In some trades, there is a further problem connected with the use of bills of lading caused by the need to present and surrender one original document to the carrier in order to obtain delivery of the goods. Ships frequently arrive at destination before an original bill of lading is available there; in such cases, the goods are often delivered to the buyer against a bill of lading guarantee issued by a bank. This is to protect the carrier if some person other than the person to whom the goods were delivered is the rightful holder of the original bill of lading.

This practice - or rather malpractice - defeats the whole bill of lading system, which depends for its validity on the firm principle that under no circumstances should the goods be delivered except in return for an original bill of lading. If that principle is not strictly followed, one can no longer say that the "bill of lading represents the goods". Then the whole system collapses.

■ Non-negotiable transport documents

In recent years, transport documents other than bills of lading for carriage of goods by sea have been increasingly used. These documents in the so-called "waybill system" are similar to those used for modes of transport other than carriage by sea and when no original document is required to obtain the goods from the carrier at destination. It is sufficient that the consignee be named and that he can properly identify himself, as in the widespread use of air waybills (AWBs) and waybills for international road and rail carriage.

Such documents cannot be used, however, for transferring rights to the goods by the transfer of the document; they are therefore called non-negotiable. They bear various names such as "liner waybills", "ocean waybills", "data freight receipts", "cargo key receipts" or "sea waybills". Although in such transport documents a buyer or a bank has been named as consignee, the seller and the seller alone enters into a contractual relationship with the carrier when the seller has contracted for carriage. The carrier takes instructions from his contracting party - the seller - and from no one else.

■ Payment against sea waybills requires caution!

If the buyer has paid for the goods in advance, or a bank wishes to use the goods as security for a loan extended to the buyer, it is not sufficient that the buyer or the bank be named as consignee in a non-negotiable document. This is true because the seller by new instructions to the carrier could replace the named consignee with someone else. To protect the buyer or the bank it is therefore necessary that the original instructions from the seller to the carrier to deliver the goods to the named consignee be irrevocable.

It follows that a seller should avoid trade terms such as CFR and CIF obliging him to present an onboard bill of lading whenever practical difficulties are involved in obtaining and using such documents. It also follows that the buyer should not pay for the goods, and the bank should not rely on security in the goods, merely by accepting transport documents naming the buyer and the bank respectively as consignees, unless such instructions to the carrier are made irrevocable.

■ The problems of replacing bills of lading by EDI

Apart from the need to agree on a method for using EDI and adopting international message standards, there should be no particular problems when replacing transport documents by electronic messages. However, it is difficult to replace the bill of lading because it is not only proof of the delivery of the goods to the carrier but also a legal symbol often expressed by the principle that "the bill of lading represents the goods".

As noted, the fundamental principle behind the "negotiable" status of the bill of lading stems from the carrier's obligation to deliver the goods to the holder of one original bill of lading and to no one else. Consequently, the possession of the bill of lading has controlled the rightful delivery of the goods to the entitled party at destination.

How can this be replaced by an electronic message? The solution is to obtain the agreement of all parties concerned. First, they must agree to communicate electronically. Second, the agreement must take a particular form with respect to the replacement of bills of lading. The carrier must agree only to deliver the goods as instructed by the party having the right to give him delivery instructions. While, as noted above, this right has traditionally been tied to the possession of the original bill of lading, it would now be vested instead in the person whom the carrier has authorised to give him electronic instructions.

■ The CMI Rules for Electronic Bills of Lading

At its World Paris Conference in June 1990, the CMI adopted Rules for Electronic Bills of Lading based on a system of electronic instructions to the carrier from the entitled party, who in principle enjoys the same rights against the carrier as the traditional bill of lading holder. (See Appendix)

■ The private key for electronic transmissions

To prevent abuse of EDI in international trade, each electronic transmission must be authenticated by reference to a so-called private key which is secret and available only to one party at a time. No one other than the so-called "holder of the private key" should be able to communicate with the carrier for the purpose of instructing him to pass the right to a new holder. Once the carrier passes the right, the private key is cancelled and a new private key issued to the new holder. Through the use of this technique, successive transfers of the right can be achieved in the same way as the right to obtain the goods at destination can pass from one party to another by the transfer of the bill of lading.

IV. SELLER'S AND BUYER'S OBLIGATIONS: AN OVERVIEW

■ Incoterms CFR and CIF A8 and EDI

Incoterms 1990, in the trade terms CFR and CIF, section A8, have taken the development of EDI into consideration. They have done this first by maintaining the traditional principle that, unless otherwise agreed, the transport document must enable the buyer to sell the goods in transit by the transfer of the document to a subsequent buyer. But they have indicated that the transfer could also be made by notification to the carrier. In the former case, the negotiable bill of lading is expressly referred to. In the latter, reference is made to a system of notification. In any event, a mere notification to the carrier is not sufficient to replace a bill of lading.

Therefore, parties wishing to replace the bill of lading by electronic messages must necessarily refer to a system, such as the CMI Rules for Electronic Bills of Lading, to enable the buyer to obtain the goods from the carrier at destination and to transfer the rights to the goods to a subsequent buyer while they are still being carried.

It follows that the use of EDI requires a particular agreement and a well-developed system following internationally agreed standards (UN/EDIFACT and UNCID), and that the replacement of bills of lading by electronic messages can only be implemented by reference to a notification system such as the CMI Rules for Electronic Bills of Lading.

■ The on board bill of lading under CFR and CIF

In the CFR and CIF terms, reference is made to the on board bill of lading, since under those terms the seller has not fulfilled his delivery obligation until the goods have been placed on board the ship. The bill of lading is critical for the buyer if he intends to sell the goods to another buyer while they are still being carried (sale "afloat"). In these circumstances transferring the original or the set of originals of the bill of lading can be used to transfer title of the goods to the other party.

■ Transport document as proof of delivery

Although under the F-terms the buyer must arrange and pay for the carriage - meaning that he enters into a direct contractual relationship with the carrier - the transport document can still be given by the carrier to the seller as proof that the seller has delivered the goods to him. If it is, the transport document will not only constitute evidence of the contract of carriage but also proof of delivery of the goods to the carrier.

Indeed the seller - in his capacity as a shipper in the contract of carriage - frequently receives the bill of lading from the carrier as a proof of delivery of the goods. This often happens, even though from a strictly legal viewpoint it is the buyer who should have received the bill of lading as evidence of the contract made with the carrier, so that the buyer can take delivery of the goods at destination in return for it.

This is further clarified in A8 of the F-terms, which stipulates that the seller must render the buyer, at the buyer's risk and expense, every assistance in obtaining the transport document if the document is not identical with the document proving delivery of the goods to the carrier. Since the possession of the bill of lading is required for the right to give instructions to the carrier and to obtain the cargo from him at destination, it is extremely important that the buyer receive this document from the seller, unless it has been given directly to him by the carrier.

■ Documents required to obtain delivery under D-terms

Under the D-terms the situation is different from that described in the preceding paragraphs, since the seller has not fulfilled his delivery obligation until the goods have actually arrived in the country of destination. Nevertheless, the buyer could still require a document to enable him to obtain the goods from the carrier at the agreed point of delivery. This may well be the case if the goods have been sold DES, in which case the buyer takes delivery from the ship, normally requiring him to surrender an original bill of lading.

The terms DEQ, DDU and DDP may be different in this respect, since the goods under these terms would have been placed on the quay or taken to an interior point in the country of destination. But this does not necessarily mean that they have left the custody of the carrier, and a bill of lading may still be required to obtain them.

Transport documents for carriage by sea

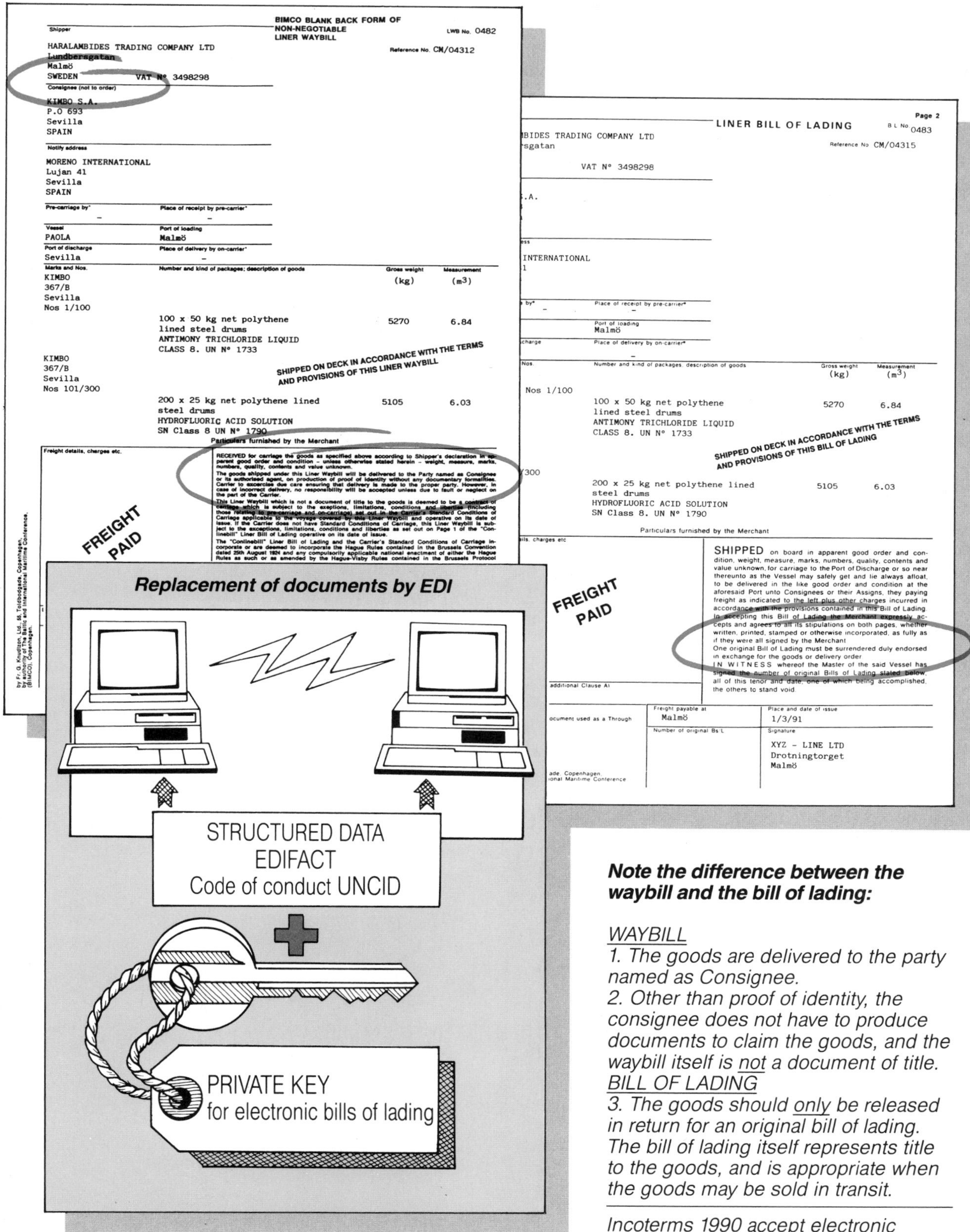

BIMCO BLANK BACK FORM OF NON-NEGOTIABLE LINER WAYBILL

LWB No. 0482

Reference No. CM/04312

Shipper
HARALAMBIDES TRADING COMPANY LTD
Lundbergsgatan
Malmö
SWEDEN VAT N° 3498298

Consignee (not to order)
KIMBO S.A.
P.O 693
Sevilla
SPAIN

Notify address
MORENO INTERNATIONAL
Lujan 41
Sevilla
SPAIN

Pre-carriage by* –
Place of receipt by pre-carrier* –

Vessel: PAOLA
Port of loading: Malmö

Port of discharge: Sevilla
Place of delivery by on-carrier* –

Marks and Nos.	Number and kind of packages; description of goods	Gross weight (kg)	Measurement (m3)
KIMBO 367/B Sevilla Nos 1/100	100 x 50 kg net polythene lined steel drums ANTIMONY TRICHLORIDE LIQUID CLASS 8. UN N° 1733	5270	6.84
KIMBO 367/B Sevilla Nos 101/300	200 x 25 kg net polythene lined steel drums HYDROFLUORIC ACID SOLUTION SN Class 8 UN N° 1790	5105	6.03

SHIPPED ON DECK IN ACCORDANCE WITH THE TERMS AND PROVISIONS OF THIS LINER WAYBILL

Particulars furnished by the Merchant

Freight details, charges etc.

FREIGHT PAID

RECEIVED for carriage the goods as specified above according to Shipper's declaration in apparent good order and condition – unless otherwise stated herein – weight, measure, marks, numbers, quality, contents and value unknown.

The goods shipped under this Liner Waybill will be delivered to the Party named as Consignee or its authorised agent, on production of proof of identity without any documentary formalities. Carrier to excercise due care ensuring that delivery is made to the proper party. However, in case of incorrect delivery, no responsibility will be accepted unless due to fault or neglect on the part of the Carrier.

This Liner Waybill which is not a document of title to the goods is deemed to be a contract of carriage which is subject to the exeptions, limitations, conditions and liberties (including those relating to pre-carriage and on-carriage) set out in the Carrier's Standard Conditions of Carriage applicable to the voyage covered by this Liner Waybill and operative on its date of issue. If the Carrier does not have Standard Conditions of Carriage, this Liner Waybill is subject to the exceptions, limitations, conditions and liberties as set out on Page 1 of the "Conlinebill" Liner Bill of Lading operative on its date of issue.

The "Conlinebill" Liner Bill of Lading and the Carrier's Standard Conditions of Carriage incorporate or are deemed to incorporate the Hague Rules contained in the Brussels Convention dated 25th August 1924 and any compulsorily applicable national enactment of either the Hague Rules as such or as amended by the Hague-Visby Rules contained in the Brussels Protocol

by Fr. G. Knudtzon, Ltd., 55, Toldbodgade, Copenhagen, by authority of The Baltic and International Maritime Conference, (BIMCO), Copenhagen.

LINER BILL OF LADING

Page 2

B L No 0483

Reference No CM/04315

...BIDES TRADING COMPANY LTD
...sgatan
VAT N° 3498298

...A.

...INTERNATIONAL
...1

Place of receipt by pre-carrier* –
Port of loading: Malmö
Place of delivery by on-carrier* –

Marks and Nos.	Number and kind of packages; description of goods	Gross weight (kg)	Measurement (m3)
Nos 1/100	100 x 50 kg net polythene lined steel drums ANTIMONY TRICHLORIDE LIQUID CLASS 8. UN N° 1733	5270	6.84
...300	200 x 25 kg net polythene lined steel drums HYDROFLUORIC ACID SOLUTION SN Class 8. UN N° 1790	5105	6.03

SHIPPED ON DECK IN ACCORDANCE WITH THE TERMS AND PROVISIONS OF THIS BILL OF LADING

Particulars furnished by the Merchant

FREIGHT PAID

SHIPPED on board in apparent good order and condition, weight, measure, marks, numbers, quality, contents and value unknown, for carriage to the Port of Discharge or so near thereunto as the Vessel may safely get and lie always afloat, to be delivered in the like good order and condition at the aforesaid Port unto Consignees or their Assigns, they paying freight as indicated to the left plus other charges incurred in accordance with the provisions contained in this Bill of Lading. In accepting this Bill of Lading the Merchant expressly accepts and agrees to all its stipulations on both pages, whether written, printed, stamped or otherwise incorporated, as fully as if they were all signed by the Merchant.
One original Bill of Lading must be surrendered duly endorsed in exchange for the goods or delivery order.
IN WITNESS whereof the Master of the said Vessel has signed the number of original Bills of Lading stated below, all of this tenor and date, one of which being accomplished, the others to stand void.

Freight payable at: Malmö
Place and date of issue: 1/3/91
Number of original Bs/L
Signature: XYZ – LINE LTD, Drotningtorget, Malmö

Note the difference between the waybill and the bill of lading:

WAYBILL
1. The goods are delivered to the party named as Consignee.
2. Other than proof of identity, the consignee does not have to produce documents to claim the goods, and the waybill itself is not a document of title.
BILL OF LADING
3. The goods should only be released in return for an original bill of lading. The bill of lading itself represents title to the goods, and is appropriate when the goods may be sold in transit.

Incoterms 1990 accept electronic equivalents for transport documents.

■ **Delivery orders**
Sometimes the goods may have been discharged in bulk, and the buyer has to remove his goods from a larger consignment. One bill of lading could then cover the whole consignment, even though the consignment is intended for several buyers. In these cases, it is customary to split the bill of lading into parts by issuing individual so-called delivery orders; these are specifically referred to in section A8 of all D-terms except DAF. (Normally under DAF there is no physical delivery of the goods to the buyer at the "D point", but the carriage continues without interruption to the final destination. This is evidenced by the stipulation in DAF A8 that the seller must provide the buyer at his request, risk and expense with a through document of transport, normally obtainable in the country of dispatch.)

Sections A4 and B4:
The seller's obligation to deliver and the buyer's obligation to take delivery

■ **Delivery at the seller's premises**
As noted, contracts requiring the buyer to take delivery of the goods at the seller's premises do not normally cause any particular problems in practice. The facilities at the seller's place will determine whether the cargo will be delivered at a ramp where a driver could place his lorry and where forklift trucks can be used by the seller's personnel to place the goods on the lorry. However, it may not be easy to determine how much stowing of the goods on the lorry should be performed by the driver and how much by the seller's personnel. This necessarily depends on the circumstances and is not resolved by the rule of interpretation in EXW A4, which simply states that the goods should be placed "at the disposal of the buyer".

■ **Delivery at the buyer's premises**
The same problem could arise under DDU and DDP, when it can be very difficult to determine exactly how the seller should arrange to hand over the goods to the buyer. Here again, A4 only stipulates that the goods should be placed "at the disposal of the buyer".

■ **Delivery at the border under DAF A4**
Although the same expression, "at the disposal of the buyer", is used in DAF A4, there will usually not be a "physical" delivery of the goods at the frontier of the buyer's country, unless it is necessary for some reason to have them stored in a warehouse for customs or other purposes pending the loading of the goods on a railway wagon or other means of conveyance for on-carriage.

■ **Delivery at the waterfront under DES and DEQ**
Under the terms DES and DEQ the cargo will be made available to the buyer in the ship and on the quay respectively. How the cargo should be received at these points (pumping installations, silos, adjoining railway tracks, cargo terminals, etc.) will depend on the circumstances.

■ **The buyer's acceptance of the seller's handing over for carriage**
As noted, there are different customs for handing over the cargo to the carrier. Under the C-terms, when the seller arranges and pays for the carriage, the seller will deliver the cargo to the carrier in the absence of the buyer. Consequently, there will be no physical delivery of the cargo directly to the buyer.

But the buyer must accept that the cargo is handed over to the carrier as stipulated in A4 of the C-terms and be content with the proof of the delivery which the seller must give him according to A8. This is because the C-terms evidence shipment contracts under which in principle the seller fulfils his delivery obligation at the place of dispatch or shipment. What happens to the cargo after the seller has fulfilled his delivery obligation is at the risk and expense of the buyer.

■ The buyer's obligation to receive the goods from the carrier

Nevertheless, it is also important to note that the buyer has an obligation to the seller to receive the goods from the carrier at the named place or port of destination (B4). If a buyer refuses to honour his obligation to pay for the goods in return for a bill of lading where applicable and thereby fails to collect the goods from the carrier, the seller could incur expenses due under the contract of carriage he has concluded with the carrier. These costs will then be included in the seller's claim for damages as a result of the buyer's breach of his contractual obligation.

Sections A5 and B5: The transfer from seller to buyer of the risk of loss of or damage to the goods

Whenever "transfer of risks" is referred to in Incoterms A5 and B5, the expression "loss of or damage to the goods" is used. This means physical loss of or damage to the cargo and does not include other risks such as the risk of delay or non-fulfilment of the contract for other reasons.

■ The "price risk"

If the risk referred to in Incoterms materialises, the buyer has to pay the price even though he does not receive the goods in contractual condition or at all.

This is the so-called "price risk". However, damage to the goods may depend upon circumstances attributable to the seller: For example, the seller may have inadequately packaged the goods. If so, the damage will not have resulted from a transportation risk, and the buyer is then entitled not only to avoid paying for the goods but also to hold the seller responsible for breach of contract.

Incoterms do not specifically deal with other consequences if the seller has not fulfilled his delivery obligation, such questions being left to the applicable law or to the stipulations in the contract of sale. But in the absence of any provisions in the contract, fulfilment of the seller's delivery obligation also means that any further risks or expenses are for the account of the buyer.

Consequently, while under the C-terms the seller has to pay the normal costs of carriage to the carrier, the buyer has to bear any additional costs resulting from circumstances occurring after the seller has fulfilled his delivery obligation. These may include, for example, extra costs for an unexpected transshipment caused by political events or adverse weather conditions which render the previously agreed routing inaccessible.

However, if such events occur before the seller has fulfilled his delivery obligation but after he has entered into the contract of sale, the extent to which (if at all) he can escape his duty to perform the contract will depend on the other terms of the contract or on the applicable law. Thus the "price risk" should not be confused with the risk of breach of the contract of sale (caused by delay, non-fulfilment, etc.). The remedies available to the affected party for these breaches are not dealt with in Incoterms.

■ Premature transfer of risk

In some cases, the risk can be transferred from the seller to the buyer even before the seller has fulfilled his delivery obligation. This could happen as a result of (1) the buyer's failure to do what is required of him to enable the seller to deliver the goods to him, or (2) the buyer's failure to take delivery of the goods (B5).

Therefore, the buyer must give such notice to the seller as the latter requires to prepare the delivery (B7) or the buyer must nominate the carrier under F-terms and accept the goods from the carrier as agreed. Moreover, a buyer having undertaken under DDU to clear the goods for import must fulfil his obligation to do this within the agreed time so the seller can proceed with the on-carriage of the goods to destination as intended. If the buyer fails to do this, he must bear all additional risks of loss of or damage to the goods resulting from his failure (B5).

■ **Appropriation of the goods to the contract**

The premature passing of the risk as noted in the above paragraphs cannot occur unless it can be ascertained that the goods are intended for the buyer and appropriated to the contract of sale made with him. Or as expressed in the Incoterms B5 clauses, the goods must have been "clearly set aside or otherwise identified as the contract goods". This appropriation is normally achieved as soon as the goods have been prepared for carriage, since it would then have been necessary to mark them and/or to name the consignee. But it may be that the goods are to be carried in bulk without such marking or naming of the consignee as would amount to appropriation. Then the risk will not pass until effective appropriation has been made - e.g. until the issuance of separate bills of lading or delivery orders for parts of the bulk consignment.

■ **Using *force majeure* clauses to protect the seller from the "breach of contract risk"**

A seller who has undertaken to deliver the goods at a point outside of his control - e.g. when the goods are to be delivered under D-terms - should consider the need to protect himself (usually by so-called *force majeure* or other relief clauses) against the risk of having to provide substitute goods instead of those lost or damaged, or to make other agreed restitution. Otherwise, he could face damages for breach of contract if he fails to do this in time or at all.

Section A3b: The seller's insurance obligation

CIF and CIP are the only Incoterms related directly to insurance cover. This is because it is important for the buyer to obtain insurance when he has left the responsiblity of arranging the contract of carriage and paying the freight to the seller. The seller is then presumed to be in a better position to arrange insurance than the buyer. This could still be the case if the goods are to be carried in chartered ships or if they consist of larger consignments of commodities. But with manufactured goods, sellers and buyers usually have lasting arrangements with their insurers for exports and imports. Therefore, separate insurance arrangements for each shipment would be unnecessary. This being so, there is no reason to impose an insurance obligation on one party to the benefit of the other, since the better solution is to leave the question of insurance to the parties themselves.

■ **Freedom of insurance restricted**

As of 1991, sellers or buyers in more than 40 countries could be compelled to take out insurance in their own country to minimise expenditure in foreign currencies and/or to support the domestic insurance industry. In these cases a buyer may be ordered to contract for imports on CFR or CPT terms instead of letting the seller arrange the insurance according to CIF or CIP. Conversely, a seller in any of these countries could be obliged to sell the goods on CIF or CIP terms for the same reasons.

Sections A7, B7 and A10, B10: Notices

■ **Conditions for the buyer giving notice**

If there is no specified date or place agreed in the contract and the buyer is entitled to determine

- the time and/or place when and where he should take delivery under EXW or D-terms;
- the nomination of the carrier and delivery time under F-terms; or
- the time for shipping the goods and/or the destination under C-terms,

the buyer has to give the seller sufficient and timely notice (B7).

■ **Conditions for the seller giving notice**

Conversely, the seller must give the buyer sufficient notice of

- when and where the goods will be placed at the buyer's disposal under EXW;
- when and where the goods have been delivered to the carrier under F- and C-terms; and
- when and where the goods are expected to arrive under D-terms so that the buyer can take appropriate measures in time to receive them (A7).

■ Information relating to insurance

When under CIF and CIP the seller has to take out insurance for the benefit of the buyer, he (the seller) may require information about particulars of the goods which do not appear in the contract of sale. He may also need to be informed about the buyer's wishes for extended or additional insurance. The buyer must then inform the seller accordingly (B10). When the buyer intends to take out insurance himself, or is obliged to do so under his country's regulations, he may also require additional information from the seller, who must then give such information to the buyer upon request (A10).

■ Sufficient notice

There are no special requirements in Incoterms that notice be given in a particular form (by letter, telex or telefax). Incoterms only state that notice must be "sufficient". If the parties have agreed to communicate electronically, notice may be given by EDI.

■ Failure to give sufficient notice

Failure to give sufficient notice would constitute a breach of contract which could lead to serious consequences, e.g. it could give the other party the right to cancel the contract. Incoterms only deal with two particular aspects of late or insufficient notice, namely

- the premature passing of the risk (B5) and
- the liability to pay additional costs (B6).

For the premature passing of the risk as well as for the liability to pay additional costs, the parties must be able to ascertain the goods to which the risk or the additional costs relate. This can only be done if the goods can be appropriated to the contract of sale, i.e. if they are clearly set aside for the buyer or otherwise identified as being intended for him.

Sections A6, B6, A3b, AI0 and BI0:
Division of costs between the parties

Division of costs is a most important element in every contract of sale. The parties must know not only who does what but also how costs resulting therefrom should be divided between them. In most cases the fact that a party must do something means that he must also bear the resulting costs, unless otherwise agreed. But there are many exceptions to this principle and uncertainties arise, particularly with respect to services performed by other parties [e.g. stevedores engaged for loading and discharge or costs which cannot clearly be attributed to either the buyer's or the seller's functions, such as (a) "semi-official" charges debited on the exportation or importation of the goods, or (b) charges for their storage pending shipment or delivery]. Also, difficulties arise with respect to the division of costs whenever additional costs are caused by unexpected events, e.g. hindrances causing a ship to deviate or to remain in a seaport longer than expected.

■ Main principle of distribution of costs

The main principle of the division of costs is clear enough: The seller has to pay costs necessary for the goods to reach the agreed point of delivery and the buyer has to pay any further costs after that point. But as noted, it is not always easy to implement this principle in practice, since the detailed distribution of functions under the various trade terms is not and cannot be fully defined in Incoterms. Instead, failing precise stipulations in the contract of sale, guidance must be sought from other criteria such as commercial practices used earlier by the same parties or the custom of the trade.

■ The four main categories of costs

The costs referred to in Incoterms can be grouped in four main categories. These include elements relating to

- dispatch, carriage and delivery;
- customs clearance for export and import;
- services or assistance rendered by one party to the other in addition to what the assisting party is required to do under the respective trade term; and
- insurance.

■ Costs related to dispatch, carriage and delivery
This category is by far the most important, since it includes costs relating to
- loading at the seller's premises;
- pre-carriage in the country of exportation;
- making of the contract (booking the cargo for shipment and issuing the relevant transport documents);
- warehousing, storage and handling charges pending dispatch of the cargo from the country of exportation;
- hire of transportation equipment and appliances in the country of exportation;
- the main international carriage;
- warehousing, storage and handling charges subsequent to discharge in the country of importation;
- hire of transportation equipment and appliances in the country of importation;
- on-carriage in the country of importation; and
- unloading at the buyer's premises.

■ Costs for export and import clearance
With respect to costs for export and import clearance, a firm distinction should be made between duties, VAT and other official charges and the cost for the clearance itself, which is frequently performed by freight forwarders in their capacity as customs brokers. Clearing of the goods will also include costs to obtain licences, certificates, consular invoices, permits, authorisations, legalisation as well as costs for inspection, customs warehouse charges, customs declarations and freight forwarders' service charges.

■ Costs for services and assistance
This category relates only to costs which one party may be entitled to claim from the other for services or assistance rendered upon request for the clearing of the goods. These include the seller's assistance for the buyer's export clearance under EXW and FAS (A2) and the buyer's assistance for the seller's clearing of the goods under DEQ and DDP (B2). They may also include costs incurred in obtaining documents which the other party could require for the clearance (A10 and B10 respectively).

■ Costs of insurance
This category is only relevant when the seller has contracted on CIF or CIP terms requiring that he take out insurance for the benefit of the buyer and also that he pay the premium. Any additional insurance (extended cover or protection against added risks such as war, riots, civil commotions, strikes or other labour disturbances) taken out by the seller at the buyer's request has to be paid for by the buyer, unless otherwise agreed in the contract of sale.

■ Cost distribution systems
In certain cases - e.g. freight forwarding services using a pre-arranged cost distribution system such as Combiterms in the Scandinavian countries (see annexes) - it may be possible to obtain the more detailed breakdown needed to avoid uncertainty and disputes between the parties over costs. These disputes often concern minor costs, but the time, effort and money spent in resolving the disputes can be out of all proportion.

The parties are therefore advised either to specify the division of such costs which does not clearly follow from the trade term itself or to agree to apply a pre-arranged cost distribution system. An agreement to use a cost distribution system should be clearly mentioned in conjunction with the trade term by adding the phrase "Incoterms 1990 with cost distribution according to ... ".

Incoterms 1990

COST/RISK DISTRIBUTION DISPLAY

The following display indicates how the seller's and buyer's cost/risk responsibilities vary from one Incoterm to another.

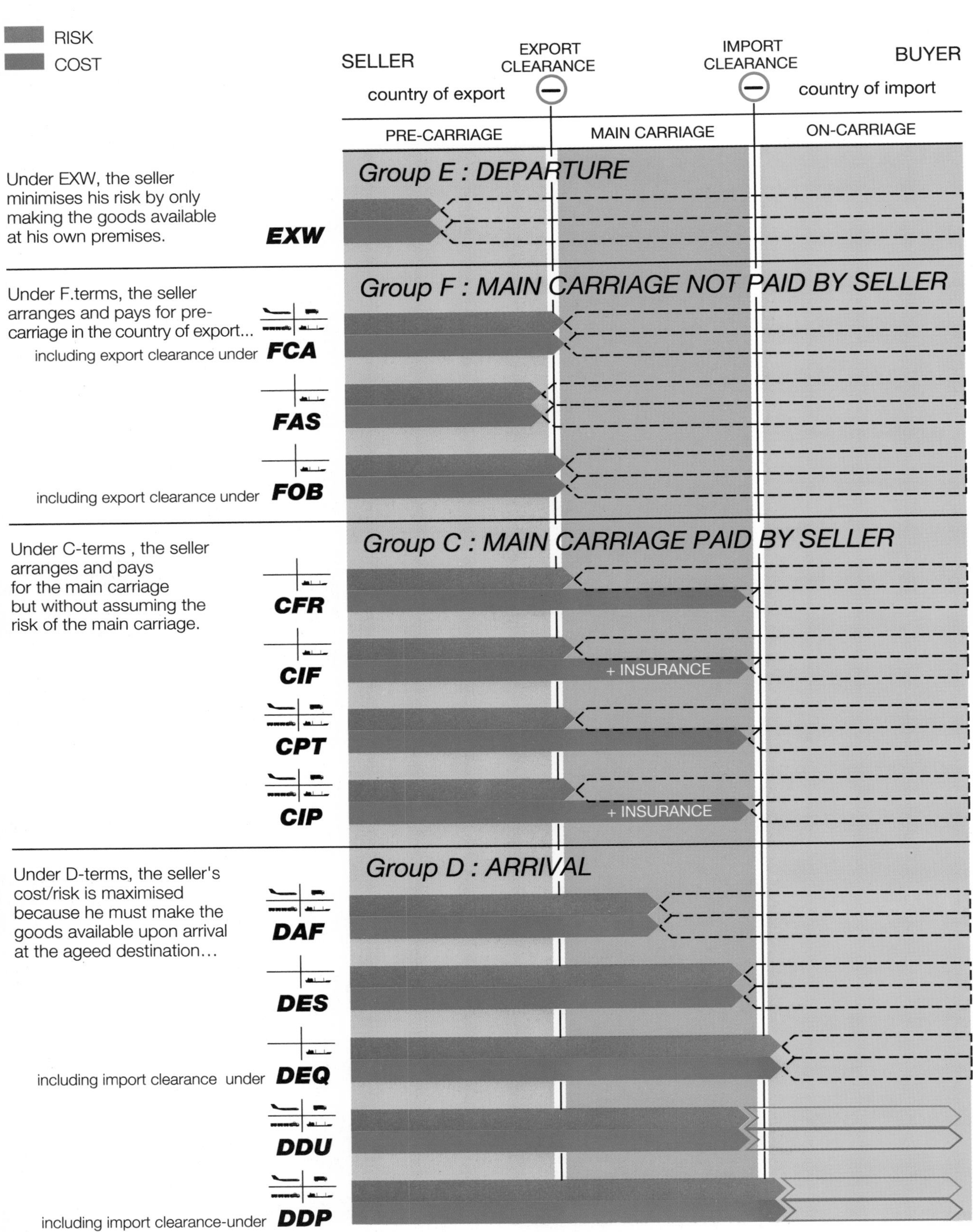

RISK
COST
SELLER
country of export
EXPORT CLEARANCE
IMPORT CLEARANCE
BUYER
country of import
PRE-CARRIAGE
MAIN CARRIAGE
ON-CARRIAGE
Group E : DEPARTURE
Under EXW, the seller minimises his risk by only making the goods available at his own premises.
EXW
Group F : MAIN CARRIAGE NOT PAID BY SELLER
Under F.terms, the seller arranges and pays for pre-carriage in the country of export...
including export clearance under FCA
FAS
including export clearance under FOB
Group C : MAIN CARRIAGE PAID BY SELLER
Under C-terms , the seller arranges and pays for the main carriage but without assuming the risk of the main carriage.
CFR
CIF
+ INSURANCE
CPT
CIP
+ INSURANCE
Group D : ARRIVAL
Under D-terms, the seller's cost/risk is maximised because he must make the goods available upon arrival at the ageed destination...
DAF
DES
including import clearance under DEQ
DDU
including import clearance-under DDP

PART II

GOING THROUGH THE 13 INCOTERMS:

A SECTION-BY-SECTION ANALYSIS

EX WORKS
(... named place)

A SELLER'S PRIMARY DUTY

- Deliver the goods at his premises (**A4**)

DOCUMENTS

Required documents

- Commercial invoice (**A1**)
- Buyer's receipt (**B8**)

NOTE:
All documents may be replaced by EDI messages

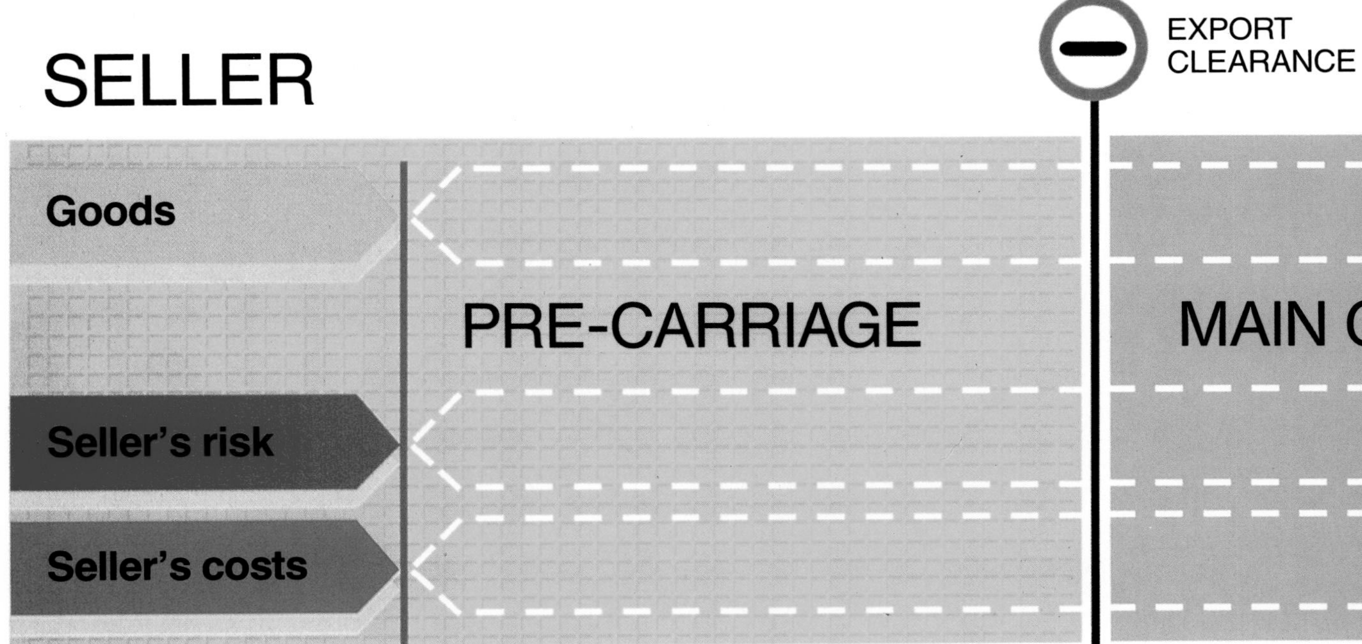

Ex works" means that the seller fulfils his obligation to deliver when he has made the goods available at his premises (i.e. works, factory, warehouse, etc.) to the buyer. In particular, he is not responsible for loading the goods on the vehicle provided by the buyer or for clearing the goods for export, unless otherwise agreed. The buyer bears all costs and risks involved in taking the goods from the seller's premises to the desired destination. This term thus represents the minimum obligation for the seller. This term should not be used when the buyer cannot carry out directly or indirectly the export formalities. In such circumstances, the FCA term should be used.

B BUYER'S PRIMARY DUTIES

- Take delivery of the goods at the seller's premises (**B4**)
- Make all arrangements at his own cost and risk to bring the goods to the destination (**B2, B6**)

tional documents

Other documents needed for export or transit of the goods through another country or for import clearance (**A10**)

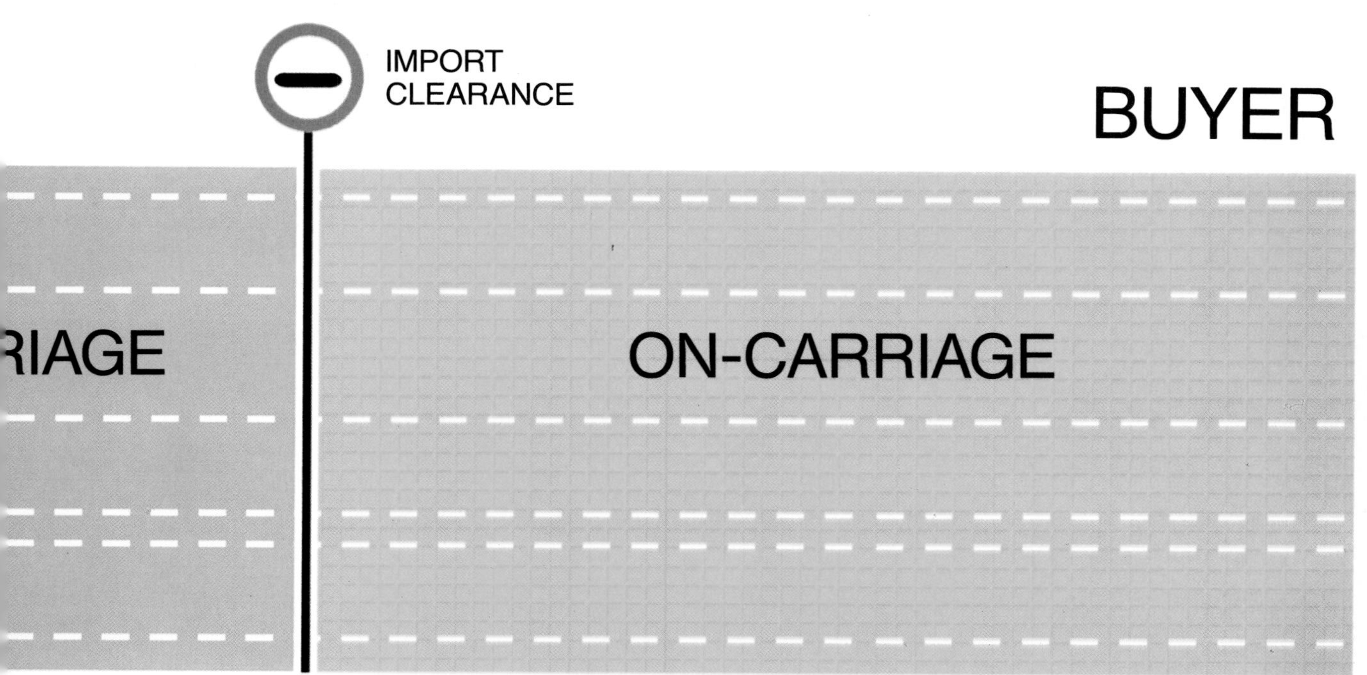

EX WORKS
(... named place)

A THE SELLER MUST

A1 Provision of goods in conformity with the contract

Provide the goods and the commercial invoice, or its equivalent electronic message, in conformity with the contract of sale and any other evidence of conformity which may be required by the contract.

Comments

The seller must provide the goods in conformity with the contract. It is also usual practice that the seller, in order to be paid, has to invoice the buyer. In addition, the seller must submit any other evidence stipulated in the contract itself that the goods conform with the contract.

This text only serves as a reminder of the seller's main obligation under the contract of sale.

A2 Licences, authorisations and formalities

Render the buyer, at the latter's request, risk and expense, every assistance in obtaining any export licence or other official authorisation necessary for the exportation of the goods.

Comments

Under EXW and FAS it is the buyer's obligation to obtain export as well as import licences or other official authorisations. It is therefore the seller under this term who should render the necessary assistance and the buyer who should bear any cost involved.

A3 Contract of carriage and insurance

a) Contract of carriage
No obligation.

b) Contract of insurance
No obligation.

Comments

Since the goods are made available to the buyer at the seller's premises, the seller has no obligation to contract for carriage or insurance.

A4 Delivery

Place the goods at the disposal of the buyer at the named place of delivery on the date or within the period stipulated or, if no such place or time is stipulated, at the usual place and time for delivery of such goods.

Comments

Under EXW the seller only has to make the goods available to the buyer at the named place of delivery in the seller's own country, which is usually at the seller's premises. Therefore, this term represents the seller's minimum obligation; delivery at the buyer's premises in the buyer's country would represent the seller's maximum obligation, e.g. DDU, DDP. Exactly how delivery should be performed is not specified, but this normally follows what has been done in previous dealings between the same parties or from the custom of the trade.

Frequently, the seller assists the buyer by bringing the goods onto a ramp from which they can be loaded on an arriving vehicle. The seller may also assist the buyer with the loading of the goods on the vehicle, e.g. by using a fork-lift truck. If it is intended that the seller assist the buyer as above, this could be made clear by the parties' adding the words "loaded upon departing vehicle" after EXW in the contract of sale.

A5 Transfer of risks

Subject to the provisions of B.5., bear all risks of loss of or damage to the goods until such time as they have been placed at the disposal of the buyer in accordance with A.4.

Comments

All Incoterms are based on the same principle that the risk of loss of or damage to the goods is transferred from the seller to the buyer when the seller has fulfilled his delivery obligation according to A4.

All Incoterms, in conformity with the general principle of CISG (Convention on the International Sale of Goods), connect the transfer of the risk with the delivery of the goods and not with other circumstances, such as the passing of ownership or the time of the conclusion of the contract. Neither Incoterms nor CISG deal with transfer of title to the goods or other property rights with respect to the goods.

The passing of risk of loss of or damage to the goods concerns the risk of fortuitous events (accidents) and does not include loss or damage caused by the seller or the buyer, e.g. through inadequate packing or marking of the goods. Therefore, even if damage occurs subsequent to the transfer of the risk, the seller may still be responsible if the damage could be attributed to the fact that the goods were not delivered in conformity with the contract (See A1 and the comments to A9).

A5 of all Incoterms starts with the phrase "subject to the provisions of B5". This means that there are exceptions to the main rule in the circumstances described in B5 which may result in a premature passing of the risk because of the buyer's failure properly to fulfil his obligations (See the comments to B5).

A6 Division of costs

Subject to the provisions of B.6., pay all costs relating to the goods until such time as they have been placed at the disposal of the buyer in accordance with A.4.

Comments

As is the case with the transfer of the risk of loss of or damage to the goods, all Incoterms follow the same rule, that the division of costs occurs at the delivery point. All costs occurring before the seller has fulfilled his obligation to deliver according to A4 are for his account, while further costs are for the account of the buyer (See the comments to B6). This rule is made subject to the provisions of B6, which indicates that the buyer may have to bear additional costs incurred by his failure to give appropriate notice to the seller.

Since under EXW the seller's obligation is limited to placing the goods at the disposal of the buyer, all further costs have to be borne by the buyer once the goods have been placed at his disposal. The seller has no duty to bear any costs incurred for export clearance, since under B2 this is the buyer's obligation.

A7 Notice to the buyer

Give the buyer sufficient notice as to when and where the goods will be placed at his disposal.

Comments

The seller must give the buyer sufficient notice as to when the goods will be available at the agreed or chosen delivery point, so that the buyer can make preparations in time to take delivery according to B4. There is no stipulation in Incoterms spelling out the consequences of the seller's failure to give such notice. But it follows from Incoterms that the seller's failure constitutes a breach of contract. This means that the seller could be held responsible for such a breach, according to the law applicable to the contract of sale.

A8 Proof of delivery, transport document or equivalent electronic message

No obligation.

Comments

Since the seller makes the goods available at his premises, or at a named place of delivery in his own country, no particular proof of delivery is required.

A9 Checking - packaging - marking

Pay the costs of those checking operations (such as checking quality, measuring, weighing, counting) which are necessary for the purpose of placing the goods at the disposal of the buyer.

Provide at his own expense packaging (unless it is usual for the particular trade to make the goods of the contract description available unpacked) which is required for the transport of the goods, to the extent that the circumstances relating to the transport (e.g. modalities, destination) are made known to the seller before the contract of sale is concluded. Packaging is to be marked appropriately.

Comments

It is necessary for the buyer to ensure that the seller has duly fulfilled his obligation with respect to the condition of the goods. This is particularly important if the buyer is called upon to pay for the goods before he has received and checked them. However, the seller has no duty to arrange and pay for inspection of the goods before shipment, unless this has been specifically agreed in the contract of sale.

The goods must also be adequately packed. But the seller may not know the buyer's intentions concerning the mode of transport and the ultimate destination. There is a considerable difference between a short journey to an adjoining country and an intercontinental carriage by sea, which may expose the goods to the risk of breakage or corrosion from humidity and condensation.

The seller is only obliged to pack the goods for a long and difficult carriage if he knows that this will actually occur. Therefore, it is advisable for the buyer to inform the seller accordingly, or, better still, to specify the required packaging in the contract of sale.

A10 Other obligations

Render the buyer at the latter's request, risk and expense, every assistance in obtaining any documents or equivalent electronic messages issued or transmitted in the country of delivery and/or of origin which the buyer may require for the exportation and/or importation of the goods and, where necessary, for their transit through another country.

Provide the buyer, upon request, with the necessary information for procuring insurance.

Comments

Since it is for the buyer to do whatever is necessary with respect to export, transit and import clearance, he may well need the seller's assistance to obtain documents (e.g. a certificate of origin, health certificate, clean report of finding, import licence) or equivalent EDI messages issued or transmitted in the country of delivery or importation. But any cost incurred by the seller in rendering this assistance must be reimbursed to him by the buyer, according to B10.

Also, the seller may be requested to provide the buyer with information relating to the goods which the buyer may require for insurance purposes, if this information does not follow from the description of the goods in the contract of sale.

B THE BUYER MUST

B1 Payment of the price

Pay the price as provided in the contract of sale.

Comments

The buyer must pay the price agreed in the contract of sale. B1 constitutes a reminder of this main obligation, which corresponds with the seller's obligation to provide the goods in conformity with the contract of sale, as stipulated in A1.

B2 Licences, authorisations and formalities

Obtain at his own risk and expense any export and import licence or other official authorisation and carry out all customs formalities for the exportation and importation of the goods and, where necessary, for their transit through another country.

Comments

Since the seller only makes the goods available to the buyer in the country of dispatch, it is for the buyer to do whatever is necessary with respect to the clearance of the goods for export, transit and import. A prohibition of export or import will not relieve the buyer from his obligation under the contract of sale. However, contracts of sale frequently contain "relief clauses" to the benefit of both parties in such cases. These clauses may stipulate that the affected party will be given the benefit of an extension of time to fulfil his obligation or, under the worst circumstances, the right to avoid the contract. It may also be possible to obtain such relief under the law applicable to the contract of sale.

Before accepting the obligation to clear the goods for export, the buyer should ascertain that the regulations of the seller's country do not prevent him as a non-resident from applying for an export licence or from performing whatever tasks are necessary to clear the goods for export. Normally, no such difficulties will be encountered, since measures in this regard can be taken by freight forwarders (customs brokers) on the buyer's behalf. If the buyer wishes to avoid the obligation to clear the goods for export, the words "cleared for export" could be added after EXW.

B3 Contract of carriage

No obligation.

Comments

The buyer has no obligation to the seller under the contract of sale to contract for carriage, except as required in order to take delivery according to B4. This is made clear by the words "no obligation" in B3. But he can nevertheless arrange for carriage <u>in his own interest</u>.

B4 Taking delivery

Take delivery of the goods as soon as they have been placed at his disposal in accordance with A.4.

Comments

The buyer must take delivery of the goods when they have been placed at his disposal at the agreed time and place as stipulated in A4. His failure to do so will not relieve him from his obligation to pay the price and could result in a premature passing of the risk of loss of or damage to the goods or make him liable to pay additional costs according to B5 and B6.

B5 Transfer of risks

Bear all risks of loss of or damage to the goods from the time they have been placed at his disposal in accordance with A.4.

Should he fail to give notice in accordance with B. 7., bear all risks of loss of or damage to the goods from the agreed date or the expiry date of any period fixed for taking delivery provided, however, that the goods have been duly appropriated to the contract, that is to say clearly set aside or otherwise identified as the contract goods.

Comments

According to the main rule, while the seller under A5 bears the risk of loss of or damage to the goods until the delivery point, the buyer has to bear the risk thereafter. The delivery point is different under the different terms. In EXW and all D-terms the goods are simply placed "at the disposal of the buyer" at the relevant point, while under the F- and C-terms the delivery point is related to the handing over of the goods to the carrier in the country of dispatch or shipment (See the comments to A4 of these terms). In the terms used for goods intended to be carried by sea, reference is made to delivery alongside the named vessel (FAS A4) or delivery onboard the vessel (FOB, CFR, CIF).

Consequences of buyer's failure to give notice

While the seller under EXW and all D-terms can transfer the risk by his own act of placing the goods at the buyer's disposal, he may be prevented from doing so by the buyer's failure to give notice according to B7. This can occur when it is the buyer's responsibility to determine (1) the time within a stipulated period when the goods are to be made available or (2) the place of delivery (See the comments to B7). The failure to perform these tasks results in a premature passing of the risk: It is not acceptable that the buyer should be able to delay the delivery and the passing of the risk longer than contemplated when the contract of sale was made. Therefore, his failure to notify according to B7 will cause the risk to pass "from the agreed date or the expiry date of any period fixed for taking delivery".

Appropriation and the passing of risk

The risk, however, cannot pass until the goods "have been duly appropriated to the contract". If the goods are unascertained - i.e. goods of a certain kind which the seller will deliver to his various buyers - appropriation occurs only when the goods are "clearly set aside or otherwise identified as the contract goods".

B6 Division of costs

Pay all costs relating to the goods from the time they have been placed at his disposal in accordance with A.4.

Pay any additional costs incurred by failing either to take delivery of the goods when they have been placed at his disposal, or to give appropriate notice in accordance with B. 7. provided, however, that the goods have been duly appropriated to the contract, that is to say clearly set aside or otherwise identified as the contract goods.

Pay all duties, taxes and other official charges as well as the costs of carrying out customs formalities payable upon exportation and importation of the goods and, where necessary, for their transit through another country.

Reimburse all costs and charges incurred by the seller in rendering assistance in accordance with A.2.

Comments

Although the seller's obligation is limited to placing the goods at the disposal of the buyer at the seller's own premises, EXW A4 does not indicate exactly how this should be done. In practice, the seller will often assist the buyer by bringing the goods onto a ramp from which they can be loaded on a vehicle for carriage from the seller's place. Or the seller may assist the buyer with the loading of the goods on this vehicle, e.g. by placing them on the vehicle by the use of a fork-lift truck. In these cases, sellers will not usually debit their buyers with costs for work performed by the seller's own personnel and/or for the use of the seller's own equipment. However, if the goods are to be taken from an independent warehouse and the seller stands to incur external costs, he would, according to the main principle of B6, be entitled to debit such costs to the buyer.

Normally, the extent to which the seller will assist the buyer free of charge in removing the goods from the seller's premises will be determined from previous dealings between the same parties or from the custom of the trade. If, however, the parties agree that the seller should perform the loading of the goods, the words "loaded upon departing vehicle" may be added after EXW in the contract of sale.

Notice and appropriation

Whenever the buyer is entitled to determine the time or place of taking delivery, his failure to notify the seller according to B7 will not only cause the risk of loss of or damage to the goods to pass prematurely but will also make him liable to pay any additional costs caused thereby, e.g. extra costs for storage and insurance. However, this liability only occurs if the goods have been identified as the contractual goods (See the comments concerning "appropriation" under B5).

Buyer clears goods for export

Under EXW the buyer has to clear the goods for export. Consequently, he will have to pay "all duties, taxes and other official charges as well as the costs of carrying out customs formalities" and reimburse the seller for any assistance the seller provides in performing these tasks.

B7 Notice to the seller

Whenever he is entitled to determine the time within a stipulated period and/or the place of taking delivery, give the seller sufficient notice thereof.

Comments

As discussed in the comments to B5 and B6, the failure of the buyer to notify the seller of the time for shipping the goods or the destination - when the buyer in the contract of sale has been given the option to determine these matters - may cause the risk of the loss of or damage to the goods to pass before the goods have been delivered according to A4. In addition, it can make the buyer liable to pay any additional costs incurred by the seller as a result of the buyer's failure.

B8 Proof of delivery, transport document or equivalent electronic message

Provide the seller with appropriate evidence of having taken delivery.

Comments

The buyer should provide the seller with a customary receipt for the goods. This receipt could be indicated on a packing list or with some other document which could constitute "appropriate evidence".

B9 Inspection of goods

Pay, unless otherwise agreed, the costs of pre-shipment inspection (including inspection mandated by the authorities of the country of exportation).

Comments

As noted in the comments to A9, the buyer has to pay for any costs of checking the goods, unless the contract determines that these costs should be wholly or partly borne by the seller. In some cases, the contract may provide that the costs should be borne by the seller if the inspection reveals that the goods do not conform with the contract.

Pre-shipment inspection

In some countries, where import licences or permission to obtain foreign currency for the payment of the price may be required, the authorities may demand an inspection of the goods before shipment, to ensure that the goods are in conformity with the contract. (This is usually called pre-shipment inspection, PSI.) If this is the case, the inspection is normally arranged by instructions from the authorities to an inspection company, which they appoint. The costs following from this inspection have to be paid by the authorities. Any reimbursement to the authorities for the inspection costs, however, must be made by the buyer, unless otherwise specifically agreed between the buyer and the seller.

B10 Other obligations

Pay all costs and charges incurred in obtaining the documents or equivalent electronic messages mentioned in A.10. and reimburse those incurred by the seller in rendering his assistance in accordance therewith.

Comments

As discussed in the comments to A10, the seller has to render the buyer assistance in obtaining the documents or electronic messages which may be required for the transit and importation of the goods. However, this assistance is rendered at the buyer's risk and expense. Therefore, B10 stipulates that the buyer must pay all costs and charges incurred in obtaining these documents or electronic messages. He will also have to reimburse the seller for the seller's costs in rendering his assistance in these matters.

FREE CARRIER
(... named place)

A SELLER'S PRIMARY DUTIES

- Deliver the goods at the named point into the custody of the carrier named by the buyer (**A4**)
- Provide export clearance (export licence, pay export taxes and fees, if required) (**A2**)
- Provide evidence of delivery of the goods to the carrier (**A8**)

DIFFERENCE FROM *FOB*

As mentioned in the brief description of the term, FREE CARRIER (FCA) is based on the same main principle as FOB. However, the seller fulfills his obligations by delivering the goods at the named point into t

DOCUMENTS

Required documents

- Commercial invoice (**A1**)
- Usual document evidencing delivery of the goods to the carrier (**A8**)
- Export licence (**A2**)

NOTE:
All documents may be replaced by EDI messages

Goods

PRE-CARRIAGE

MAIN

Seller's risk

Seller's costs

Critical point

ee Carrier" means that the seller fulfils his obligation to iver when he has handed over the goods, cleared for ort, into the charge of the carrier named by the buyer at named place or point. If no precise point is indicated by buyer, the seller may choose within the place or range ulated where the carrier shall take the goods into his rge. When, according to commercial practice, the seller's istance is required in making the contract with the carrier ch as in rail or air transport) the seller may act at the er's risk and expense.

s term may be used for any mode of transport, including ltimodal transport.

rrier" means any person who, in a contract of carriage, lertakes to perform or to procure the performance of carriage by rail, road, sea, air, inland waterway or by a combination of such modes. If the buyer instructs the seller to deliver the cargo to a person, e.g. a freight forwarder who is not a "carrier", the seller is deemed to have fulfilled his obligation to deliver the goods when they are in the custody of that person.

"Transport terminal" means a railway terminal, a freight station, a container terminal or yard, a multi-purpose cargo terminal or any similar receiving point.

"Container" includes any equipment used to unitise cargo, e.g. all types of containers and/or flats, whether ISO accepted or not, trailers, swap bodies, ro-ro equipment, igloos, and applies to all modes of transport.

tody of the carrier nominated the buyer. The risk of loss of lamage to the goods is isferred from the seller to the er when the goods have been delivered and not at the ship's as in FOB.

tional documents

ther documents needed for ansit of the goods through nother country or for import earance (**A10**)

B BUYER'S PRIMARY DUTIES

- Nominate carrier (**B3**)
- Contract for the carriage and pay the freight (**B3** but see **A3a**)

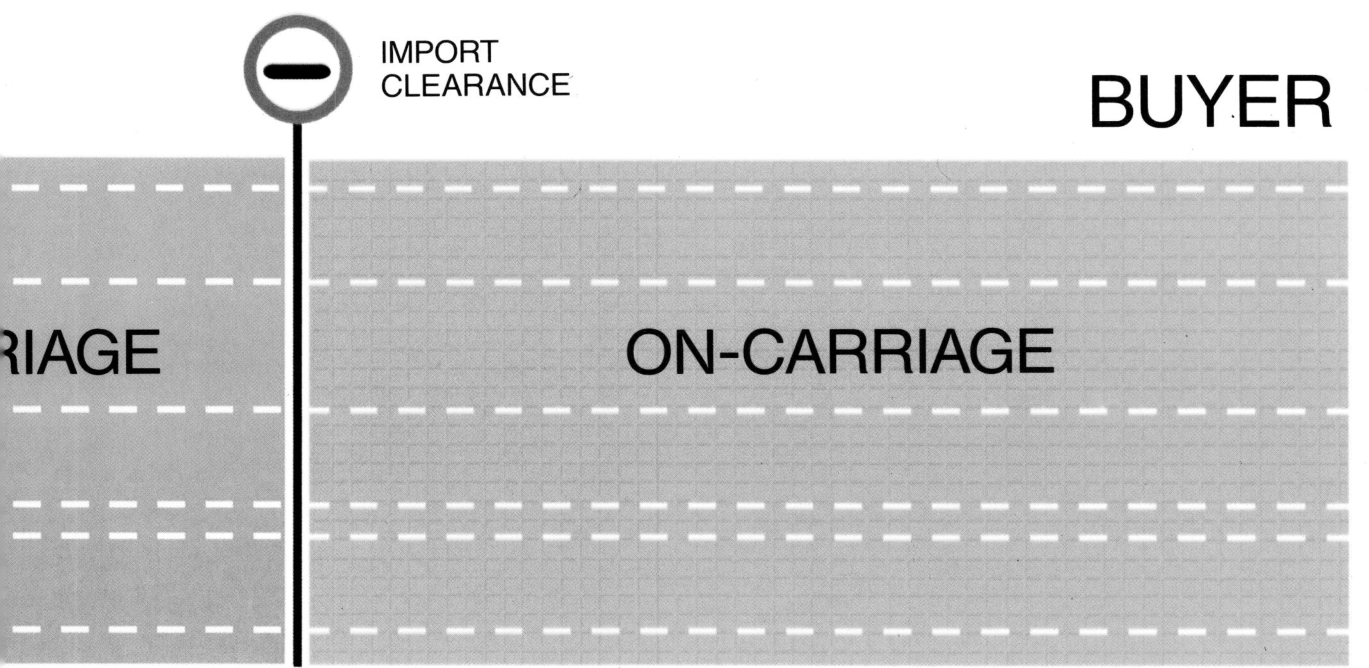

Group F: **Main carriage not paid by seller**

FCA FREE CARRIER
(... named place)

A THE SELLER MUST

A1 Provision of goods in conformity with the contract

Provide the goods and the commercial invoice, or its equivalent electronic message, in conformity with the contract of sale and any other evidence of conformity which may be required by the contract.

Comments

The seller must provide the goods in conformity with the contract. It is also usual practice that the seller, in order to be paid, has to invoice the buyer. In addition, the seller must submit any other evidence stipulated in the contract itself that the goods conform with the contract.

This text only serves as a reminder of the seller's main obligation under the contract of sale.

A2 Licences, authorisations and formalities

Obtain at his own risk and expense any export licence or other official authorisation and carry out all customs formalities necessary for the exportation of the goods.

Comments

The seller has to clear the goods for export and assume any risk or expense which this involves. Consequently, if there is an export prohibition or if there are particular taxes on the export of the goods - and if there are other government-imposed requirements which may render the export of the goods more expensive than contemplated - all of these risks and costs must be borne by the seller. However, contracts of sale usually contain particular provisions which the seller may invoke to protect himself in the event of these contingencies. Under the 1980 Convention on International Sale of Goods (CISG) and corresponding provisions in various national Sale of Goods Acts, unforeseen or reasonably unforeseeable export prohibitions may relieve the seller from his obligations under the contract of sale.

A3 Contract of carriage and insurance

a) Contract of carriage
No obligation. However, if requested by the buyer or if it is commercial practice and the buyer does not give an instruction to the contrary in due time, the seller may contract for carriage on usual terms at the buyer's risk and expense. The seller may decline to make the contract and, if he does, shall promptly notify the buyer accordingly.

b) Contract of insurance
No obligation.

Comments

The F-terms all mean that the seller's obligation is limited to handing over the goods to the carrier nominated by the buyer. Consequently, the seller has no obligation to contract for carriage. Nevertheless, if arranging for the carriage is not difficult and if the freight rate would be more or less the same regardless of whether the seller or the buyer contracts with the carrier, it is often more practical for the seller to contract for carriage at the buyer's risk and expense. This explains why, in many cases, a commercial practice has developed to this effect.

It should be stressed, however, that the seller has no obligation to contract for carriage as noted above and that the buyer does not have to let him do so. If there is a commercial practice between the two parties, then under F-terms the seller may contract for carriage as an additional service to the buyer, unless the buyer in due time has instructed the seller not to do so.

Therefore, if it is possible for the buyer to obtain a better freight rate than the seller, or if there are other reasons for him to exercise his right to contract for carriage (e.g. government directions), he must inform the seller accordingly, preferably when the contract of sale is made. Otherwise, problems and additional expenses may follow if both parties contract for carriage assuming that the other party did not.

Conversely, the seller must promptly inform the buyer if for some reason he does not wish to follow the buyer's request to contract for carriage or to adhere to commercial practice. Otherwise, additional expenses and risks may occur as a result of the failure to arrange for carriage in due time. In any event, the seller does not incur any risk in complying with the buyer's request or with commercial practice, since whatever he does or intends to do is at the buyer's risk and expense.

If transport becomes temporarily unavailable or more expensive, the buyer under all F-terms has to bear these risks.

The seller, even under F-terms, has to contract for any carriage required to reach the place where the parties have agreed that the goods should be handed over for carriage, as for example, when the goods are to be carried from an inland point to an ocean carrier to be named by the buyer. This pre-carriage would be for the seller's account.

A4 Delivery

Deliver the goods into the custody of the carrier or another person (e.g. a freight forwarder) named by the buyer, or chosen by the seller in accordance with A.3.a), at the named place or point (e.g. transport terminal or other receiving point) on the date or within the period agreed for delivery and in the manner agreed or customary at such point. If no specific point has been agreed, and if there are several points available, the seller may select the point at the place of delivery which best suits his purpose. Failing precise instructions from the buyer, the seller may deliver the goods to the carrier in such a manner as the transport mode of that carrier and the quantity and/or nature of the goods may require.

Delivery to the carrier is completed:

I) In the case of rail transport when the goods constitute a wagon load (or a container load carried by rail) the seller has to load the wagon or container in the appropriate manner. Delivery is completed when the loaded wagon or container is taken over by the railway or by another person acting on its behalf.

When the goods do not constitute a wagon or container load, delivery is completed when the seller has handed over the goods at the railway receiving point or loaded them into a vehicle provided by the railway.

II) In the case of road transport when loading takes place at the seller's premises, delivery is completed when the goods have been loaded on the vehicle provided by the buyer.

When the goods are delivered to the carrier's premises, delivery is completed when they have been handed over to the road carrier or to another person acting on his behalf.

III) In the case of transport by inland waterway when loading takes place at the seller's premises, delivery is completed when the goods have been loaded on the carrying vessel provided by the buyer.

When the goods are delivered to the carrier's premises, delivery is completed when they have been handed over to the inland waterway carrier or to another person acting on his behalf.

IV) In the case of sea transport when the goods constitute a full container load (FCL), delivery is completed when the loaded container is taken over by the sea carrier. When the container has been carried to an operator of a transport terminal acting on behalf of the carrier, the goods shall be deemed to have been taken over when the container has entered into the premises of that terminal.

When the goods are less than a container load (LCL), or are not to be containerised, the seller has to carry them to the transport terminal. Delivery is completed when the goods have been handed over to the sea carrier or to another person acting on his behalf.

V) In the case of air transport, delivery is completed when the goods have been handed over to the air carrier or to another person acting on his behalf.

VI) In the case of unnamed transport, delivery is completed when the goods have been handed over to the carrier or to another person acting on his behalf.

VII) In the case of multimodal transport, delivery is completed when the goods have been handed over as specified in I) - VI), as the case may be.

Comments

FCA, as first presented in Incoterms 1980 (where it was referred to as FRC), was primarily intended to solve the particular problems arising from changed cargo handling techniques, such as containerisation or other means of assembling parcel cargo in transportation units before the vehicle of transport arrived. Therefore, FCA can be used instead of FOB, the latter of which is intended to be used in cases where the seller tenders the goods over the ship's rail. By using FCA instead of FOB, the point of delivery is moved from the ship's rail to the prior point where the goods are delivered to the carrier, either at his cargo terminal or to a vehicle sent to pick up the goods after they have been containerised or otherwise assembled in transportation units at the seller's premises.

Changes from 1980 Incoterms

In the 1980 version of Incoterms, FCA (then called FRC) could be used for any mode of transport, even though the specific terms for rail and air carriage (FOR/FOT and FOB Airport) were available for these modes. Now that FOR/FOT and FOB Airport have been removed from Incoterms 1990, the ICC believed that FCA should spell out in more detail how the goods are handed over for transport. This allows the multipurpose character of FCA to be demonstrated more effectively.

However, it must be borne in mind that all F-terms require the buyer to arrange and pay for the carriage, and the manner in which the seller hands over the goods for carriage necessarily depends upon the kind of contract of carriage the buyer has made.

Stipulations on handing over and delivery advisable in contract of sale

It is vital for the seller to know at the time he makes his offer what he may be required to do according to the contract of sale, since this may well affect his costs and should therefore be reflected in the price. Ideally, in the contract of sale the parties should agree on a precise point for the delivery of the goods to the carrier and make clear how the goods should be handed over to him, e.g. by naming the carrier's cargo terminal and specifying if the goods should be delivered containerised or not.

Even as early as when the seller makes his offer, it may be possible to know whether the buyer should arrange with the carrier to send a container or vehicle to the seller's premises.

If this is known, it is advisable for the parties to stipulate in the contract of sale that the goods should be handed over for carriage at the seller's premises. If at the time the contract of sale is concluded, the buyer wishes to have the option later to decide (1) the point where the goods should be handed over for carriage or (2) the mode of transport, it is important to determine the extent of the buyer's options concerning these matters and the time within which he must exercise them. If the buyer is not given options but a place where the carrier has several receiving points is mentioned in the contract, the seller "may select the point at the place of delivery which best suits his purpose".

Normally, it would follow from the mode of transport and the carrier's receiving point exactly how the goods should be handed over for carriage. But, as noted in the preceding paragraph, there may be different alternatives for the handing over, and, failing precise stipulations or instructions in the contract of sale, the goods may be handed over to the carrier "in such manner as the transport mode of that carrier and the quantity and/or nature of the goods may require".

The quantity and nature of the goods will determine whether the goods should be containerised by the seller as homogeneous cargo in one full load in a so-called FCL-container, or by the carrier at his cargo terminal as parcel cargo together with cargo from other shippers in a so-called LCL-container.

Who is a carrier?

Since the carrier under FCA is named by the buyer, it is normally not necessary to decide whether the entity named can be regarded as a "carrier" according to the law applicable to the contract of sale and the contract of carriage. The seller merely has to accept the buyer's nomination. Therefore, the buyer is not compelled to name someone who has the status of a carrier in a legal sense; he could also name "another person (e.g. a freight forwarder)".

It has been deemed important specifically to mention freight forwarders, since in practice it may be difficult to decide whether the forwarder should be regarded as a "carrier" (e.g. when he actually performs the carriage or assumes liability as a so-called contracting carrier) or merely as an agent without the status of a "carrier".

However, the problem of deciding whether the person engaged for the carriage is a "carrier" in the legal sense may arise whenever the seller chooses this person in accordance with A3. The seller must then "contract for carriage on usual terms at the buyer's risk and expense" and, unless otherwise agreed, arrange a contract of carriage and not merely a contract of forwarding agency.

A contract of carriage may be entered into with organisations which do not physically perform the carriage as long as they assume liability as carriers for the carriage; (See Article 25 of the ICC Uniform Rules for Documentary Credits 1983, which specifically refers to the FIATA Combined Transport Bill of Lading ["FBL"], a freight forwarder document evidencing the forwarder's status as contracting carrier).

Delivery for carriage

While it is impossible to foresee and to define delivery for carriage for different kinds of carriers operating in different places under widely differing conditions, FCA A4 nevertheless sets forth some general principles to determine when "delivery to the carrier is completed".

The goods need not necessarily be handed over to the carrier himself; they can also be handed over to "a person acting on his behalf", as is often the case. From a legal viewpoint this clarification is superfluous, since a person can act on someone else's behalf when he is duly authorised to do so. But the ICC deemed it appropriate to make this clear, to avoid any unnecessary misunderstandings.

A5 Transfer of risks

Subject to the provisions of B.5., bear all risks of loss of or damage to the goods until such time as they have been delivered in accordance with A.4.

Comments

All Incoterms are based on the same principle that the risk of loss of or damage to the goods is transferred from the seller to the buyer when the seller has fulfilled his delivery obligation according to A4. A5 of FOB, CFR and CIF further specifies that the risk is transferred when the goods "have passed the ship's rail at the named port of shipment".

All Incoterms, in conformity with the general principle of CISG (Convention on the International Sale of Goods) connect the transfer of the risk with the delivery of the goods and not with other circumstances, such as the passing of ownership or the time of the conclusion of the contract. Neither Incoterms nor CISG deal with transfer of title to the goods or other property rights with respect to the goods.

The passing of risk for loss of or damage to the goods concerns the risk of fortuitous events (accidents) and does not include loss or damage caused by the seller or the buyer, e.g. through inadequate packing or marking of the goods. Therefore, even if damage occurs subsequent to the transfer of the risk, the seller may still be responsible if the damage could be attributed to the fact that the goods were not delivered in conformity with the contract (See A1 and the comments to A9).

A5 of all Incoterms starts with the phrase "subject to the provisions of B5". This means that there are exceptions to the main rule in the circumstances described in B5 which may result in a premature passing of the risk because of the buyer's failure properly to fulfil his obligations (See the comments to B5).

A6 Division of costs

Subject to the provisions of B.6.

- pay all costs relating to the goods until such time as they have been delivered to the carrier in accordance with A.4.;
- pay the costs of customs formalities as well as all duties, taxes, and other official charges payable upon exportation.

Comments

As is the case with the transfer of the risk of loss of or damage to the goods, all Incoterms follow the same rule, that the division of costs occurs at the delivery point. All costs occurring before the seller has fulfilled his obligation to deliver according to A4 are for his account, while further costs are for the account of the buyer (See the comments to B6). This rule is made subject to the provisions of B6, which indicates that the buyer may have to bear additional costs incurred by his failure to give appropriate notice to the seller.

Since the seller's obligation is limited to handing over the goods to the carrier named by the buyer, all further costs have to be borne by the buyer once the goods have been delivered in this way. The seller must, however, pay the costs of customs formalities as well as all duties, taxes and other official charges payable upon exportation.

A7 Notice to the buyer

Give the buyer sufficient notice that the goods have been delivered into the custody of the carrier. Should the carrier fail to take the goods into his charge at the time agreed, the seller must notitfy the buyer accordingly.

Comments

The seller must give the buyer sufficient notice as to when the goods will be available at the agreed or chosen delivery point, so that the buyer can make preparations in time to take delivery according to B4. There is no stipulation in Incoterms spelling out the consequences of the seller's failure to give such notice. But it follows from Incoterms that the seller's failure constitutes a breach of contract. This means that the seller could be held responsible for such a breach, according to the law applicable to the contract of sale.

The seller must also inform the buyer if the carrier fails to take the goods into his charge at the time agreed. There is no similar stipulation in the other Incoterms, since, under all C- and D-terms, the consequences of any failure of the carrier to take the goods into his charge have to be borne by the seller. Under EXW and other F-terms, the buyer is assumed to have full control of the carrier he names. The duty to notify according to FCA follows from FCA A3a, according to which the seller may contract for carriage at the buyer's risk and expense. Consequently, he has to notify the buyer if something goes wrong.

A8 Proof of delivery, transport document or equivalent electronic message

Provide the buyer at the seller's expense, if customary, with the usual document in proof of delivery of the goods in accordance with A.4.

Unless the document referred to in the preceding paragraph is the transport document, render the buyer at the latter's request, risk and expense, every assistance in obtaining a transport document for the contract of carriage (for example, a negotiable bill of lading, a non-negotiable sea waybill, an inland waterway document, an air waybill, a railway consignment note, a road consignment note, or a multimodal transport document).

When the seller and the buyer have agreed to communicate electronically, the document referred to in the preceding paragraph may be replaced by an equivalent electronic data interchange (EDI) message.

Comments

Since the seller has to hand over the goods for carriage, the carrier normally gives him a receipt which is usually identical to the transport document. If so, that document serves not only as evidence of the contract of carriage - which under F-terms is made by or on behalf of the buyer - but also as evidence of the delivery of the goods to the carrier.

If, however, the seller receives a document other than the transport document - for example, a so-called mate's receipt when the goods have been loaded onboard a ship chartered by the buyer - he should, upon the buyer's request, assist the buyer to obtain the transport document. This assistance is rendered at the buyer's risk and expense.

Whenever the parties have agreed to communicate electronically, documents may be replaced by EDI messages.

A9 Checking - packaging - marking

Pay the costs of those checking operations (such as checking quality, measuring, weighing, counting) which are necessary for the purpose of delivering the goods to the carrier.

Provide at his own expense packaging (unless it is usual for the particular trade to send the goods of the contract description unpacked) which is required for the transport of the goods, to the extent that the circumstances relating to the transport (e.g. modalities, destination) are made known to the seller before the contract of sale is concluded. Packaging is to be marked appropriately.

Comments

It is necessary for the buyer to ensure that the seller has duly fulfilled his obligation with respect to the condition of the goods. This is particularly important if the buyer is called upon to pay for the goods before he has received and checked them. However, the seller has no duty to arrange and pay for inspection of the goods before shipment, unless this has been specifically agreed in the contract of sale.

The goods must also be adequately packed. But the seller may not know the buyer's intentions concerning the mode of transport and the ultimate destination. There is a considerable difference between a short journey to an adjoining country and an intercontinental carriage by sea, which may expose the goods to the risk of breakage or corrosion from humidity and condensation.

The seller is only obliged to pack the goods for a long and difficult carriage if he knows that this will actually occur. Therefore, it is advisable for the buyer to inform the seller accordingly, or, better still, to specify the required packaging in the contract of sale.

A10 Other obligations

Render the buyer at the latter's request, risk and expense, every assistance in obtaining any documents or equivalent electronic messages (other than those mentioned in A.8.) issued or transmitted in the country of delivery and/or of origin which the buyer may require for the importation of the goods and, where necessary, for their transit through another country.

Provide the buyer, upon request, with the necessary information for procuring insurance.

Comments

Since it is for the buyer to do whatever is necessary with respect to transit and import clearance, he may well need the seller's assistance to obtain documents (e.g. a certificate of origin, health certificate, clean report of finding, import licence) or equivalent EDI messages issued or transmitted in the country of delivery and/or of origin. But any cost incurred by the seller in rendering this assistance must be reimbursed to him by the buyer, according to B10.

Also, the seller may be requested to provide the buyer with information relating to the goods which the buyer may require for insurance purposes, if this information does not follow from the description of the goods in the contract of sale.

FREE CARRIER

(... named place)

B THE BUYER MUST

B1 Payment of the price

Pay the price as provided in the contract of sale.

Comments

The buyer must pay the price agreed in the contract of sale. B1 constitutes a reminder of this main obligation, which corresponds with the seller's obligation to provide the goods in conformity with the contract of sale, as stipulated in A1.

B2 Licences, authorisations and formalities

Obtain at his own risk and expense any import licence or other official authorisation and carry out all customs formalities for the importation of the goods and, where necessary, for their transit through another country.

Comments

Since the seller fulfils his obligations by handing over the goods for carriage and clearing the goods for export, the buyer has to take care of any necessary transit formalities and clear the goods for import. These obligations of the buyer are specifically mentioned in B2.

B3 Contract of carriage

Contract at his own expense for the carriage of the goods from the named place, except as provided for in A.3.a).

Comments

Under all F-terms the buyer has the obligation to contract for carriage, though the seller may, as an additional service, arrange for carriage at the buyer's risk and expense. However, the contract for carriage starts "from the named place" and any prior carriage (pre-carriage) would have to be arranged by the seller (See A3).

B4 Taking delivery

Take delivery of the goods in accordance with A.4.

Comments

The buyer must take delivery of the goods when they have been placed at his disposal at the agreed time and place as stipulated in A4. His failure to do so will not relieve him from his obligation to pay the price and could result in a premature passing of the risk of loss of or damage to the goods or make him liable to pay additional costs according to B5 and B6.

B5 Transfer of risks

Bear all risks of loss of or damage to the goods from the time they have been delivered in accordance with A.4.

Should he fail to give notice in accordance with B.7., or should the carrier named by him fail to take the goods into his charge, bear all risks of loss of or damage to the goods from the agreed date or the expiry date of any period stipulated for delivery provided, however, that the goods have been duly appropriated to the contract, that is to say, clearly set aside or otherwise identified as the contract goods.

Comments

According to the main rule, while the seller under A5 bears the risk of loss of or damage to the goods until the delivery point, the buyer has to bear the risk thereafter. The delivery point is different under the different terms. In EXW and all D-terms the goods are simply placed "at the disposal of the buyer" at the relevant point, while under the F- and C-terms the delivery point is related to the handing over of the goods to the carrier in the country of dispatch or shipment (See the comments to A4 of these terms). In the terms used for goods intended to be carried by sea, reference is made to delivery alongside the named vessel (FAS A4) or delivery onboard the vessel (FOB, CFR, CIF).

The seller cannot - as under EXW and the D-terms - cause the goods to be delivered and the risk to pass unless he receives instructions or contracts for carriage himself when requested by the buyer or unless he acts according to commercial practice (See the comments to FCA A3a). When the buyer is responsible for making the contract of carriage and nominating the carrier and that carrier fails to take the goods into his charge, the buyer incurs the same liability as he would incur if he failed properly to nominate the carrier or to notify the seller of matters required for handing over the goods for carriage.

Appropriation and premature passing of risk

For risk to pass prematurely, it is required that the goods be able to be identified as the contract goods (i.e. they have to be "appropriated to the contract"). When the goods have been prepared for dispatch they have also normally been appropriated to the contract. But a failure of the buyer to give sufficient notice of the date or period of shipment according to B7 causes the seller to defer his preparations. If so, it may not be possible to identify some goods stored at the seller's premises or in an independent cargo terminal as the contract goods on the "agreed date or the expiry date of any period stipulated for delivery". The risk would then not pass until the appropriation has been made.

B6 Division of costs

Pay all costs relating to the goods from the time when they have been delivered in accordance with A.4.

Pay any additional costs incurred, either because he fails to name the carrier, or the carrier named by him fails to take the goods into his charge at the agreed time, or because he has failed to give appropriate notice in accordance with B.7. provided, however, that the goods have been duly appropriated to the contract, that is to say, clearly set aside or otherwise identified as the contract goods.

Pay all duties, taxes and other official charges as well as the costs of carrying out customs formalities payable upon importation of the goods and, where necessary, for their transit through another country.

Comments

Under FCA the seller fulfils his delivery obligation according to A4 by handing over the goods to the carrier. The buyer must pay the freight and other costs occurring subsequent to the delivery of the goods to the carrier.

Since the buyer has to contract for carriage he would also have to pay any additional costs incurred because "the carrier named by him fails to take the goods into his charge".

Whenever the buyer is entitled to determine the time or place of taking delivery, his failure to notify the seller according to B7 would not only cause the risk of loss of or damage to the goods to pass prematurely but would also make him liable to pay any additional costs caused thereby, e.g. extra costs for storage and insurance.

The liability to pay additional costs as noted above only occurs if the goods have been identified as the contract goods (See the comments on "appropriation" in B5).

B7 Notice to the seller

Give the seller sufficient notice of the name of the carrier and, where necessary, specify the mode of transport, as well as the date or period for delivering the goods to him and, as the case may be, the point within the place where the goods should be delivered to the carrier.

Comments

As discussed in the comments to B5 and B6, the failure of the buyer to notify the seller of the time for shipping the goods or the destination - when the buyer in the contract of sale has been given the option to determine these matters - may cause the risk of the loss of or damage to the goods to pass before the goods have been delivered according to A4. In addition, it can make the buyer liable to pay any additional costs incurred by the seller as a result of the buyer's failure.

The buyer's notice should inform the seller of the name of the carrier as well as of any further particulars relating to the delivery of the goods for carriage (such as the mode of transport and the exact point and time for the delivery) unless, of course, the carrier has been chosen by the seller according to A3.

B8 Proof of delivery, transport document or equivalent electronic message

Accept the proof of delivery in accordance with A.8.

Comments

The seller has to provide proof of delivery, and the buyer must accept that proof if it conforms with the contract and with the requirements of A8 (See comments to A8). If the buyer rejects the document giving proof (e.g. by instructions to a bank not to pay the seller under a documentary credit), he commits a breach of contract which would give the seller remedies available for the breach under the contract of sale (e.g. a right to cancel the contract or to claim damages for breach). However, the buyer is not obliged to accept a document which does not provide adequate proof of delivery, e.g. if there are notations on the document showing that the goods are defective or if the document indicates that the goods have been provided in less than the agreed quantity. The document is then considered to be "unclean".

B9 Inspection of goods

Pay, unless otherwise agreed, the costs of pre-shipment inspection except when mandated by the authorities of the country of exportation.

Comments

As noted in the comments to A9, the buyer has to pay for any costs of checking the goods, unless the contract determines that these costs should be wholly or partly borne by the seller. In some cases, the contract may provide that the costs should be borne by the seller if the inspection reveals that the goods do not conform with the contract.

In some countries, where import licences or permission to obtain foreign currency for the payment of the price may be required, the authorities may demand an inspection of the goods before shipment, to ensure that the goods are in conformity with the contract. (This is usually called pre-shipment inspection, PSI.) If this is the case, the inspection is normally arranged by instructions from the authorities to an inspection company, which they appoint. The costs following from this inspection have to be paid by the authorities. Any reimbursement to the authorities for the inspection costs, however, must be made by the buyer, unless otherwise specifically agreed between the buyer and the seller.

B10 Other obligations

Pay all costs and charges incurred in obtaining the documents or equivalent electronic messages mentioned in A.10. and reimburse those incurred by the seller in rendering his assistance in accordance therewith and in contracting for carriage in accordance with A.3.a).

Give the seller appropriate instructions whenever the seller's assistance in contracting for carriage is required in accordance with A.3.a).

Comments

As discussed in the comments to A10, the seller has to render the buyer assistance in obtaining the documents or electronic messages which may be required for the transit and importation of the goods. However, this assistance is rendered at the buyer's risk and expense. Therefore, B10 stipulates that the buyer must pay all costs and charges incurred in obtaining these documents or electronic messages. He will also have to reimburse the seller for the seller's costs in rendering his assistance in connection with these matters or in contracting for carriage in accordance with A3.

FREE ALONGSIDE SHI

(... named port of shipment)

A SELLER'S PRIMARY DUTIES

- Deliver the goods alongside the ship (**A4**)
- Provide an "alongside" receipt (**A8**)

DIFFERENCE FROM *FOB*

While FOB requires the seller to place the goods onboard the shi FAS only requires him to place them alongside. Further, under

DOCUMENTS

Required documents

- Commercial invoice (**A1**)
- Customary clean receipt, usually mate's receipt (**A8**)

NOTE:
All documents may be replaced by EDI messages

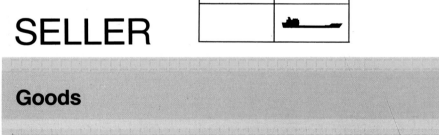

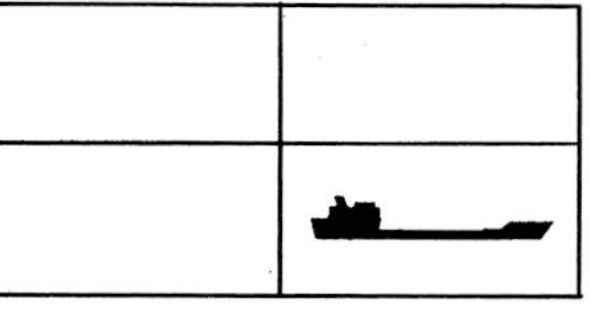

Goods

PRE-CARRIAGE

MAIN C

Seller's risk

Seller's costs

Critical point

ree Alongside Ship" means that the seller fulfils his bligation to deliver when the goods have been placed ongside the vessel on the quay or in lighters at the named ort of shipment. This means that the buyer has to bear all osts and risks of loss of or damage to the goods from that oment.

The FAS term requires the buyer to clear the goods for export. It should not be used when the buyer cannot carry out directly or indirectly the export formalities.
This term can only be used for sea or inland waterway transport.

OB, the seller must clear the oods for export, while such bligation under FAS falls upon e buyer.

ptional documents

- Other documents needed for export or transit of the goods through another country or for import clearance (**A10**)

B BUYER'S PRIMARY DUTIES

- Nominate carrier (**B3**)
- Contract for the carriage and pay the freight (**B3**)
- Provide export clearance (export licence, pay export taxes and fees, if required) (**B2**)

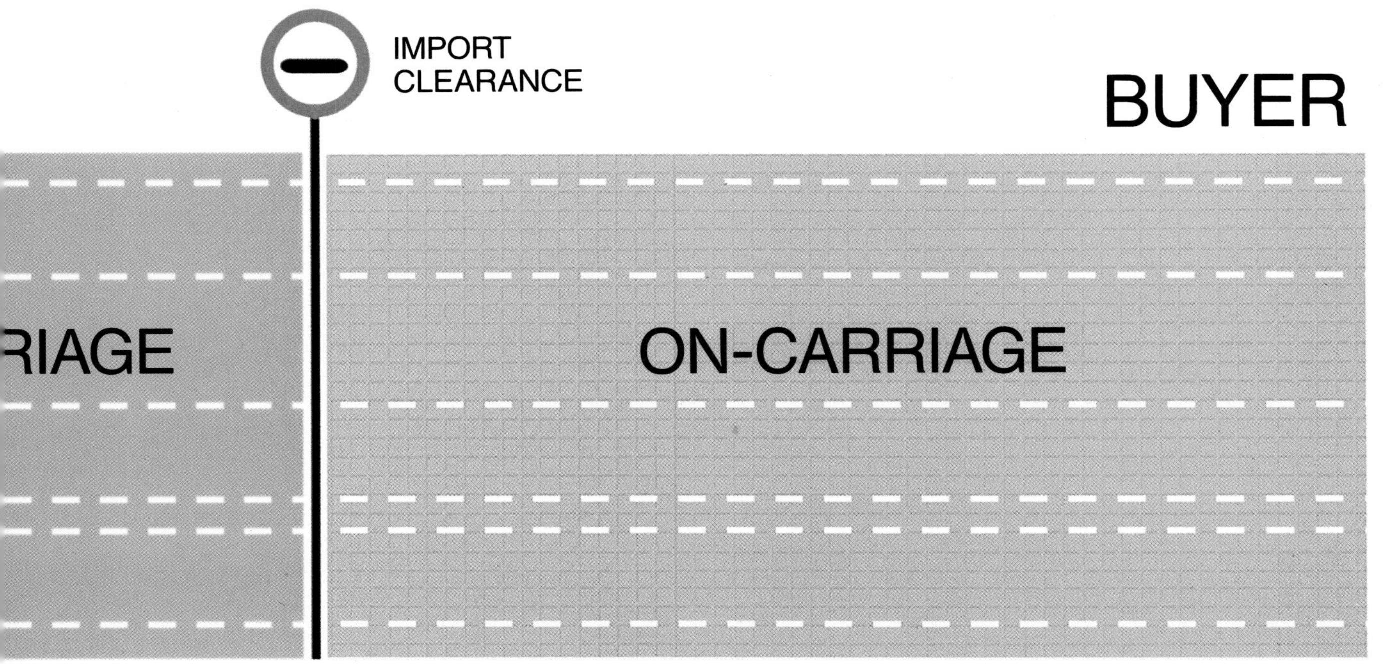

FREE ALONGSIDE SHIP

(... named port of shipment)

A THE SELLER MUST

A1 Provision of goods in conformity with the contract

Provide the goods and the commercial invoice, or its equivalent electronic message, in conformity with the contract of sale and any other evidence of conformity which may be required by the contract.

Comments

The seller must provide the goods in conformity with the contract. It is also usual practice that the seller, in order to be paid, has to invoice the buyer. In addition, the seller must submit any other evidence stipulated in the contract itself that the goods conform with the contract.

This text only serves as a reminder of the seller's main obligation under the contract of sale.

A2 Licences, authorisations and formalities

Render the buyer, at the latter's request, risk and expense, every assistance in obtaining any export licence or other official authorisation necessary for the exportation of the goods.

Comments

Under FAS it is the buyer's obligation to obtain export as well as import licences or other official authorisations. It is therefore the seller under this term who should render the necessary assistance.

A3 Contract of carriage and insurance

a) Contract of carriage
No obligation.

b) Contract of insurance
No obligation.

Comments

Since in A4 the goods should only be placed alongside the vessel named by the buyer, the seller has no obligation to contract for carriage or insurance.

A4 Delivery

Deliver the goods alongside the named vessel at the loading place named by the buyer at the named port of shipment on the date or within the period stipulated and in the manner customary at the port.

Comments

The seller fulfills his obligation to deliver the goods by placing them alongside the named vessel in the port of shipment, either on the quay or in lighters. Once this has been done any further risks and costs in loading the goods onboard are for the account of the buyer.

A5 Transfer of risks

Subject to the provisions of B.5., bear all risks of loss of or damage to the goods until such time as they have been delivered in accordance with A.4.

Comments

All Incoterms are based on the same principle that the risk of loss of or damage to the goods is transferred from the seller to the buyer when the seller has fulfilled his delivery obligation according to A4. A5 of FOB, CFR and CIF further specifies that the risk is transferred when the goods "have passed the ship's rail at the named port of shipment".

All Incoterms, in conformity with the general principle of CISG (Convention on the International Sale of Goods) connect the transfer of the risk with the delivery of the goods and not with other circumstances, such as the passing of ownership or the time of the conclusion of the contract. Neither Incoterms nor CISG deal with transfer of title to the goods or other property rights with respect to the goods.

The passing of risk for loss of or damage to the goods concerns the risk of fortuitous events (accidents) and does not include loss or damage caused by the seller or the buyer, e.g. through inadequate packing or marking of the goods. Therefore, even if damage occurs subsequent to the transfer of the risk, the seller may still be responsible if the damage could be attributed to the fact that the goods were not delivered in conformity with the contract (See A1 and the comments to A9).

A5 of all Incoterms starts with the phrase "subject to the provisions of B5". This means that there are exceptions to the main rule in the circumstances described in B5 which may result in a premature passing of the risk because of the buyer's failure properly to fulfil his obligations (See the comments to B5).

A6 Division of costs

Subject to the provisions of B.6., pay all costs relating to the goods until such time as they have been delivered in accordance with A.4.

Comments

As is the case with the transfer of the risk for loss of or damage to the goods, all Incoterms follow the same rule, that the division of costs occurs at the delivery point. All costs occurring before the seller has fulfilled his obligation to deliver according to A4 are for his account, while further costs are for the account of the buyer (See the comments to B6). This rule is made subject to the provisions of B6, which indicates that the buyer may have to bear additional costs incurred by his failure to give appropriate notice to the seller.

Since under FAS the seller's obligation is limited to delivering the goods alongside the vessel named by the buyer, all further costs have to be borne by the buyer once the goods have been made available in this manner. The seller has no duty to bear any costs incurred for export clearance, since under FAS B2 this is the buyer's obligation.

A7 Notice to the buyer

Give the buyer sufficient notice that the goods have been delivered alongside the named vessel.

Comments

The seller must give the buyer sufficient notice concerning when the goods have been placed alongside the named vessel. There is no stipulation in Incoterms spelling out the consequences of the seller's failure to give this notice. But it follows from Incoterms that the seller's failure constitutes a breach of contract. This means that the seller could be held responsible for the breach according to the law applicable to the contract of sale.

A8 Proof of delivery, transport document or equivalent electronic message

Provide the buyer at the seller's expense with the usual document in proof of delivery of the goods in accordance with A.4.

Unless the document referred to in the preceding paragraph is the transport document, render the buyer at the latter's request, risk and expense, every assistance in obtaining a transport document (for example, a negotiable bill of lading, a non-negotiable sea waybill, an inland waterway document).

When the seller and the buyer have agreed to communicate electronically, the document referred to in the preceding paragraphs may be replaced by an equivalent electronic data interchange (EDI) message.

Comments

Since the seller's obligation is limited to placing the goods alongside the named vessel, he may not always receive a receipt or a transport document from the carrier. The seller must then provide some other document to prove that the goods have been delivered. When requested by the buyer, the seller must assist the buyer to obtain the transport document or the equivalent EDI message. This assistance is at the buyer's risk and expense.

A9 Checking - packaging - marking

Pay the costs of those checking operations (such as checking quality, measuring, weighing, counting) which are necessary for the purpose of placing the goods at the disposal of the buyer.

Provide at his own expense packaging (unless it is usual for the particular trade to ship the goods of the contract description unpacked) which is required for the transport of the goods, to the extent that the circumstances relating to the transport (e.g. modalities, destination) are made known to the seller before the contract of sale is concluded. Packaging is to be marked appropriately.

Comments

The goods must also be adequately packed. But the seller may not know the buyer's intentions with respect to the ultimate destination. There is a considerable difference between a short journey to an adjoining country and an intercontinental carriage by sea, which may expose the goods to the risk of breakage or corrosion from humidity and condensation.

A10 Other obligations

Render the buyer at the latter's request, risk and expense, every assistance in obtaining any documents or equivalent electronic messages (other than those mentioned in A.8.) issued or transmitted in the country of shipment and/or of origin which the buyer may require for the exportation and/or importation of the goods and, where necessary, for their transit through another country.

Provide the buyer, upon request, with the necessary information for procuring insurance.

Comments

Since it is for the buyer to do whatever is necessary with respect to export, transit and import clearance, he may well need the seller's assistance to obtain documents (e.g. a certificate of origin, a health certificate, a clean report of finding, import licence) or equivalent EDI messages issued or transmitted in the country of delivery or importation. But any cost incurred by the seller in rendering this assistance must be reimbursed to him by the buyer, according to B10.

Also, the seller may be requested to provide the buyer with information relating to the goods which the buyer may require for insurance purposes, if this information does not follow from the description of the goods in the contract of sale.

FREE ALONGSIDE SHIP
(... named port of shipment)

B THE BUYER MUST

B1 Payment of the price

Pay the price as provided in the contract of sale.

Comments

The buyer must pay the price agreed in the contract of sale. B1 constitutes a reminder of this main obligation, which corresponds with the seller's obligation to provide the goods in conformity with the contract of sale, as stipulated in A1.

B2 Licences, authorisations and formalities

Obtain at his own risk and expense any export and import licence or other official authorisation and carry out all customs formalities for the exportation and importation of the goods and, where necessary, for their transit through another country.

Comments

Since the seller only makes the goods available to the buyer in the country of shipment, it is for the buyer to do whatever is necessary with respect to the clearance of the goods for export, transit and import. A prohibition of export or import, governmental or otherwise, will not relieve the buyer from his obligation under the contract of sale. However, contracts of sale frequently contain "relief clauses" to the benefit of both parties in such cases. These clauses may stipulate that the affected party will be given the benefit of an extension of time to fulfil his obligation or, under the worst circumstances, the right to avoid the contract. It may also be possible to obtain such relief under the law applicable to the contract of sale.

Before accepting the obligation to clear the goods for export, the buyer should ascertain that the regulations of the seller's country do not prevent him as a non-resident from applying for an export licence or from performing whatever tasks are necessary to clear the goods for export. Normally, no such difficulties will be encountered, since measures in this regard can be taken by freight forwarders (customs brokers) on the buyer's behalf. If the buyer wishes to avoid the obligation to clear the goods for export, the words "cleared for export" could be added after FAS.

B3 Contract of carriage

Contract at his own expense for the carriage of the goods from the named port of shipment.

Comments

In a strictly legal sense, the buyer under FAS has no obligation to the seller to contract for carriage except as required for the buyer to take delivery according to B4. This, however, still obliges the buyer to name and arrange for a vessel, so that the seller can deliver the goods alongside. Indeed in practice the buyer normally arranges for carriage in his own interest and does not let the ship remain in the port of loading. In this regard, FAS stipulates that the buyer must "contract at his own expense for the carriage of the goods from the named port of shipment".

B4 Taking delivery

Take delivery of the goods in accordance with A.4.

Comments

The buyer must take delivery of the goods when they have been placed alongside the vessel as stipulated in A4. His failure to do so would not relieve him from his obligation to pay the price and could further result in a premature passing of the risk of loss of or damage to the goods or make him liable to pay additional costs according to B5 and B6.

B5 Transfer of risks

Bear all risks of loss of or damage to the goods from the time they have been delivered in accordance with A.4.

Should he fail to fulfil his obligations in accordance with B.2., bear all additional risks of loss of or damage to the goods incurred thereby and should he fail to give notice in accordance with B.7., or should the vessel named by him fail to arrive on time, or be unable to take the goods, or close for cargo earlier than the stipulated time, bear all risks of loss of or damage to the goods from the agreed date or the expiry date of the period stipulated for delivery provided, however, that the goods have been duly appropriated to the contract, that is to say, clearly set aside or otherwise identified as the contract goods.

Comments

According to the main rule, while the seller under A5 bears the risk of loss of or damage to the goods until the delivery point, the buyer has to bear the risk thereafter. The delivery point is different under the different terms. In EXW and all D-terms the goods are simply placed "at the disposal of the buyer" at the relevant point, while under the F- and C-terms the delivery point is related to the handing over of the goods to the carrier in the country of dispatch or shipment (See the comments to A4 of these terms). In the terms used for goods intended to be carried by sea, reference is made to delivery alongside the named vessel (FAS A4) or delivery onboard the vessel (FOB, CFR, CIF).

Premature passing of the risk

The buyer's failure to notify the seller of the vessel name, loading place and required delivery time may result in a premature passing of the risk, as it cannot be accepted that the buyer should be able to delay the delivery and passing of the risk longer than contemplated when the contract of sale was made. Thus, his failure to notify according to B7 will cause the risk to pass "from the agreed date or the expiry date of the period stipulated for delivery".

A further problem can arise if the vessel fails to arrive in time, since in these cases the goods cannot be placed alongside as contemplated. Consequently, a premature passing of the risk could occur in these circumstances. The same result could also occur if the vessel is "unable to take the goods, or closes for cargo earlier than the stipulated time". In this latter case, the goods will remain at the buyer's risk.

A premature passing of the risk can also occur as a result of the buyer's failure properly to fulfil his obligation under B2 to clear the goods for export. If this happens, the goods may be exposed to risks of loss or damage longer than contemplated. These additional risks are for the account of the buyer. For risk to pass prematurely, it is required that the goods be able to be identified as the contract goods (i.e. they have to be "appropriated to the contract"). When the goods have been prepared for dispatch they have also normally been appropriated to the contract. But a failure of the buyer to give sufficient notice of the date or period of shipment according to B7 causes the seller to defer his preparations. If so, it may not be possible to identify some goods stored at the seller's premises or in an independent cargo terminal as the contract goods on the "agreed date or the expiry date of any period stipulated for delivery". The risk would then not pass until the appropriation has been made.

B6 Division of costs

Pay all costs relating to the goods from the time they have been delivered in accordance with A.4.

Pay any additional costs incurred, either because the vessel named by him has failed to arrive on time, or will be unable to take the goods, or will close for cargo earlier than the stipulated time, or because the buyer has failed to fulfil his obligations in accordance with B.2., or to give appropriate notice in accordance with B.7. provided, however, that the goods have been duly appropriated to the contract, that is to say, clearly set aside or otherwise identified as the contract goods.

Pay all duties, taxes and other official charges as well as the costs of carrying out customs formalities payable upon exportation and importation of the goods and, where necessary, for their transit through another country.

Pay all costs and charges incurred by the seller in rendering assistance in accordance with A.2.

Comments

Under FAS the seller fulfils his delivery obligation according to A4 by placing the goods alongside the vessel. The buyer must pay the freight and other costs occurring subsequently.

Since under FAS the buyer has to contract for carriage and nominate the ship, he also has to pay any additional costs incurred "because the vessel named by him has failed to arrive on time, or will be unable to take the goods, or will close for cargo earlier than the stipulated time" (See the corresponding rule for the premature passing of the risk in the comments to B5).

The failure of the buyer to notify the seller according to B7 will not only cause the risk of loss of or damage to the goods to pass prematurely, but will also make the buyer liable to pay any additional costs caused thereby, e.g. extra costs for storage and insurance.

A further problem could arise if the buyer fails to clear the goods for export, since it may then be impossible for the seller to place the goods alongside the vessel according to A4. If so, the buyer must bear any additional costs incurred by the seller, e.g. for storage and insurance of the goods pending the completion of the clearance (See the corresponding rule for the passing of the risk in the comments to B5).

For the buyer to be liable for additional costs according to B6, the goods to which these costs relate must be identifiable as the contract goods (See the comments on "appropriation under B5).

Under FAS, because the buyer has to clear the goods for export, he has to pay "all duties, taxes and other official charges as well as the costs of carrying out customs formalities" and to reimburse the seller for any assistance the seller renders him in this regard.

B7 Notice to the seller

Give the seller sufficient notice of the vessel name, loading place and required delivery time.

Comments

As discussed in the comments to B5 and B6, the failure of the buyer to notify the seller of the name of the vessel, the loading place and the required delivery time may cause the risk of the loss of or damage to the goods to pass before the goods have been delivered according to A4 and also make the buyer liable to pay any additional costs the seller incurs as a result of the buyer's failure.

B8 Proof of delivery, transport document or equivalent electronic message

Accept the proof of delivery in accordance with A.8.

Comments

The buyer must accept the seller's proof of delivery if the proof is adequate. If the buyer nevertheless rejects it (e.g. by instructions to a bank not to pay the seller under a documentary credit), he commits a breach of contract which will give the seller remedies for the breach available under the contract of sale (e.g. a right to cancel the contract or to claim damages for breach). However, the buyer is not obliged to accept a document which does not provide adequate proof of delivery. If there are notations on the document showing that the goods are defective or that they have been provided in less than the agreed quantity, the document is then considered to be "unclean".

B9 Inspection of goods

Pay, unless otherwise agreed, the costs of pre-shipment inspection (including inspection mandated by the authorities of the country of exportation).

Comments

As noted in the comments to A9, the buyer has to pay for any costs of checking the goods, unless the contract determines that these costs should be wholly or partly borne by the seller. In some cases, the contract may provide that the costs should be borne by the seller if the inspection reveals that the goods do not conform with the contract.

In some countries, where import licences or permission to obtain foreign currency for the payment of the price may be required, the authorities may demand an inspection of the goods before shipment to ensure that the goods are in conformity with the contract. (This is usually called pre-shipment inspection, PSI.) If this is the case, the inspection is normally arranged by instructions from the authorities to an inspection company, which they appoint.

The costs following from this inspection have to be paid by the authorities. Any reimbursement to the authorities for the inspection costs, however, must be made by the buyer, unless otherwise specifically agreed between the buyer and the seller.

B10 Other obligations

Pay all costs and charges incurred in obtaining the documents or equivalent electronic messages mentioned in A.10. and reimburse those incurred by the seller in rendering his assistance in accordance therewith.

Comments

As discussed in the comments to A10, the seller has to render the buyer assistance in obtaining the documents or electronic messages which may be required for the exportation, transit and importation of the goods. However, this assistance is rendered at the buyer's risk and expense. Therefore, B10 stipulates that the buyer must pay all costs and charges incurred in obtaining these documents or electronic messages. He will also have to reimburse the seller for the seller's costs in rendering his assistance in these matters.

FREE ON BOARD

(... named port of shipment)

A SELLER'S PRIMARY DUTIES

- Deliver the goods on board (**A4**)
- Provide export clearance (export licence, pay export taxes and fees, if required) (**A2**)
- Provide a clean on board receipt (**A8**)
- Pay loading costs according to the custom of the port to the extent that they are not included in the freight (**A6**)

DIFFERENCE FROM *FAS*

FAS is similar to a sale in the domestic market. Therefore, th seller does not have to arrange any export licence whilst for FC the seller must provide the exp

DOCUMENTS

Required documents

- Commercial invoice (**A1**)
- Customary clean receipt (**A8**)
- Export licence (**A2**)

NOTE:
All documents may be replaced by EDI messages

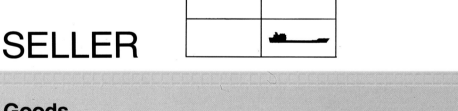

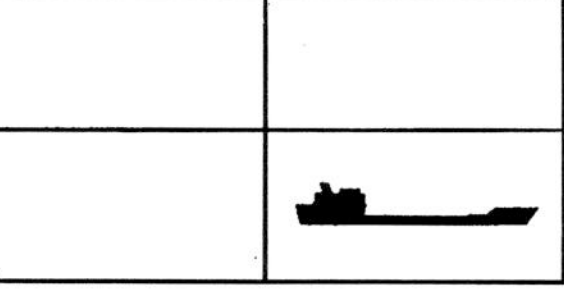

Goods

PRE-CARRIAGE

MAIN

Seller's risk

Seller's costs

Critical point

ee on Board" means that the seller fulfils his obligation deliver when the goods have passed over the ship's rail he named port of shipment. This means that the buyer s to bear all costs and risks of loss of or damage to the ods from that point.

The FOB term requires the seller to clear the goods for export.
This term can only be used for sea or inland waterway transport. When the ship's rail serves no practical purpose, such as in the case of roll-on/roll-off or container traffic, the FCA term is more appropriate to use.

nce at his own risk and must any export taxes and fees. ther, the goods must not rely be placed alongside but board the ship.

tional documents

ther documents needed for ansit of the goods through nother country or for import earance (**A10**)

B BUYER'S PRIMARY DUTIES

- Nominate carrier (**B3**)
- Contract for the carriage and pay the freight (**B3**)
- Pay loading costs to the extent that they are included in the freight (**B6**)
- Pay unloading costs (**B6**)

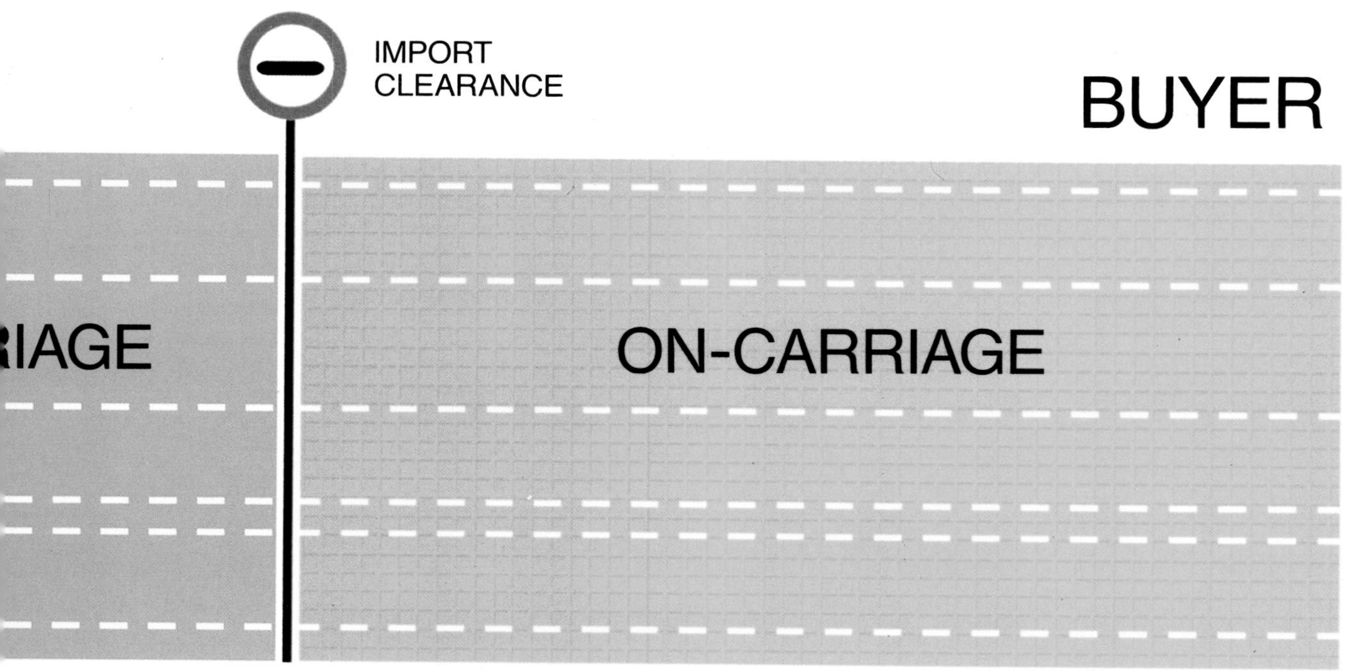

Group F: **Main carriage not paid by seller**

FREE ON BOARD

(... named port of shipment)

A THE SELLER MUST

A1 Provision of goods in conformity with the contract

Provide the goods and the commercial invoice, or its equivalent electronic message, in conformity with the contract of sale and any other evidence of conformity which may be required by the contract.

Comments

The seller must provide the goods in conformity with the contract. It is also usual practice that the seller, in order to be paid, has to invoice the buyer. In addition, the seller must submit any other evidence stipulated in the contract itself that the goods conform with the contract.

This text only serves as a reminder of the seller's main obligation under the contract of sale.

A2 Licences, authorisations and formalities

Obtain at his own risk and expense any export licence or other official authorisation and carry out all customs formalities necessary for the exportation of the goods.

Comments

The seller has to clear the goods for export and assume any risk or expense which this involves. Consequently, if there is an export prohibition or if there are particular taxes on the export of the goods - and if there are other government-imposed requirements which may render the export of the goods more expensive than contemplated - all of these risks and costs must be borne by the seller. However, contracts of sale usually contain particular provisions which the seller may invoke to protect himself in the event of these contingencies. Under the 1980 Convention on International Sale of Goods (CISG) and corresponding provisions in various national Sale of Goods Acts, unforeseen or reasonably unforeseeable export prohibitions may relieve the seller from his obligations under the contract of sale.

A3 Contract of carriage and insurance

a) Contract of carriage
No obligation.

b) Contract of insurance
No obligation.

Comments

The seller has no obligation to contract for carriage and would not be requested to do so if the FOB term is used for the carriage of full ship loads of bulk commodities.

Freight rates are often fixed according to standards determined by liner conferences. In these cases, it does not matter whether the seller or the buyer contracts for carriage; indeed, the seller or his freight forwarder can often do this more easily in the port of shipment. Nevertheless, the ICC considered it inappropriate to repeat here the reference in FCA A3 to the seller's additional service in contracting for carriage at the buyer's risk and expense, since FOB should normally not be used for carriage of general cargo unless said cargo is handed over for carriage at the ship's rail.

A4 Delivery

Deliver the goods on board the vessel named by the buyer at the named port of shipment on the date or within the period stipulated and in the manner customary at the port.

Comments

The seller's obligation to place the goods onboard the ship in due time is the essence of the FOB term. Through the centuries the ship's rail has assumed an inordinate importance as an imaginary border between the seller's and the buyer's territory. But using the ship's rail as a point for the division of functions, costs and risks between the parties is not, and never has been, quite appropriate. To divide the functions between the parties while the goods are swinging across the ship's rail seems inexact. In the words of an often cited English court decision: "Only the most enthusiastic lawyer could watch with satisfaction the spectacle of liabilities shifting uneasily as the cargo sways at the end of a derrick across a notional perpendicular projecting from the ship's rail."

The reference in FOB A4 to "the manner customary at the port" highlights the problem of using the passing of the ship's rail as the guiding factor in practice. The parties in these circumstances will have to follow the custom of the port regarding the actual measures to be taken in delivering the goods onboard. Usually the task is performed by stevedoring companies, and the practical problem normally lies in deciding who should bear the costs of their services.

The seller's obligation to place the goods onboard may be extended by a phrase added to FOB, e.g. "FOB stowed" or "FOB stowed and trimmed". Though these additional words are primarily intended to make sure the seller has to pay all of the loading costs, it is doubtful whether they are also intended to move the "delivery point" to the extent that the seller would be considered to have failed to fulfil his delivery obligation until the loading, stowing and trimming have been completed (See comments to FOB A5, A6 and FOB B5, B6).

A5 Transfer of risks

Subject to the provisions of B.5., bear all risks of loss of or damage to the goods until such time as they have passed the ship's rail at the named port of shipment.

Comments

All Incoterms are based on the same principle that the risk of loss of or damage to the goods is transferred from the seller to the buyer when the seller has fulfilled his delivery obligation according to A4. A5 of FOB, CFR and CIF further specifies that the risk is transferred when the goods "have passed the ship's rail at the named port of shipment".

All Incoterms, in conformity with the general principle of CISG (Convention on the International Sale of Goods) connect the transfer of the risk with the delivery of the goods and not with other circumstances, such as the passing of ownership or the time of the conclusion of the contract. Neither Incoterms nor CISG deal with transfer of title to the goods or other property rights with respect to the goods.

The passing of risk for loss of or damage to the goods concerns the risk of fortuitous events (accidents) and does not include loss or damage caused by the seller or the buyer, e.g. through inadequate packing or marking of the goods. Therefore, even if damage occurs subsequent to the transfer of the risk, the seller may still be responsible if the damage could be attributed to the fact that the goods were not delivered in conformity with the contract (See A1 and the comments to A9).

A5 of all Incoterms starts with the phrase "subject to the provisions of B5". This means that there are exceptions to the main rule in the circumstances described in B5 which may result in a premature passing of the risk because of the buyer's failure properly to fulfil his obligations (See the comments to B5).

A6 Division of costs

Subject to the provisions of B.6.

- pay all costs relating to the goods until such time as they have passed the ship's rail at the named port of shipment;
- pay the costs of customs formalities necessary for exportation as well as all duties, taxes and other official charges payable upon exportation.

Comments

As is the case with the transfer of the risk of loss of or damage to the goods, all Incoterms follow the same rule, that the division of costs occurs at the delivery point. All costs occurring before the seller has fulfilled his obligation to deliver according to A4 are for his account, while further costs are for the account of the buyer (See the comments to B6). This rule is made subject to the provisions of B6, which indicates that the buyer may have to bear additional costs incurred by his failure to give appropriate notice to the seller.

The seller must pay the costs of customs formalities necessary for exportation as well as all duties, taxes and other official charges payable upon exportation.

A7 Notice to the buyer

Give the buyer sufficient notice that the goods have been delivered on board.

Comments

The seller must give the buyer sufficient notice concerning when the goods have been delivered onboard. There is no stipulation in Incoterms spelling out the consequences of the seller's failure to give this notice. But it follows from Incoterms that the seller's failure constitutes a breach of contract. This means that the seller could be held responsible for the breach according to the law applicable to the contract of sale.

A8 Proof of delivery, transport document or equivalent electronic message

Provide the buyer at the seller's expense with the usual document in proof of delivery in accordance with A.4.

Unless the document referred to in the preceding paragraph is the transport document, render the buyer, at the latter's request, risk and expense, every assistance in obtaining a transport document for the contract of carriage (for example, a negotiable bill of lading, a non-negotiable sea waybill, an inland waterway document, or a multimodal transport document).

Where the seller and the buyer have agreed to communicate electronically, the document referred to in the preceding paragraph may be replaced by an equivalent electronic data interchange (EDI) message.

Comments

Since the seller has to hand over the goods for carriage, the carrier normally gives him a receipt which is usually identical to <u>the transport document</u>. If so, that document serves not only as evidence of the contract of carriage - which under F-terms is made by or on behalf of the buyer - but also as evidence of the delivery of the goods to the carrier.

If, however, the seller receives a document other than the transport document - for example, a so-called mate's receipt when the goods have been loaded onboard a ship chartered by the buyer - he should, upon the buyer's request, assist the buyer to obtain the transport document. This assistance is rendered at the buyer's risk and expense.

Whenever the parties have agreed to communicate electronically, documents may be replaced by EDI messages.

A9 Checking - packaging - marking

Pay the costs of those checking operations (such as checking quality, measuring, weighing, counting) which are necessary for the purpose of delivering the goods in accordance with A.4.

Provide at his own expense packaging (unless it is usual for the particular trade to ship the goods of the contract description unpacked) which is required for the transport of the goods, to the extent that the circumstances relating to the transport (e.g. modalities, destination) are made known to the seller before the contract of sale is concluded. Packaging is to be marked appropriately.

Comments

The goods must also be adequately packed. But the seller may not know the buyer's intentions with respect to the ultimate destination. There is a considerable difference between a short journey to an adjoining country and an intercontinental carriage by sea, which may expose the goods to the risk of breakage or corrosion from humidity and condensation.

A10 Other obligations

Render the buyer at the latter's request, risk and expense, every assistance in obtaining any documents or equivalent electronic messages (other than those mentioned in A.8.) issued or transmitted in the country of shipment and/or of origin which the buyer may require for the importation of the goods and, where necessary, for their transit through another country.

Provide the buyer, upon request, with the necessary information for procuring insurance.

Comments

It is for the buyer to do whatever is necessary with respect to transit and import clearance. He may also need the seller's assistance to obtain documents (e.g. a certificate of origin, a health certificate, a clean report of finding, an import licence) or equivalent EDI messages issued or transmitted in the country of shipment and/or origin. But any cost incurred by the seller in rendering this assistance must be reimbursed to him by the buyer, according to B10.

Also, the seller may be requested to provide the buyer with information relating to the goods which the buyer may require for insurance purposes, if this information does not follow from the description of the goods in the contract of sale.

FREE ON BOARD

(... named port of shipment)

B THE BUYER MUST

B1 Payment of the price

Pay the price as provided in the contract of sale.

Comments

The buyer must pay the price agreed in the contract of sale. B1 constitutes a reminder of this main obligation, which corresponds with the seller's obligation to provide the goods in conformity with the contract of sale, as stipulated in A1.

B2 Licences, authorisations and formalities

Obtain at his own risk and expense any import licence or other official authorisation and carry out all customs formalities for the importation of the goods and, where necessary, for their transit through another country.

Comments

The buyer must take care of the import clearance and bear any costs and risks in connection with it. Therefore, an import prohibition will not relieve the buyer of his obligation to pay for the goods, unless there is a particular "relief clause" in the contract of sale which he invokes to obtain this relief. Such clauses may provide for the extension of time or the right to avoid the contract under the applicable law (See the comments to A2).

B3 Contract of carriage

Contract at his own expense for the carriage of the goods from the named port of shipment.

Comments

The buyer has to contract for carriage so that the goods can be placed onboard. However, the seller - as in FCA A3 - may assist the buyer in contracting for carriage (See the comments to A3). If so, the assistance is rendered at the buyer's risk and expense.

B4 Taking delivery

Take delivery of the goods in accordance with A.4.

Comments

The buyer must take delivery of the goods when they have been placed onboard the vessel named by the buyer at the named port of shipment. His failure to do so will not relieve him of his obligation to pay the price and could further result in a premature passing of the risk of loss of or damage to the goods, or make him liable to pay additional costs according to B5 and B6.

B5 Transfer of risks

Bear all risks of loss of or damage to the goods from the time they have passed the ship's rail at the named port of shipment.

Should he fail to give notice in accordance with B.7., or should the vessel named by him fail to arrive on time, or be unable to take the goods, or close for cargo earlier than the stipulated time, bear all risks of loss of or damage to the goods from the agreed date or the expiry date of the period stipulated for delivery provided, however, that the goods have been duly appropriated to the contract, that is to say, clearly set aside or otherwise identified as the contract goods.

Comments

According to the main rule, while the seller under A5 bears the risk of loss of or damage to the goods until the delivery point, the buyer has to bear the risk thereafter. The delivery point is different under the different terms. In EXW and all D-terms the goods are simply placed "at the disposal of the buyer" at the relevant point, while under the F- and C-terms the delivery point is related to the handing over of the goods to the carrier in the country of dispatch or shipment (See the comments to A4 of these terms). In the terms used for goods intended to be carried by sea, reference is made to delivery alongside the named vessel (FAS A4) or delivery onboard the vessel (FOB, CFR, CIF).

Premature passing of risk

The buyer's failure to notify the seller of the vessel name, loading place and required delivery time may result in a premature passing of the risk, as it cannot be accepted that the buyer should be able to delay the delivery and passing of the risk longer than contemplated when the contract of sale was made. Thus, his failure to notify according to B7 will cause the risk to pass "from the agreed date or the expiry date of the period stipulated for delivery".

A further problem could arise if the vessel is not named or if it fails to arrive in time, since then the goods cannot be placed onboard as contemplated. Moreover, a premature passing of the risk could occur in these circumstances. B5 also stipulates that the same could result if the vessel is "unable to take the goods, or close for cargo earlier than the stipulated time".

For risk to pass prematurely, it is required that the goods are able to be identified as the contract goods (i.e. they have to be "appropriated to the contract"). When the goods have been prepared for dispatch they have also usually been appropriated to the contract. But a failure of the buyer to give sufficient notice of the date or period of shipment according to B7 causes the seller to defer his preparations. If so, it may not be possible to identify some goods stored at the seller's premises or in an independent cargo terminal or on the quay as the contract goods on the "agreed date or the expiry date of any period stipulated for delivery". The risk would then not pass until the appropriation has been made.

B6 Division of costs

Pay all costs relating to the goods from the time they have passed the ship's rail at the named port of shipment.

Pay any additional costs incurred, either because the vessel named by him has failed to arrive on time, or is unable to take the goods, or will close for cargo earlier than the stipulated date, or because the buyer has failed to give appropriate notice in accordance with B.7. provided, however, that the goods have been duly appropriated to the contract, that is to say, clearly set aside or otherwise identified as the contract goods.

Pay all duties, taxes and other official charges as well as the costs of carrying out customs formalities payable upon importation of the goods and, where necessary, for their transit through another country.

Comments

Under FOB the seller fulfils his delivery obligation according to A4 by placing the goods onboard the vessel at the loading place.

Since under FOB the buyer has to contract for carriage and nominate the ship, he also has to pay any additional costs incurred "because the vessel named by him has failed to arrive on time, or will be unable to take the goods, or will close for cargo earlier than the stipulated time" (See the corresponding rule for the premature passing of the risk in the comments to B5).

The failure of the buyer to notify the seller according to B7 would not only cause the risk of loss of or damage to the goods to pass prematurely but would also make the buyer liable to pay any additional costs caused thereby, e.g. extra costs for storage and insurance.

For the buyer to be liable for additional costs according to B6, the goods to which these costs relate must be identifiable as the contract goods (See the comments on "appropriation" under B5).

Under FOB, because the buyer has to clear the goods for import, he has to pay "all duties, taxes and other official charges as well as the costs of carrying out customs formalities" and to reimburse the seller for any assistance the seller renders him in this regard.

B7 Notice to the seller

Give the seller sufficient notice of the vessel name, loading point and required delivery time.

Comments

As discussed in the comments to B5 and B6, the failure of the buyer to notify the seller of the name of the vessel, the loading place and the required delivery time may cause the risk of the loss of or damage to the goods to pass before the goods have been delivered according to A4 and also make the buyer liable to pay any additional costs the seller incurs as a result of the buyer's failure.

B8 Proof of delivery, transport document or equivalent electronic message

Accept the proof of delivery in accordance with A.8.

Comments

The buyer must accept the seller's proof of delivery if the proof is adequate. If the buyer nevertheless rejects it (e.g. by instructions to a bank not to pay the seller under a documentary credit), he commits a breach of contract which will give the seller remedies for the breach available under the contract of sale (e.g. a right to cancel the contract or to claim damages for breach). However, the buyer is not obliged to accept a document which does not provide adequate proof of delivery. If there are notations on the document showing that the goods are defective or that they have been provided in less than the agreed quantity, the document is then considered to be "unclean".

B9 Inspection of goods

Pay, unless otherwise agreed, the costs of pre-shipment inspection except when mandated by the authorities of the country of export.

Comments

As noted in the comments to A9, the buyer has to pay for any costs of checking the goods, unless the contract determines that these costs should be wholly or partly borne by the seller. In some cases, the contract may provide that the costs should be borne by the seller if the inspection reveals that the goods do not conform with the contract.

In some countries, where import licences or permission to obtain foreign currency for the payment of the price may be required, the authorities may demand an inspection of the goods before shipment, to ensure that the goods are in conformity with the contract. (This is usually called pre-shipment inspection, PSI.) If this is the case, the inspection is normally arranged by instructions from the authorities to an inspection company, which they appoint. The costs following from this inspection have to be paid by the authorities. Any reimbursement to the authorities for the inspection costs, however, must be made by the buyer, unless otherwise specifically agreed between the buyer and the seller.

B10 Other obligations

Pay all costs and charges incurred in obtaining the documents or equivalent electronic messages mentioned in A.10. and reimburse those incurred by the seller in rendering his assistance in accordance therewith.

Comments

As discussed in the comments to A10, the seller has to render the buyer assistance in obtaining the documents or electronic messages which may be required for the transit and importation of the goods. However, this assistance is rendered at the buyer's risk and expense. Therefore, B10 stipulates that the buyer must pay all costs and charges incurred in obtaining these documents or electronic messages. He will also have to reimburse the seller for the seller's costs in rendering his assistance.

Group C : Main carriage paid by seller

COST AND FREIGHT
(... named port of destination)

A SELLER'S PRIMARY DUTIES

- Contract for the carriage and pay the freight to the named port of destination (**A3a**)
- Deliver the goods on board (**A4**)
- Provide export clearance (export licence, pay export taxes and fees, if required) (**A2**)
- Furnish the buyer with the invoice and a clean transport document (e.g. bill of lading, sea waybill) (**A1, A8**)
- Pay loading costs (**A6**)
- Pay unloading costs to the extent that they are included in the freight (**A6**)

DIFFERENCE FROM *FOB*

Under CFR the seller must contract for the carriage of the goods to the port of destination

DOCUMENTS

Required documents
- Commercial invoice (**A1**)
- Transport document (**A8**)
- Export licence (**A2**)

NOTE:
All documents may be replaced by EDI messages

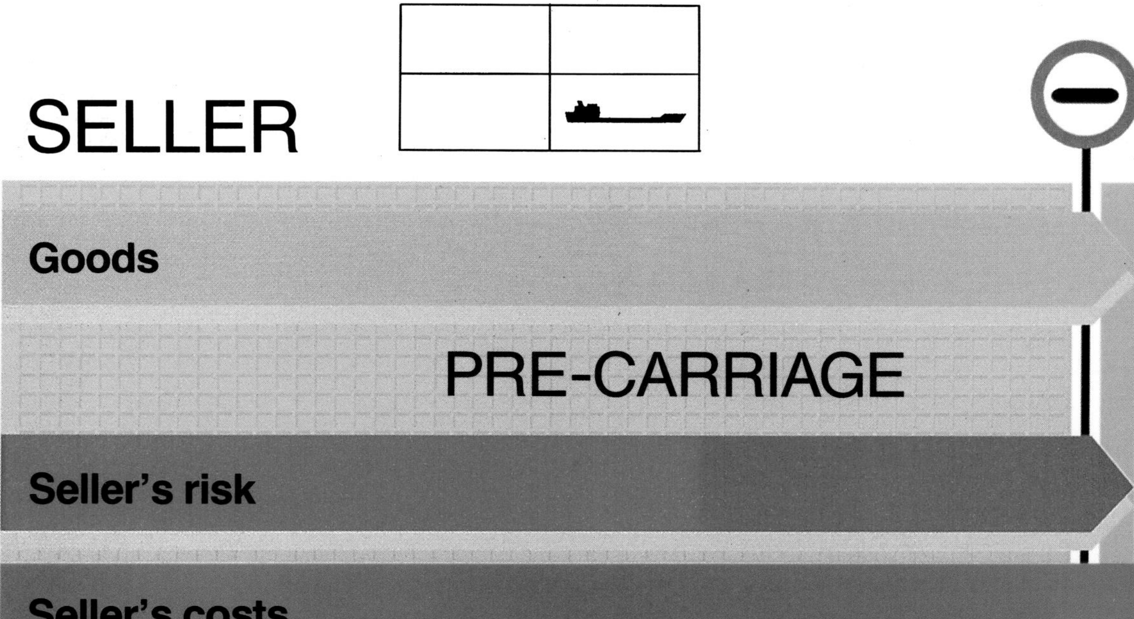

Cost and Freight" means that the seller must pay the osts and freight necessary to bring the goods to the named ort of destination but the risk of loss of or damage to the oods, as well as any additional costs due to events ccurring after the time the goods have been delivered on oard the vessel, is transferred from the seller to the buyer hen the goods pass the ship's rail in the port of shipment.

The CFR term requires the seller to clear the goods for export.
This term can only be used for sea and inland waterway transport. When the ship's rail serves no practical purpose, such as in the case of roll-on/roll-off or container traffic, the CPT term is more appropriate to use.

amed in the sales contract and ay the freight.

ptional documents

- Other documents needed for transit of the goods through another country or for import clearance (**A10**)

B BUYER'S PRIMARY DUTIES

- Accept delivery of the goods upon shipment, when the invoice and the transport document are tendered to him, and receive the goods from the carrier at the named port of destination (**B4**)
- Pay unloading costs to the extent that they are not included in the freight (**B6**)

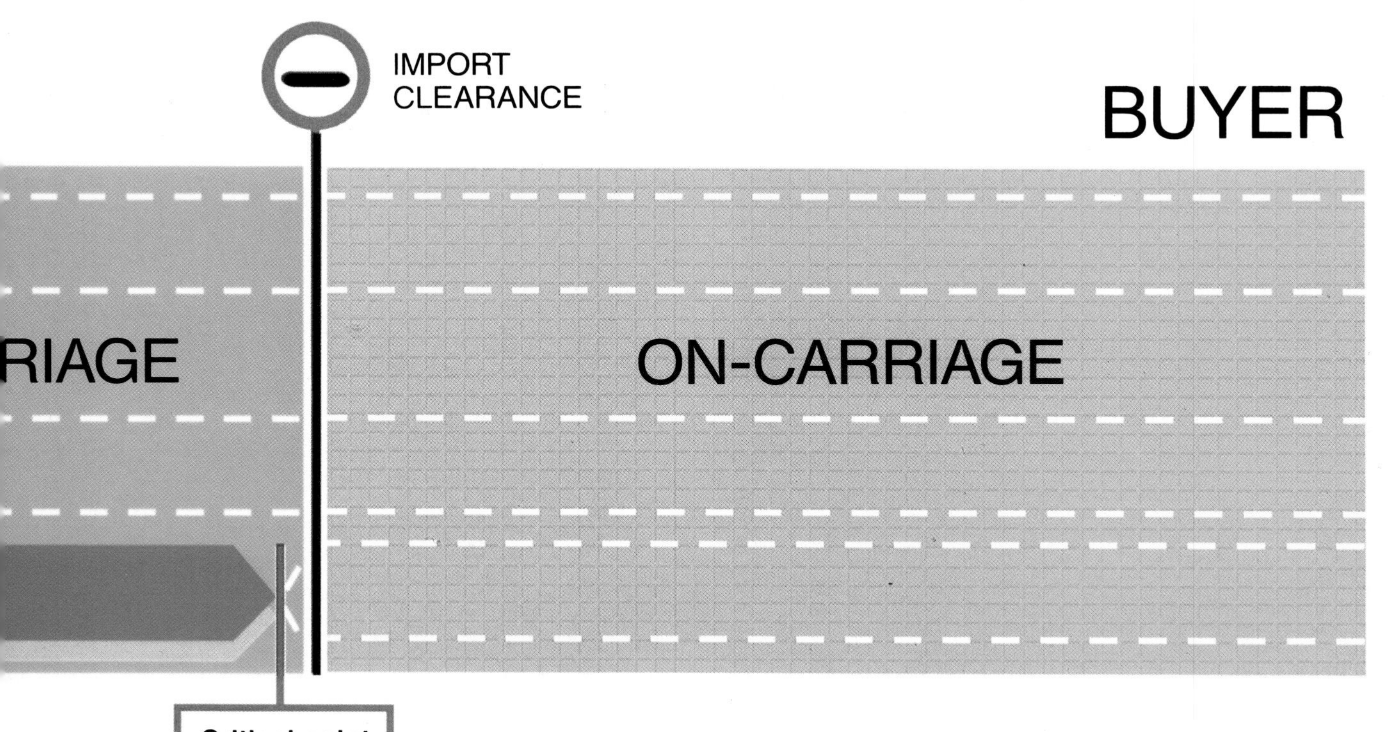

COST AND FREIGHT
(... named port of destination)

A THE SELLER MUST

A1 Provision of goods in conformity with the contract

Provide the goods and the commercial invoice, or its equivalent electronic message, in conformity with the contract of sale and any other evidence of conformity which may be required by the contract.

Comments

The seller must provide the goods in conformity with the contract. It is also usual practice that the seller, in order to be paid, has to invoice the buyer. In addition, the seller must submit any other evidence stipulated in the contract itself that the goods conform with that contract.

This text only serves as a reminder of the seller's main obligation under the contract of sale.

A2 Licences, authorisations and formalities

Obtain at his own risk and expense any export licence or other official authorisation and carry out all customs formalities necessary for the exportation of the goods.

Comments

The seller has to clear the goods for export and assume any risk or expense which this involves. Consequently, if there is an export prohibition or if there are particular taxes on the export of the goods - and if there are other government-imposed requirements which may render the export of the goods more expensive than contemplated - all of these risks and costs must be borne by the seller. However, contracts of sale usually contain particular provisions which the seller may invoke to protect himself in the event of these contingencies. Under the 1980 Convention on International Sale of Goods (CISG) and corresponding provisions in various national Sale of Goods Acts, unforeseen or reasonably unforeseeable export prohibitions may relieve the seller from his obligations under the contract of sale.

A3 Contract of carriage and insurance

a) Contract of carriage
Contract on usual terms at his own expense for the carriage of the goods to the named port of destination by the usual route in a seagoing vessel (or inland waterway vessel as appropriate) of the type normally used for the transport of goods of the contract description.

b) Contract of insurance
No obligation.

Comments

Although the CFR seller fulfils his obligations by shipping the goods (See section A4 below), he has to arrange and pay for the contract of carriage to the named port of destination. Unless the contract contains specific stipulations as to the nature of the contract of carriage, the seller may contract "on usual terms" and for carriage "by the usual route".

The CFR term can only be used for sea and inland waterway transport. (Section A8 requires the seller to provide a negotiable bill of lading, which is not possible to obtain for modes of transport other than carriage of goods by sea.) But the vessel need not necessarily be "seagoing", since the CFR term may also be used for carriage by inland waterways. In this latter case, an "inland waterway vessel" may be used.

The vessel should be of a kind normally used for the transport of the goods of the contract description. It may be unacceptable, for example, to arrange for the carriage of containerised cargo on deck if the ship is not designed for carriage of containers, since the carriage may then expose the cargo to additional risks and even render the insurance cover ineffective.

Differences between goods carried in liner trade and bulk cargoes carried in chartered ships

There is a considerable difference between goods normally carried in so-called liner trade and bulk cargoes, which are normally carried in chartered ships. In most cases, it should be clear what kind of carriage the seller should arrange, since break bulk cargo now is normally containerised or otherwise carried by regular transport in transportation units (flats, pallets, etc.) from port to port.

In these cases, the carrier frequently undertakes to carry the goods, not only from port to port but from an interior point in the country of shipment to an interior point in the country of destination. It is then inappropriate to use the CFR term and the parties are advised to use the CPT term instead (See the comments on CPT).

When it is uncertain whether the goods should be carried by regular shipping lines or by chartered ships, it is advisable that the matter be specifically dealt with in the contract of sale. It often happens that carriage by chartered ships is permitted, but that the carriage must nevertheless be contracted for on "liner terms". If so, the freight costs would ordinarily include loading and unloading costs. A charter party, however, may well provide that these costs should be "free" to the carrier. This is the so-called FIO-clause - which stands for "Free In" and "Free Out".

In any case, the expression "liner terms" is vague and ambiguous, and it is recommended that the parties specifically deal with the conditions of the contract of carriage in the contract of sale when carriage is not to be arranged by regular, well-known shipping lines.

A4 Delivery

Deliver the goods on board the vessel at the port of shipment on the date or within the period stipulated.

Comments

As noted above, delivery under the CFR term occurs at the moment the goods are placed onboard the vessel at the port of shipment. Thus, the CFR term, like the FOB term, is evidence of a shipment contract. Since the point of destination is mentioned after CFR, e.g. "CFR London" by a seller in New York, the legal nature of a CFR contract is frequently misunderstood by traders. This is quite understandable, because the critical point where the seller fulfills his obligation is usually omitted. CFR contracts do not usually provide that shipment shall take place at a particular port, e.g. "CFR London shipment from New York", since this would restrict the seller's options to ship the goods from alternative ports of shipment.

It must be emphasised that the CFR term, as distinguished from the FOB term, contains two critical points. The first represents the point at which delivery takes place upon shipment according to A4, namely when the goods are placed onboard the vessel. The second represents the point at destination, up to which the seller shall arrange for carriage of the goods.

Avoid stipulating date of delivery at destination

One essential point of the CFR term is sometimes ignored in commercial practice. When, for example, the contract stipulates that delivery should take place not later than a specified date at destination (e.g. "arrival London not later than ..."), this kind of stipulation defeats the object of the CFR term and leaves room for different interpretations of the contract.

One option would be to interpret this stipulation to mean that the parties have agreed on an arrival contract rather than a shipment contract. If that is the case, the seller is not considered to have fulfilled the contract until the goods have actually arrived at destination. If in such a case the goods are delayed because of casualties after shipment or are even lost, the seller would not be free from his obligations under the contract of sale - unless, of course, he has the protection of a particular relief clause or force majeure clause in the contract of sale. Such a contract is of course different from a CFR contract under which the seller fulfills the contract in the port of shipment.

The other option would be to interpret the stipulation in a way which would allow the basic nature of the CFR contract to supersede the particular wording the parties use, even in cases when the parties have stipulated that the goods should arrive before a particular date at destination. If that is done, the contract would be interpreted to mean that the goods must arrive before the stipulated date, unless something happens to the shipment as the result of subsequent events. Of course, under CFR these events are at the risk of the buyer.

Since it is uncertain which of these options will be used to interpret CFR with this or similar language added, the parties are strongly advised to abstain from using such additions.

A5 Transfer of risks

Subject to the provisions of B.5., bear all risks of loss of or damage to the goods until such time as they have passed the ship's rail at the port of shipment.

Comments

All Incoterms are based on the same principle that the risk of loss of or damage to the goods is transferred from the seller to the buyer when the seller has fulfilled his delivery obligation according to A4. A5 of FOB, CFR and CIF further specifies that the risk is transferred when the goods "have passed the ship's rail at the named port of shipment".

All Incoterms, in conformity with the general principle of CISG, connect the transfer of the risk with the delivery of the goods and not with other circumstances, such as the passing of ownership or the time of the conclusion of the contract. As noted, neither Incoterms nor CISG deal with transfer of title to the goods or other property rights with respect to the goods.

The passing of risk of loss of or damage to the goods concerns the risk of fortuitous events (accidents) and does not include loss or damage caused by the seller or the buyer, e.g. inadequate packing or marking of the goods. Therefore, even if damage occurs subsequent to the transfer of the risk, the seller may still be responsible if the damage could be attributed to the fact that the goods were not delivered in conformity with the contract (See A1 and the comments to A9).

A5 of all Incoterms starts with the phrase "subject to the provisions of B5". This means that there are exceptions to the main rule concerning the passing of risk under the circumstances mentioned in B5, which may result in a premature passing of the risk because of the buyer's failure properly to fulfil his obligations (See the comments to B5).

A6 Division of costs

Subject to the provisions of B. 6.

- pay all costs relating to the goods until they have been delivered in accordance with A.4. as well as the freight and all other costs resulting from A.3.a), including costs of loading the goods on board and any charges for unloading at the port of discharge which may be levied by regular shipping lines when contracting for carriage;
- pay the costs of customs formalities necessary for exportation as well as all duties, taxes and other official charges payable upon exportation.

Comments

As is the case with the transfer of the risk of loss of or damage to the goods, all Incoterms follow the same rule, that the division of costs occurs at the delivery point. All costs occurring before the seller has fulfilled his obligation to deliver according to A4 are for his account, while further costs are for the account of the buyer (See the comments to B6). This rule is made subject to the provisions of B6, which indicates that the buyer may have to bear additional costs incurred by his failure to give appropriate notice to the seller.

A7 Notice to the buyer

Give the buyer sufficient notice that the goods have been delivered on board the vessel as well as any other notice required in order to allow the buyer to take measures which are normally necessary to enable him to take the goods.

Comments

The seller must give the buyer sufficient notice that the goods have been delivered onboard the vessel, as well as other relevant information, so that the buyer can make preparations in time to take delivery according to B4. There is no stipulation in Incoterms spelling out the consequences of the seller's failure to give such notice. But it follows from Incoterms that the seller's failure constitutes a breach of contract. This means that the seller could be held responsible for the breach according to the law applicable to the contract of sale.

A8 Proof of delivery, transport document or equivalent electronic message

Unless otherwise agreed, at his own expense provide the buyer without delay with the usual transport document for the agreed port of destination.

This document (for example, a negotiable bill of lading, a non-negotiable sea waybill or an inland waterway document) must cover the contract goods, be dated within the period agreed for shipment, enable the buyer to claim the goods from the carrier at destination and, unless otherwise agreed, enable the buyer to sell the goods in transit by the transfer of the document to a subsequent buyer (the negotiable bill of lading) or by notification to the carrier.

When such a transport document is issued in several originals, a full set of originals must be presented to the buyer. If the transport document contains a reference to a charter party, the seller must also provide a copy of this latter document. Where the seller and the buyer have agreed to communicate electronically, the document referred to in the preceding paragraphs may be replaced by an equivalent electronic data interchange (EDI) message.

Comments

It is of vital importance for the buyer to know that the seller has fulfilled his obligation to deliver the goods onboard the ship. The transport document usually constitutes proof of such delivery.

Non-negotiable transport documents

Generally, it suffices for the parties to refer to the "usual transport document" obtained from the carrier when the goods are handed over to him. But in maritime carriage different documents can be used. While traditionally negotiable bills of lading were used for carriage of goods by sea, other documents have appeared in recent years, e.g. transport documents which are non-negotiable and similar to those used for other modes of transport. These alternative documents have different names - "liner waybills", "ocean waybills", "cargo quay receipts", "data freight receipts" or "sea waybills". The term "sea waybill" is frequently used to include all of the various non-negotiable transport documents used for carriage of goods by sea.

Unfortunately, international conventions and national laws do not yet provide specific regulations for these non-negotiable transport documents. (The exception is in the United States, where a non-negotiable bill of lading is recognised; this is the so-called "straight bill of lading".) For this reason, the Comité Maritime International (CMI) in June 1990 adopted Uniform Rules for Sea Waybills. The parties should refer to these Rules in the contract of carriage to avoid any legal uncertainties stemming from the use of non-negotiable documents (See Appendix).

Sale of goods in transit

In most cases, goods intended for carriage by regular shipping lines will not be the subject of a further sale in transit. But with respect to goods intended to be carried in chartered ships the situation is frequently quite different. For example, when commodities are sold on the spot market, they are often sold many times before they reach destination. In these cases the negotiable bill of lading has traditionally been very important, since the possession of the paper document enables the subsequent buyer to claim the goods from the carrier at destination. He does this by surrendering the original bill of lading to the carrier in exchange for the goods.

However, when no sale of the goods in transit is intended, there is no need to use a bill of lading if the buyer's right to claim the goods from the carrier at destination is ensured by other means such as by reference in the contract to the CMI Uniform Rules for Sea Waybills.

A buyer intending to sell the goods in transit to a subsequent buyer has the right under CFR and CIF terms to claim a negotiable bill of lading from his seller. This sale in transit can also be arranged, however, without a bill of lading. It can occur if the parties involved use a system which calls upon the carrier to follow instructions to hold the goods at the disposition of subsequent buyer(s).

EDI and the bill of lading

Section A8 takes into account that the parties may wish to engage in so-called "paperless trading". If the parties have agreed to communicate electronically, the requirement that a paper document be presented is no longer compulsory.

Needless to say, the traditional bill of lading is out of step with the modern development towards "paperless trading". For this reason, the CMI in June 1990 designed the "Uniform Rules for Electronic Bills of Lading", which cover situations in which EDI messages between the parties involved are intended to replace the need for the traditional paper bill of lading (See Appendix).

These Uniform Rules are based on EDI messages to the carrier which serve the same purpose as the words "notification to the carrier" in A8. Parties which have not agreed to use the "Uniform Rules for Electronic Bills of Lading", however, have to continue the traditional practice of requiring negotiable bills of lading.

Risk of maritime fraud when issuing several original bills of lading

Unfortunately, the malpractice of issuing bills of lading in several originals has persisted despite the fact that it creates a considerable risk of maritime fraud. A buyer paying for the goods directly or through a bank must therefore ensure that he receives all originals of the bill of lading, if several originals have been issued.

Bills of lading issued upon request of a charterer

When bills of lading are issued upon the request of a charterer by the owner of a chartered ship, the bill of lading may refer to the terms of the charter party (e.g. "all other terms as per charter party"). In these cases, the seller must also provide a copy of the charter party, so the buyer can ascertain the carrier's rights and obligations.

A9 Checking - packaging - marking

Pay the costs of those checking operations (such as checking quality, measuring, weighing, counting) which are necessary for the purpose of delivering the goods in accordance with A.4.

Provide at his own expense packaging (unless it is usual for the particular trade to ship the goods of the contract description unpacked) which is required for the transport of the goods arranged by him. Packaging is to be marked appropriately.

Comments

It is necessary for the buyer to ensure that the seller has duly fulfilled his obligation with respect to the condition of the goods. This is particularly important if the buyer is called upon to pay for the goods before he has received and checked them. However, the seller has no duty to arrange and pay for inspection of the goods before shipment, unless this has been specifically agreed in the contract of sale.

The goods must also be adequately packed. Since the seller arranges the carriage, he is in a good position to decide the packing required for the transport of the goods. The goods should also be marked in accordance with applicable standards and regulations.

A10 Other obligations

Render the buyer at the latter's request, risk and expense, every assistance in obtaining any documents or equivalent electronic messages (other than those mentioned in A.8.) issued or transmitted in the country of shipment and/or of origin which the buyer may require for the importation of the goods and, where necessary, for their transit through another country.

Provide the buyer, upon request, with the necessary information for procuring insurance.

Comments

The seller has the obligation to clear the goods for export, but he has no obligation after shipment to bear any costs and risks connected either with the transit through another country or with import clearance of the goods at destination. However, he has the duty to render assistance to the buyer in obtaining any documents (e.g. a certificate of origin, a health certificate, a clean report of findings, an import licence) or equivalent electronic messages which may be required for these purposes. The buyer, however, must reimburse the seller for any expenses which the seller might have incurred in connection with this assistance. Moreover, if something goes wrong, the buyer will have to assume the risk.

Also, the seller may be requested to provide the buyer with such information relating to the goods as the buyer may require for insurance purposes, if this information does not follow from the description of the goods in the contract of sale.

COST AND FREIGHT

(... named port of destination)

B THE BUYER MUST

B1 Payment of the price

Pay the price as provided in the contract of sale.

Comments

The buyer must pay the price agreed in the contract of sale. B1 constitutes a reminder of this main obligation, which corresponds with the seller's obligation to provide the goods in conformity with the contract of sale, as stipulated in A1.

B2 Licences, authorisations and formalities

Obtain at his own risk and expense any import licence or other official authorisation and carry out all customs formalities for the importation of the goods and, where necessary, for their transit through another country.

Comments

The buyer must take care of the import clearance and bear any costs and risks in connection with it. Therefore, an import prohibition will not relieve the buyer of his obligation to pay for the goods, unless there is a particular "relief clause" in the contract of sale which he invokes to obtain this relief. Such clauses may provide for the extension of time or the right to avoid the contract under the applicable law (See the comments to A2).

The buyer must also do whatever may be needed to pass the goods through a third country after they have been shipped (dispatched) from the seller's country, and he must assume any cost and risk in connection with these matters.

B3 Contract of carriage

No obligation.

Comments

Although B3 merely stipulates "No obligation" for the buyer, on-carriage from the port of destination is necessary in most cases, and it is the buyer's responsibility to do whatever is required for this purpose. But the seller is not concerned with the further carriage of the goods and the buyer has no obligation to the seller in this respect. The words "No obligation" mean that whatever the buyer does is in his own interest and is not covered by the contract of sale.

B4 Taking delivery

Accept delivery of the goods when they have been delivered in accordance with A.4. and receive them from the carrier at the named port of destination.

Comments

Here, the two critical points under a CFR sale appear again. Since the seller fulfills his obligation by delivering the goods onboard the vessel at the port of shipment (A4), it is for the buyer to accept such delivery under B4. But the buyer also has a further obligation to receive the goods from the carrier at the named port of destination. This is not something he does only in his own interest (as in B3) but is an obligation to the seller, who has concluded the contract of carriage with the carrier.

Unless the buyer frees the goods from the ship when they duly arrive, the seller may incur additional costs debited to him by the carrier. These costs must be borne by the buyer if he is in breach of his obligation to receive the goods from the carrier.

Charter party loading and discharge

In the charter party trade, problems frequently arise in ports of loading as well as in ports of discharge when the time for loading and discharging the cargo exceeds the "free" time according to the charter party terms (the so-called "lay-time"). In these cases, the charterer has to pay particular compensation (so-called "demurrage") to the owner.

Needless to say, it is vital for sellers and buyers to agree, not only in the charter party but also in the contract of sale, how much time should be available for loading and discharge respectively, and which of the parties should bear the costs of any demurrage charged by the shipowner. Charter parties may also provide that the shipowner should pay compensation if the time of loading and/or discharge is less than a certain stipulated time This is so-called dispatch, or despatch, money. If this is the case, it is also important to stipulate in the contract of sale which of the parties should be entitled to this compensation.

B5 Transfer of risks

Bear all risks of loss of or damage to the goods from the time they have passed the ship's rail at the port of shipment.

Should he fail to give notice in accordance with B.7., bear all risks of loss of or damage to the goods from the agreed date or the expiry date of the period fixed for shipment provided, however, that the goods have been duly appropriated to the contract, that is to say, clearly set aside or otherwise identified as the contract goods.

Comments

According to the main rule, while the seller under A5 bears the risk of loss of or damage to the goods until the delivery point, the buyer has to bear the risk thereafter. The delivery point is different under the different terms. In EXW and all D-terms the goods are simply placed "at the disposal of the buyer" at the relevant point, while under the F- and C-terms the delivery point is related to the handing over of the goods to the carrier in the country of dispatch or shipment (See the comments to A4 of these terms). In the terms used for goods intended to be carried by sea, reference is made to delivery alongside the named vessel (FAS A4) or delivery onboard the vessel (FOB, CFR, CIF).

Since the seller is relieved from any further risk of loss of or damage to the goods when they have passed the ship's rail, it follows that the buyer has to assume these risks subsequent to the passing of that critical point. According to the terms of the contract of sale, the buyer may be given the option to determine the time for shipping the goods. This option may also include the right to later name the port to which the goods should be shipped. In these cases, it is necessary that the seller be given timely and sufficient notice (See comments to B7).

Premature transfer of risk

If the buyer fails to give appropriate notice to the seller, he could be exposed to additional costs and risks if the goods have to be stored in the port of loading pending shipping instructions. B5 stipulates that in these cases the risk may be transferred from the seller to the buyer before the time when the goods have passed the ship's rail. This is an important exception to the main rule.

This premature transfer of the risks could occur at one of two points: Either (l) when, as a result of the buyer's failure to give sufficient notice, the goods cannot be shipped at an agreed date or (2) on the expiry date, in cases when the buyer has been given a period during which to determine the time for shipment.

In accordance with the general principle of Incoterms, this premature transfer of the risks will never occur until the goods have been duly appropriated to the contract. In other words, the goods have to be clearly set aside or otherwise identified as the contract goods for the premature transfer of the risks to occur.

B6 Division of costs

Subject to the provisions of A.3., pay all costs relating to the goods from the time they have been delivered in accordance with A.4. and, unless such costs and charges have been levied by regular shipping lines when contracting for carriage, pay all costs and charges relating to the goods whilst in transit until their arrival at the port of destination, as well as unloading costs including lighterage and wharfage charges.

Should he fail to give notice in accordance with B.7., pay the additional costs thereby incurred for the goods from the agreed date or the expiry date of the period fixed for shipment provided, however, that the goods have been duly appropriated to the contract, that is to say, clearly set aside or otherwise identified as the contract goods.

Pay all duties, taxes and other official charges as well as the costs of carrying out customs formalities payable upon importation of the goods and, where necessary, for their transit through another country.

Comments

While the seller has to pay all costs required to bring the goods to the port of shipment and to deliver the goods onboard the vessel (as well as unloading charges at the port of discharge, provided they have been included in the freight), the buyer has to pay any further costs which may arise after the seller has delivered the goods onboard the vessel. In this sense, the transfer of the risk also determines the division of costs; if something occurs as a result of contingencies after shipment - such as strandings, collisions, strikes, government directions, hindrances because of ice or other weather conditions - any additional costs charged by the carrier as a result of these contingencies, or otherwise occurring, will be for the account of the buyer.

The buyer is only free from paying the further costs if these costs "have been levied by regular shipping lines when contracting for carriage". This does not mean, however, that the buyer must pay for costs and charges payable under the contract of carriage in the ordinary course of events (for example, when the shipper has been given credit by the carrier, i.e. so-called "collect freight").

Failure to give notice and buyer's additional costs

The failure to give appropriate notice in accordance with B7 not only results in a premature transfer of the risks (See comments to B5) but also imposes on the buyer the responsibility to pay any additional costs as a consequence. In this case, the obligation to pay these additional costs only occurs if the goods have been duly appropriated to the contract (as discussed in the comments to B5).

Buyer's duties in clearing goods for import

As noted in the comments to B2, the buyer has the duty to clear the goods for import; it is then established in B6 that he has to pay the costs arising from the clearance ("duties, taxes and other official charges as well as the costs of carrying out customs formalities"). The buyer also has to pay any duties, taxes and other charges arising in connection with the transit of the goods through another country after they have been delivered by the seller in accordance with A4.

B7 Notice to the seller

Whenever he is entitled to determine the time for shipping the goods and/or the port of destination, give the seller sufficient notice thereof.

Comments

As discussed in the comments to B5 and B6, the failure of the buyer to notify the seller of the time for shipping the goods or the destination - when the buyer in the contract of sale has been given the option to determine these matters - may cause the risk of the loss of or damage to the goods to pass before the goods have been delivered according to A4. In addition, it can make the buyer liable to pay any additional costs incurred by the seller as a result of the buyer's failure.

B8 Proof of delivery, transport document or equivalent electronic message

Accept the transport document in accordance with A.8. if it is in conformity with the contract.

Comments

The buyer has to accept the transport document if it conforms with the contract and with the requirements of A8 (See the comments to A8). If the buyer rejects the transport document (e.g. by instructions to a bank not to pay the seller under a documentary credit), he commits a breach of contract, which would give the seller remedies available for such a breach under the contract of sale.

These remedies could include, for example, a right to cancel the contract or to claim damages for breach. However, the buyer is not obliged to accept a document which does not provide adequate proof of delivery, e.g. one which has notations on it showing that the goods are defective or that they have been provided in less than the agreed quantity. In these cases, the document is termed "unclean".

B9 Inspection of goods

Pay, unless otherwise agreed, the costs of pre-shipment inspection except when mandated by the authorities of the country of exportation.

Comments

As noted in the comments to A9, the buyer has to pay for any costs of checking the goods, unless the contract determines that these costs should be wholly or partly borne by the seller. In some cases, the contract may provide that the costs should be borne by the seller if the inspection reveals that the goods do not conform with the contract.

In some countries, where import licences or permission to obtain foreign currency for the payment of the price may be required, the authorities may demand an inspection of the goods before shipment, to ensure that the goods are in conformity with the contract. (This is usually called pre-shipment inspection, PSI.) If this is the case, the inspection is normally arranged by instructions from the authorities to an inspection company, which they appoint. The costs following from this inspection have to be paid by the authorities. Any reimbursement to the authorities for the inspection costs, however, must be made by the buyer, unless otherwise specifically agreed between the buyer and the seller.

B10 Other obligations

Pay all costs and charges incurred in obtaining the documents or equivalent electronic messages mentioned in A. 10. and reimburse those incurred by the seller in rendering his assistance in accordance therewith.

Comments

As discussed in the comments to A10, the seller has to render the buyer assistance in obtaining the documents or electronic messages which may be required for the transit and importation of the goods. However, this assistance is rendered at the buyer's risk and expense. Therefore, B10 stipulates that the buyer must pay all costs and charges incurred in obtaining these documents or electronic messages. He will also have to reimburse the seller for the seller's costs in rendering his assistance in these matters.

Group C : Main carriage paid by seller

COST, INSURANCE AND FREIGHT

(... named port of destination)

A SELLER'S PRIMARY DUTIES

- Contract for the carriage and pay the freight to the named port of destination (**A3a**)
- Deliver the goods on board (**A4**)
- Provide export clearance (export licence, pay export taxes and fees, if required) (**A2**)
- Contract for the insurance of the goods during the carriage and pay the insurance premium (**A3b**)
- Furnish the buyer with the invoice, a clean transport document and a cargo insurance policy certificate (**A1, A8** and **A3b**)
- Pay loading costs (**A6**)
- Pay unloading costs to the extent that they are included in the freight (**A6**)

DIFFERENCE FROM *CFR*

The only difference between CF
and CIF is that under the latter

DOCUMENTS

Required documents

- Commercial invoice (**A1**)
- Transport document (**A8**)
- Export licence (**A2**)
- Insurance policy (**A3b**)

NOTE:
All documents may be replaced by EDI messages

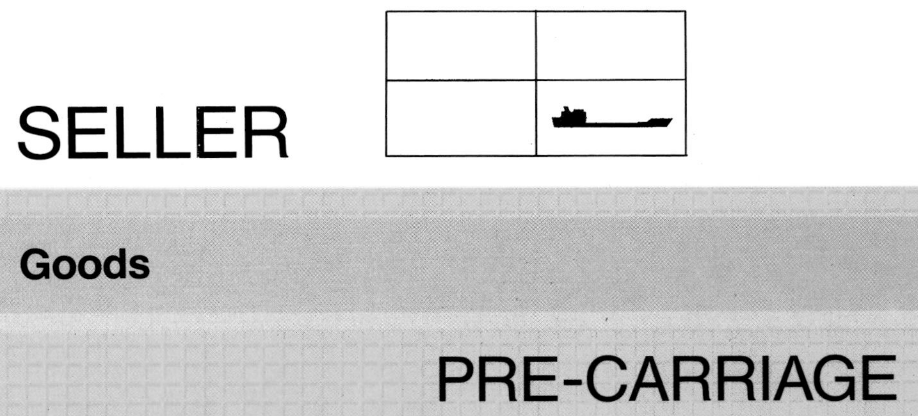

ost, Insurance and Freight" means that the seller has the me obligations as under CFR but with the addition that has to procure marine insurance against the buyer's risk loss of or damage to the goods during the carriage. The ller contracts for insurance and pays the insurance emium.

e buyer should note that under the CIF term the seller is only required to obtain insurance on minimum coverage. The CIF term requires the seller to clear the goods for export.

This term can only be used for sea and inland waterway transport. When the ship's rail serves no practical purpose such as in the case of roll-on/roll-off or container traffic, the CIP term is more appropriate to use.

m the seller has the added igation to procure insurance.

tional documents

)ther documents needed for ansit of the goods through nother country or for import learance (**A10**)

B BUYER'S PRIMARY DUTIES

- Accept delivery of the goods upon shipment, when the invoice, the cargo insurance policy or other evidence of insurance cover and the transport document are tendered to him, and receive the goods from the carrier at the named port of destination (**B4**)
- Pay unloading costs to the extent that they are not included in the freight (**B6**)

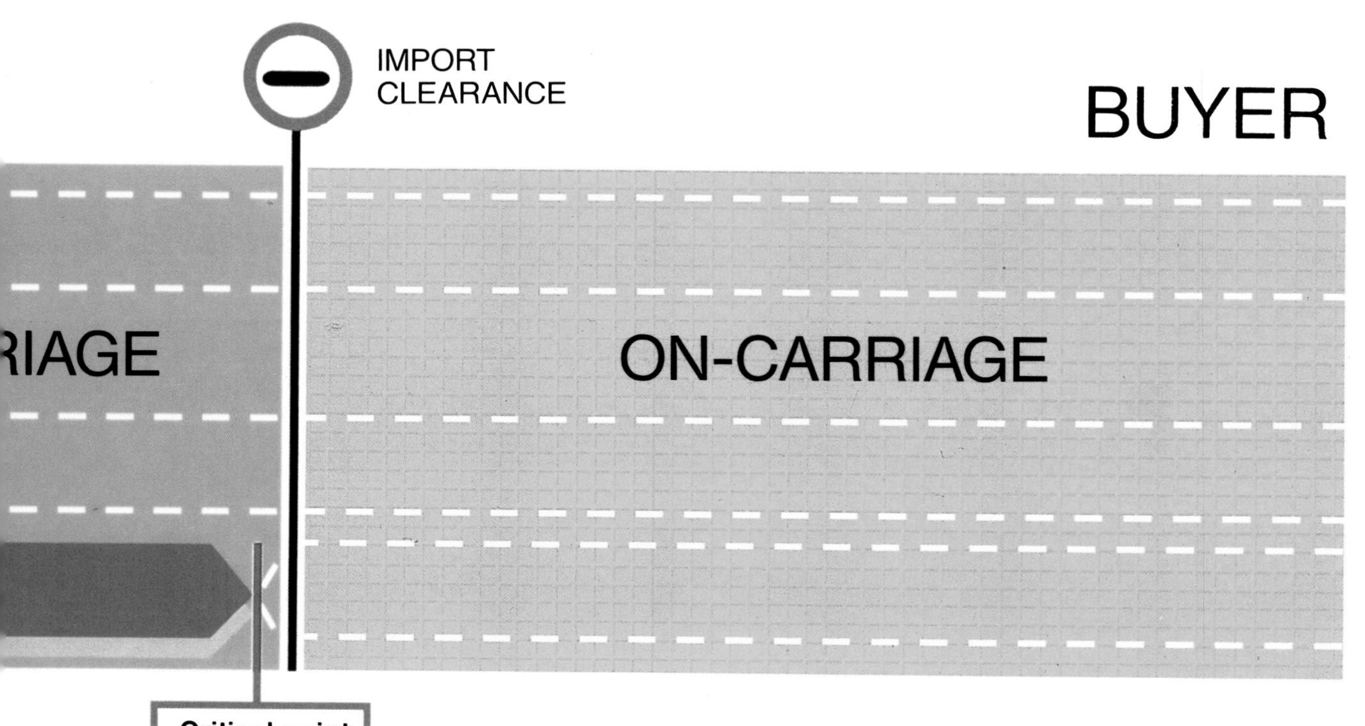

Group C: **Main carriage paid by seller**

CIF

COST, INSURANCE AND FREIGHT

(... named port of destination)

The CFR and CIF terms are identical with only one exception, which is the requirement under CIF for the seller to provide cargo insurance. Therefore, readers wishing to read comments on CIF may use all of the comments on CFR, with the additions below.

A THE SELLER MUST

A1, A2, A4 to A10

(See the comments to CFR A1, A2, A4 to A10)

A3 Contract of carriage and insurance

a) Contract of carriage
Contract on usual terms at his own expense for the carriage of the goods to the named port of destination by the usual route in a seagoing vessel (or inland waterway vessel as appropriate) of the type normally used for the transport of goods of the contract description.

b) Contract of insurance
Obtain at his own expense cargo insurance as agreed in the contract, that the buyer, or any other person having an insurable interest in the goods, shall be entitled to claim directly from the insurer and provide the buyer with the insurance policy or other evidence of insurance cover.

The insurance shall be contracted with underwriters or an insurance company of good repute and, failing express agreement to the contrary, be in accordance with minimum cover of the Institute Cargo Clauses (Institute of London Underwriters) or any similar set of clauses. The duration of insurance cover shall be in accordance with B.5. and B.4. When required by the buyer, the seller shall provide at the buyer's expense war, strikes, riots and civil commotion risk insurances if procurable. The minimum insurance shall cover the price provided in the contract plus ten per cent (i.e. 110 %) and shall be provided in the currency of the contract.

Comments

The only difference between the CFR and the CIF term is that the latter requires the seller to also obtain and pay for cargo insurance. This is particularly important for the buyer, since under CIF the risk for loss of or damage to the goods will pass from the seller to the buyer when the goods pass the ship's rail at the port of shipment (See A5 under CFR).

In addition, it is vital for the buyer to be given the right to claim against the insurer independently of the seller. For this purpose it may be necessary to provide the buyer with the insurance policy under which the insurer makes his undertaking directly to the buyer.

Seller need only provide "minimum cover"

It is important to note that the seller only has to provide for so-called "minimum cover". Such limited cover is only suitable for bulk cargoes, which normally do not suffer loss or damage in transit unless something happens to the ship as well as to the cargo (strandings, collisions, fire etc). The buyer and seller are therefore advised to agree that the seller should provide a more suitable insurance cover. The buyer should then specify the extended cover he prefers.

The insurance cover according to the so-called Institute Cargo Clauses is available in categories A, B and C. The C category provides the minimum cover, and the cover is extended progressively in categories B and A. However, even the most extended cover in A does not provide for what is misleadingly called "all-risk insurance". Furthermore, there are other important exceptions which category A insurance does not cover, e.g. cases when the loss of the goods has been caused by insolvency or fraud, or when financial loss has been incurred by delay in delivery.

Duration of insurance cover

The duration of the insurance cover must coincide with the carriage and must protect the buyer from the moment he has to bear the risk of loss of or damage to the goods (i.e. from the moment the goods pass the ship's rail at the port of shipment). It must extend until the goods arrive at the agreed port of destination.

Some risks require additional cover

Some particular risks require additional insurance, and if the buyer requests it, the seller must arrange this additional cover at the buyer's expense - e.g. insurance against the risks of war, strikes, riots and civil commotions - if this cover can possibly be arranged.

Amount of the insurance cover

The amount of the insurance should correspond to the price provided in the contract plus 10 per cent. The additional 10 per cent is intended to cover the average profit which buyers of goods expect from the sale. The insurance should be provided in the same currency as stipulated in the contract for the price of the goods. Consequently, if the price of the goods is to be paid in convertible currency, the seller may not provide insurance in other than convertible currency.

(See also the comments to CFR A3a)

COST, INSURANCE AND FREIGHT
(... named port of destination)

B THE BUYER MUST

B1 to B9
(See the comments to CFR B1 to B9)

B10 Other obligations

Pay all costs and charges incurred in obtaining the documents or equivalent electronic messages mentioned in A. 10. and reimburse those incurred by the seller in rendering his assistance in accordance therewith.

Provide the seller, upon request, with the necessary information for procuring insurance.

Comments

It is vital for the buyer to understand that the seller only has to take out minimum insurance cover. This cover in most cases is insufficient when manufactured goods are involved. In the contract of sale, therefore, the buyer should require the seller to take out additional cover, usually according to the Institute Clauses A or a corresponding cover. If, however, the contract does not deal with this matter at all, the seller's obligation is limited as stipulated in A 3, and the buyer has to arrange and pay for any additional insurance cover required.

In most cases the seller will know how to arrange the insurance from the contract of sale (from the invoice value of the goods, their destination, etc.). But if this is not the case, the buyer has to provide the seller, upon the latter's request, with any additional necessary information.

(See also the comments to CFR B10)

CARRIAGE PAID TO
(... named place of destination)

A SELLER'S PRIMARY DUTIES

- Contract for the carriage and pay the freight to the named place of destination (**A3a**)
- Deliver the goods into the custody of the first carrier (**A4**)
- Provide export clearance (export licence, pay export taxes and fees, if required) (**A2**)
- Furnish the buyer with the invoice and the usual transport document (**A1, A8**)

DIFFERENCE FROM *CFR*

While CFR is used for goods that are to be carried by sea, the term CPT is used irrespective of the mode of transport.

DOCUMENTS

Required documents

- Commercial invoice (**A1**)
- Usual transport document (**A8**)
- Export licence (**A2**)

NOTE:
All documents may be replaced by EDI messages

Goods

PRE-CARRIAGE

MAIN C

Seller's risk

Seller's costs

Critical point

rriage paid to..." means that the seller pays the freight he carriage of the goods to the named destination. The of loss of or damage to the goods, as well as any itional costs due to events occurring after the time the ds have been delivered to the carrier, is transferred from seller to the buyer when the goods have been delivered the custody of the carrier.
rrier" means any person who, in a contract of carriage, ertakes to perform or to procure the performance of carriage, by rail, road, sea, air, inland waterway or by a combination of such modes.
If subsequent carriers are used for the carriage to the agreed destination, the risk passes when the goods have been delivered to the first carrier.
The CPT term requires the seller to clear the goods for export.
This term may be used for any mode of transport including multimodal transport.

B BUYER'S PRIMARY DUTIES

- Accept delivery of the goods when they are delivered to the first carrier and when the invoice and, if customary, the usual transport document are tendered to him, and receive the goods from the carrier at the named place of destination (**B4**)

onal documents

ner documents needed for nsit of the goods through other country or for import arance (**A10**)

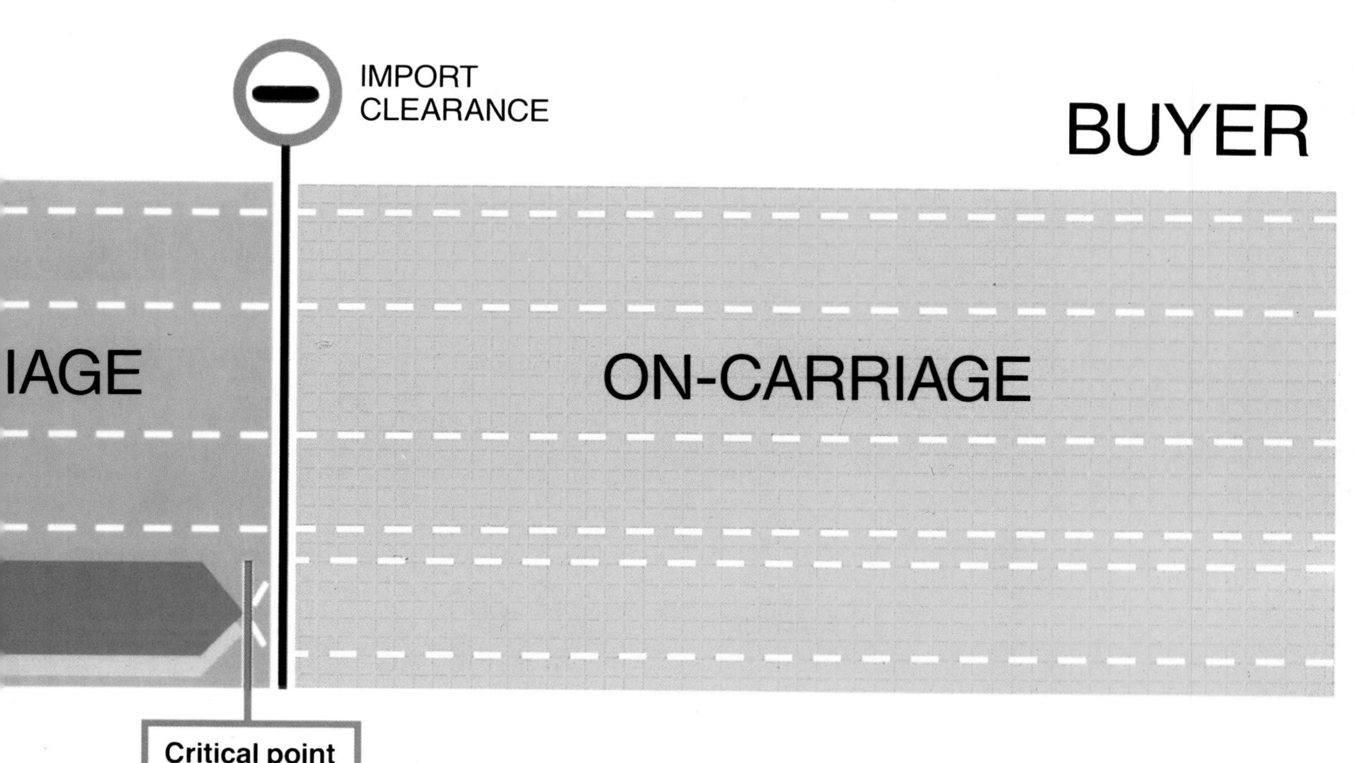

Group C: **Main carriage paid by seller**

CARRIAGE PAID TO

(... named place of destination)

A THE SELLER MUST

A1 Provision of goods in conformity with the contract

Provide the goods and the commercial invoice, or its equivalent electronic message, in conformity with the contract of sale and any other evidence of conformity which may be required by the contract.

Comments

The seller must provide the goods in conformity with the contract. It is also usual practice that the seller, in order to be paid, has to invoice the buyer. In addition, the seller must submit any other evidence stipulated in the contract itself that the goods conform with that contract.

This text only serves as a reminder of the seller's main obligation under the contract of sale.

A2 Licences, authorisations and formalities

Obtain at his own risk and expense any export licence or other official authorisation and carry out all customs formalities necessary for the exportation of the goods.

Comments

The seller has to clear the goods for export and assume any risk or expense which this involves. Consequently, if there is an export prohibition or if there are particular taxes on the export of the goods - and if there are other government-imposed requirements which may render the export of the goods more expensive than contemplated - all of these risks and costs must be borne by the seller. However, contracts of sale usually contain particular provisions which the seller may invoke to protect himself in the event of these contingencies. Under the 1980 Convention on International Sale of Goods (CISG) and corresponding provisions in various national Sale of Goods Acts, unforeseen or reasonably unforeseeable export prohibitions may relieve the seller from his obligations under the contract of sale.

A3 Contract of carriage and insurance

a) Contract of carriage
Contract on usual terms at his own expense for the carriage of the goods to the agreed point at the named place of destination by a usual route and in a customary manner. If a point is not agreed or is not determined by practice, the seller may select the point at the named place of destination which best suits his purpose.

b) Contract of insurance
No obligation.

Comments

The seller's obligation to contract for carriage is basically the same under all C-terms, in that the seller fulfills his delivery obligation upon handing over the goods for carriage in the country of shipment but with the additional obligation to arrange and pay for the carriage up to the agreed point in the country of destination. Since CFR and CIF can only be used when the goods are intended for carriage by sea or inland waterway transport, CPT and CIP respectively must be used as alternatives to CFR and CIF when the goods are intended to be carried by other modes of transport (air, road, rail, unnamed or multimodal transport). But they should also be used whenever the goods are not handed over for sea transport over the ship's rail, e.g. transport of containerised cargo or in roll on-roll off traffic when the goods are carried in railway wagons, trailers or semi-trailers on ferries.

In all C-terms, the seller must, unless otherwise agreed, contract for carriage "on usual terms" or "by a usual route". In CFR and CIF reference is made to a vessel "of the type normally used for the transport of goods of the contract description". Since CPT and CIP are not confined to sea carriage but may be used for all modes of transport, reference is not made to the vehicle of transport but instead to the "customary manner" of transportation.

A4 Delivery

Deliver the goods into the custody of the carrier or, if there are subsequent carriers, to the first carrier, for transportation to the named place of destination on the date or within the period stipulated.

Comments

While delivery under CFR and CIF must be made "onboard the vessel at the port of shipment", the goods under CPT and CIP must be delivered "into the custody of the carrier". Therefore, the delivery obligation is no longer related to the means of conveyance - the vessel - but to the carrier as such.

CPT and CIP should be the preferred terms even when in practice delivery is not intended to be made directly to a vessel. When the parties intend to use several carriers - for example, a pre-carriage by road or rail from the seller's premises at an inland point for further carriage by sea to the agreed destination - the seller has fulfilled his delivery obligation under CPT and CIP when the goods have been handed over for carriage to the first carrier. In this respect, there is an important difference between CPT and CIP on the one hand and CFR and CIF on the other.

In the latter two terms, delivery is not completed until the goods have reached a vessel at the port of shipment. Therefore, the principle that the delivery is completed when the goods have been handed over to the first carrier cannot apply under CFR and CIF unless the pre-carriage is performed by sea, e.g. by a so-called feeder ship to an oceangoing vessel for further carriage.

A5 Transfer of risks

Subject to the provisions of B.5., bear all risks of loss of or damage to the goods until such time as they have been delivered in accordance with A.4.

Comments

All Incoterms are based on the same principle that the risk of loss of or damage to the goods is transferred from the seller to the buyer when the seller has fulfilled his delivery obligation according to A4. A5 of FOB, CFR and CIF further specifies that the risk is transferred when the goods "have passed the ship's rail at the named port of shipment".

All Incoterms, in conformity with the general principle of CISG, connect the transfer of the risk with the delivery of the goods and not with other circumstances, such as the passing of ownership or the time of the conclusion of the contract. Neither Incoterms nor CISG deal with transfer of title to the goods or other property rights with respect to the goods.

The passing of risk of loss of or damage to the goods concerns the risk of fortuitous events (accidents) and does not include loss or damage caused by the seller or the buyer, e.g. inadequate packing or marking of the goods. Therefore, even if damage occurs subsequent to the transfer of the risk, the seller may still be responsible if the damage could be attributed to the fact that the goods were not delivered in conformity with the contract (See A1 and the comments to A9).

A5 of all Incoterms starts with the phrase "subject to the provisions of B5". This means that there are exceptions to the main rule concerning the passing of risk under the circumstances mentioned in B5, which may result in a premature passing of the risk because of the buyer's failure to fulfil his obligations properly (See the comments to B5).

A6 Division of costs

Subject to the provisions of B.6.

- pay all costs relating to the goods until they have been delivered in accordance with A.4. as well as the freight and all other costs resulting from A.3.a), including costs of loading the goods and any charges for unloading at the place of destination which may be included in the freight or incurred by the seller when contracting for carriage;
- pay the costs of customs formalities necessary for exportation as well as all duties, taxes or other official charges payable upon exportation.

Comments

As is the case with the transfer of the risk for loss of or damage to the goods, all Incoterms follow the same rule, that the division of costs occurs at the delivery point.

All costs occurring before the seller has fulfilled his obligation to deliver according to A4 are for his account, while further costs are for the account of the buyer (See the comments to B6). This rule is made subject to the provisions of B6, which indicates that the buyer may have to bear additional costs incurred by his failure to give appropriate notice to the seller.

A7 Notice to the buyer

Give the buyer sufficient notice that the goods have been delivered in accordance with A.4. as well as any other notice required in order to allow the buyer to take measures which are normally necessary to enable him to take the goods.

Comments

The seller must give the buyer sufficient notice that the goods have been dispatched, as well as other relevant information, so that the buyer can make preparations in time to take delivery according to B4. There is no stipulation in Incoterms spelling out the consequences of the seller's failure to give such notice. But it follows from Incoterms that the seller's failure constitutes a breach of contract. This means that the seller could be held responsible for the breach according to the law applicable to the contract of sale.

A8 Proof of delivery, transport document or equivalent electronic message

Provide the buyer at the seller's expense, if customary, with the usual transport document (for example a negotiable bill of lading, a non-negotiable sea waybill, an inland waterway document, an air waybill, a railway consignment note, a road consignment note, or a multimodal transport document).

Where the seller and the buyer have agreed to communicate electronically, the document referred to in the preceding paragraph may be replaced by an equivalent electronic data interchange (EDI) message.

Comments

In all shipment contracts - and particularly contracts under the so-called C-terms which require the seller to arrange and pay for the contract of carriage - it is vital for the buyer to know that the seller has fulfilled his obligation to perform these tasks and to deliver the goods to the carrier. The transport document constitutes proof of such delivery.

Non-negotiable transport documents

Generally, it suffices for the parties to refer to the "usual transport document" obtained by the carrier when the goods are handed over to him. But in maritime carriage, different documents can be used. While traditionally, negotiable bills of lading were used for carriage of goods by sea, other documents have appeared in recent years, e.g. transport documents which are non-negotiable and similar to those used for other modes of transport. These alternative documents have different names - "liner waybills", "ocean waybills", "cargo quay receipts", "data freight receipts" or "sea waybills". The term "sea waybill" is frequently used to include all of the various non-negotiable transport documents used for carriage of goods by sea.

Unfortunately, international conventions and national laws do not yet provide specific regulations for these non-negotiable transport documents. (The exception is in the United States, where a non-negotiable bill of lading is recognised; this is the so-called "straight bill of lading".) For this reason, the Comité Maritime International (CMI) in June 1990 adopted Uniform Rules for Sea Waybills. The parties should refer to these Rules in the contract of carriage to avoid any legal uncertainties stemming from the use of non-negotiable documents (See Appendix).

Electronic communication and the bill of lading

Section A8 takes into account that the parties may wish to engage in so-called "paperless trading". If the parties have agreed to communicate electronically, the requirement that a paper document be presented is no longer compulsory.

However, with respect to maritime carriage, particular problems arise in replacing the bill of lading with electronic communication (See the comments to CFR A8).

A9 Checking - packaging - marking

Pay the costs of those checking operations (such as checking quality, measuring, weighing, counting) which are necessary for the purpose of delivering the goods in accordance with A.4.

Provide at his own expense packaging (unless it is usual for the particular trade to send the goods of the contract description unpacked) which is required for the transport of the goods arranged by him. Packaging is to be marked appropriately.

Comments

It is necessary for the buyer to ensure that the seller has duly fulfilled his obligation with respect to the condition of the goods. This is particularly important if the buyer is called upon to pay for the goods before he has received and checked them. However, the seller has no duty to arrange and pay for inspection of the goods before shipment, unless this has been specifically agreed in the contract of sale.

The goods must also be adequately packed. Since the seller arranges the carriage, he is in a good position to decide the packing required for the transport of the goods. The goods should also be marked in accordance with applicable standards and regulations.

A10 Other obligations

Render the buyer at the latter's request, risk and expense, every assistance in obtaining any documents or equivalent electronic messages (other than those mentioned in A.8.) issued or transmitted in the country of dispatch and/or of origin which the buyer may require for the importation of the goods and, where necessary, for their transit through another country.

Provide the buyer, upon request, with the necessary information for procuring insurance.

Comments

The seller has the obligation to clear the goods for export, but he has no obligation after shipment to bear any costs and risks connected either with the transit through another country or with import clearance of the goods at destination. However, he has the duty to render assistance to the buyer in obtaining any documents or equivalent electronic messages which may be required for these purposes. The buyer, however, must reimburse the seller for any expenses which the seller might have incurred in connection with this assistance. Moreover, if something goes wrong, the buyer will have to assume the risk.

The seller may also be requested to provide the buyer with information related to the goods which the buyer requires for insurance purposes, if this information does not follow from the description of the goods in the contract of sale.

CARRIAGE PAID TO
(... named place of destination)

B THE BUYER MUST

B1 Payment of the price

Pay the price as provided in the contract of sale.

Comments

The buyer must pay the price agreed in the contract of sale. B1 constitutes a reminder of this main obligation, which corresponds with the seller's obligation to provide the goods in conformity with the contract of sale, as stipulated in A1.

B2 Licences, authorisations and formalities

Obtain at his own risk and expense any import licence or other official authorisation and carry out all customs formalities for the importation of the goods and, where necessary, for their transit through another country.

Comments

The buyer must take care of the import clearance and bear any costs and risks in connection with it. Therefore, an import prohibition will not relieve the buyer of his obligation to pay for the goods, unless there is a particular "relief clause" in the contract of sale which he invokes to obtain this relief. Such clauses may provide for the extension of time or the right to avoid the contract under the applicable law (See the comments to A2).

The buyer must also do whatever may be needed to pass the goods through a third country after they have been shipped (dispatched) from the seller's country, and he must assume any cost and risk in connection with these matters.

B3 Contract of carriage

No obligation.

Comments

Although B3 merely stipulates "No obligation" for the buyer, on-carriage from the port of destination is necessary in most cases, and it is the buyer's responsibility to do whatever is required for this purpose. But the seller is not concerned with the further carriage of the goods and the buyer has no obligation to the seller in this respect. The words "No obligation" mean that whatever the buyer does is in his own interest and is not covered by the contract of sale.

B4 Taking delivery

Accept delivery of the goods when they have been delivered in accordance with A.4. and receive them from the carrier at the named place of destination.

Comments

Here, the two critical points under the C-term appear again. Since the seller fulfills his obligation by handing over the goods to the carrier at the place of dispatch (A4), it is for the buyer to accept such delivery under B4. But the buyer also has a further obligation to receive the goods from the carrier at the named port of destination. This is not something he does only in his own interest (as in B3) but is an obligation to the seller, who has concluded the contract of carriage with the carrier.

B5 Transfer of risks

Bear all risks of loss of or damage to the goods from the time they have been delivered in accordance with A.4.

Should he fail to give notice in accordance with B.7., bear all risks of the goods from the agreed date or the expiry date of the period fixed for delivery provided, however, that the goods have been duly appropriated to the contract, that is to say, clearly set aside or otherwise identified as the contract goods.

Comments

According to the main rule, while the seller under A5 bears the risk of loss of or damage to the goods until the delivery point, the buyer has to bear the risk thereafter. The delivery point is different under the different terms. In EXW and all D-terms the goods are simply placed "at the disposal of the buyer" at the relevant point, while under the F- and C-terms the delivery point is related to the handing over of the goods to the carrier in the country of dispatch or shipment (See the comments to A4 of these terms). In the terms used for goods intended to be carried by sea, reference is made to delivery alongside the named vessel (FAS A4) or delivery on board the vessel (FOB, CFR, CIF).

The buyer's failure to give notice according to B7, which relates to the "time for dispatching the goods and/or the destination" (See the comments to B7) may result in a premature passing of the risk: It is unacceptable to allow the buyer to delay the delivery and passing of the risk longer than contemplated when the contract of sale was made. Therefore, his failure to notify according to B7 will cause the risk to pass "from the agreed date or the expiry date of the period fixed for delivery".

The risk, however, cannot pass until the goods "have been appropriated to the contract". If the goods are unascertained - i.e. goods of a certain kind which the seller will deliver to various buyers - appropriation only occurs when the goods are "clearly set aside as the contract goods".

B6 Division of costs

Subject to the provisions of A.3.a), pay all costs relating to the goods from the time they have been delivered in accordance with A.4. and, unless such costs and charges have been included in the freight or incurred by the seller when contracting for carriage in accordance with A.3.a), pay all costs and charges relating to the goods whilst in transit until their arrival at the agreed place of destination, as well as unloading costs.

Should he fail to give notice in accordance with B.7., pay the additional costs thereby incurred for the goods from the agreed date or the expiry date of the period fixed for dispatch provided, however, that the goods have been duly appropriated to the contract, that is to say, clearly set aside or otherwise identified as the contract goods.

Pay all duties, taxes and other official charges as well as the costs of carrying out customs formalities payable upon importation of the goods and, where necessary, for their transit through another country.

Comments

While the seller has to pay all costs required to bring the goods to the place of dispatch and to deliver the goods to the carrier (as well as unloading charges at the place of destination, provided they have been included in the freight), the buyer has to pay any further costs which may arise after the seller has fulfilled these obligations. In this sense, the transfer of the risk also determines the division of costs; if something occurs as a result of contingencies after shipment - such as strandings, collisions, strikes, government directions, hindrances because of ice or other weather conditions - any additional costs charged by the carrier as a result of these contingencies, or otherwise occurring, will be for the account of the buyer.

Failure to give notice and premature passing of risk

The failure to give appropriate notice in accordance with B7 not only results in a premature transfer of the risks (See comments to B5) but also imposes on the buyer the responsibility to pay any additional costs as a consequence. In this case, the obligation to pay these additional costs only occurs if the goods have been duly appropriated to the contract (as discussed in the comments to B5).

Buyer's duties in clearing goods for import

As noted in the comments to B2, the buyer has the duty to clear the goods for import; it is then established in B6 that he has to pay the costs arising from the clearance ("duties, taxes and other official charges as well as the costs of carrying out customs formalities"). The buyer also has to pay any duties, taxes and other charges arising in connection with the transit of the goods through another country after they have been delivered by the seller in accordance with A4.

B7 Notice to the seller

Whenever he is entitled to determine the time for dispatching the goods and/or the destination, give the seller sufficient notice thereof.

Comments

As discussed in the comments to B5 and B6, the failure of the buyer to notify the seller of the time for shipping the goods or the destination - when the buyer in the contract of sale has been given the option to determine these matters - may cause the risk of the loss of or damage to the goods to pass before the goods have been delivered according to A4. In addition, it can make the buyer liable to pay any additional costs incurred by the seller as a result of the buyer's failure.

B8 Proof of delivery, transport document or equivalent electronic message

Accept the transport document in accordance with A.8. if it is in conformity with the contract.

Comments

The buyer has to accept the transport document if it conforms with the contract and with the requirements of A8 (See the comments to A8). If the buyer rejects the transport document (e.g. by instructions to a bank not to pay the seller under a documentary credit), he commits a breach of contract, which would give the seller remedies available for such a breach under the contract of sale.

These remedies could include, for example, a right to cancel the contract or to claim damages for breach. However, the buyer is not obliged to accept a document which does not provide adequate proof of delivery, e.g. one which has notations on it showing that the goods are defective or that they have been provided in less than the agreed quantity. In these cases, the document is termed "unclean".

B9 Inspection of goods

Pay, unless otherwise agreed, the costs of pre-shipment inspection except when mandated by the authorities of the country of exportation.

Comments

As discussed in the comments to A9, the buyer has to pay for any costs of checking the goods unless the contract states that these costs should be borne wholly or partly by the seller. In some cases, the contract may provide that the costs should be borne by the selier if the inspection reveals that the goods do not conform with the contract.

In some countries, where import licences or permission to obtain foreign currency for the payment of the price may be required, the authorities may demand an inspection of the goods before shipment, to ensure that the goods are in conformity with the contract. (This is usually called pre-shipment inspection, PSI.) If this is the case, the inspection is normally arranged by instructions from the authorities to an inspection company, which they appoint. The costs following from this inspection have to be paid by the authorities. Any reimbursement to the authorities for the inspection costs, however, must be made by the buyer, unless otherwise specifically agreed between the buyer and the seller.

B10 Other obligations

Pay all costs and charges incurred in obtaining the documents or equivalent electronic messages mentioned in A. 10. and reimburse those incurred by the seller in rendering his assistance in accordance therewith.

Comments

As discussed in the comments to A10, the seller has to render the buyer assistance in obtaining the documents or electronic messages which may be required for the transit and importation of the goods. However, this assistance is rendered at the buyer's risk and expense. Therefore, B10 stipulates that the buyer must pay all costs and charges incurred in obtaining these documents or electronic messages. He will also have to reimburse the seller for the seller's costs in rendering his assistance in these matters.

Group C : Main carriage paid by seller

CARRIAGE AND INSURANCE PAID TO

(... named place of destination)

A SELLER'S PRIMARY DUTIES

- Contract for the carriage and pay the freight to the named place of destination (**A3a**)
- Deliver the goods into the custody of the first carrier (**A4**)
- Provide export clearance (export licence, pay export taxes and fees, if required) (**A2**)
- Contract for the insurance of the goods during the carriage and pay the insurance premium (**A3b**)
- Furnish the buyer with the invoice, the usual transport document and a cargo insurance policy or other evidence of insurance cover (**A1, A8, A3b**)

DIFFERENCE FROM *CIF*

CIF is used for goods carried sea, while CIP is used irrespective of the mode of transport.

DOCUMENTS

Required documents

- Commercial invoice (**A1**)
- Usual transport document (
- Export licence (**A2**)
- Insurance policy or certificat

NOTE:
All documents may be replaced by EDI messages

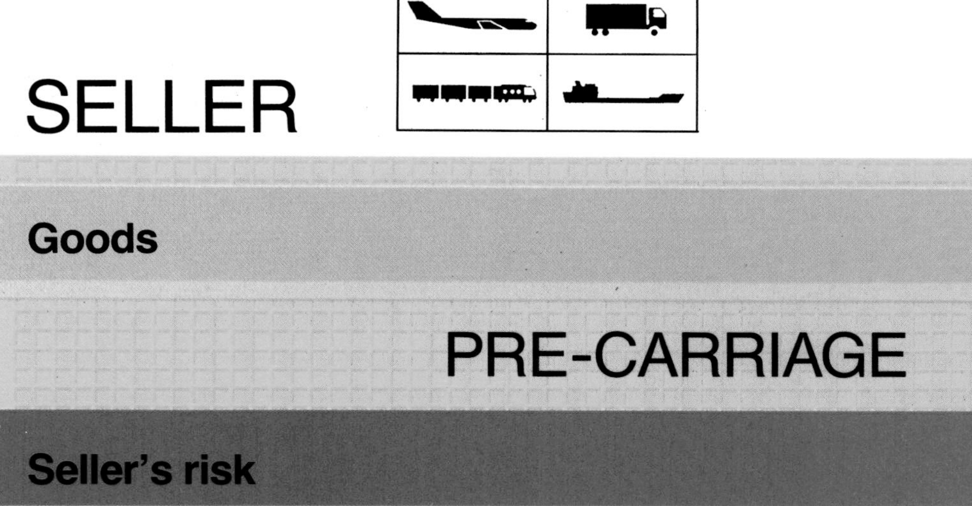

MAIN

+ INSURA

Critical point

‑arriage and insurance paid to..." means that the seller as the same obligations as under CPT but with the addition at the seller has to procure cargo insurance against the uyer's risk of loss of or damage to the goods during the arriage. The seller contracts for insurance and pays the surance premium.

The buyer should note that under the CIP term the seller is only required to obtain insurance on minimum coverage. The CIP term requires the seller to clear the goods for export. This term may be used for any mode of transport including multimodal transport.

B BUYER'S PRIMARY DUTY

- Accept delivery of the goods when they are delivered to the first carrier and when the invoice, the cargo insurance policy or other evidence of insurance cover, and, if customary, the usual transport document are tendered to him, and receive the goods from the carrier at the named place of destination (**B4**)

ptional documents

- Other documents needed for transit of the goods through another country or for import clearance (**A10**)

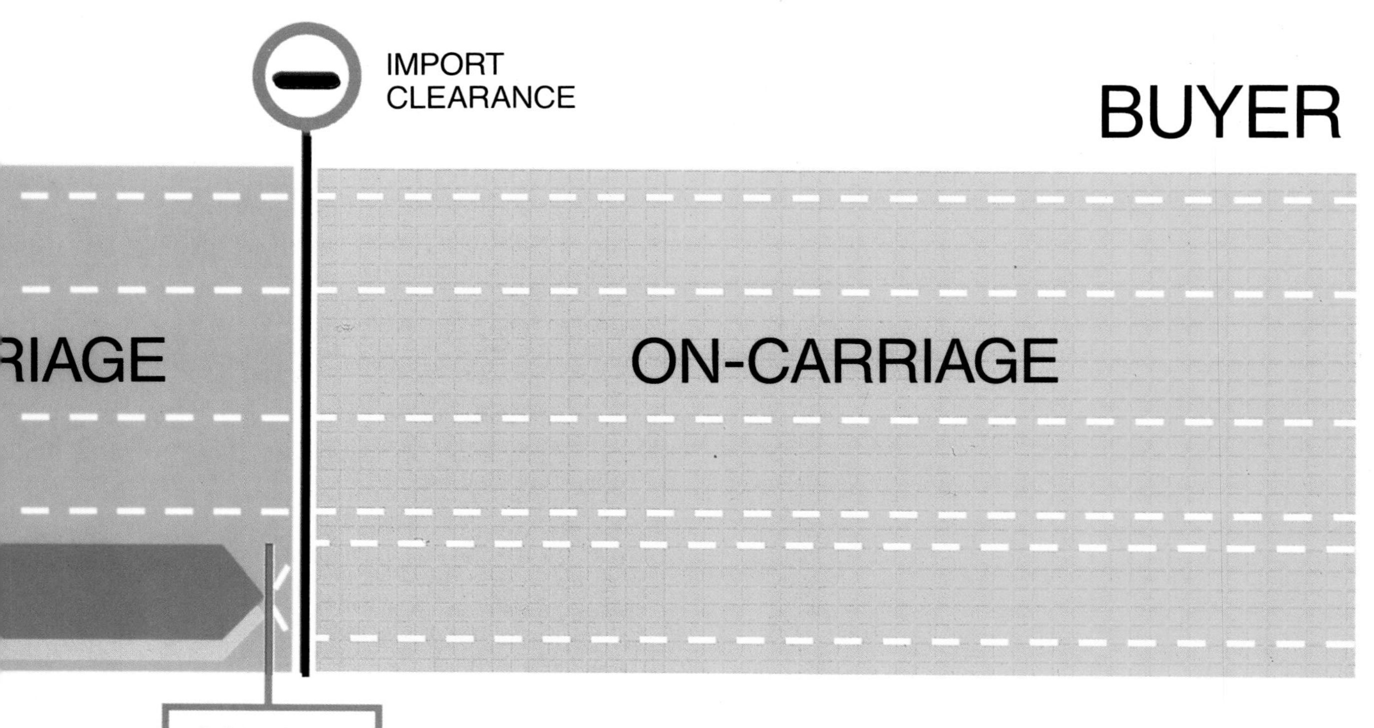

Group C: **Main carriage paid by seller**

CARRIAGE AND INSURANCE PAID TO

(... named place of destination)

The terms CIP and CPT are identical with only one exception which is the requirement under CIP for the seller to provide cargo insurance. Therefore, readers wishing to read comments on CIP should use all of the comments on CPT with the additions below.

A THE SELLER MUST

A1, A2, A4 to A10

(See the comments to CPT A1, A2, A4 to A10)

A3 Contract of carriage and insurance

a) Contract of carriage

Contract on usual terms at his own expense for the carriage of the goods to the agreed point at the named place of destination by a usual route and in a customary manner. If a point is not agreed or is not determined by practice, the seller may select the point at the named place of destination which best suits his purpose.

b) Contract of insurance

Obtain at his own expense cargo insurance as agreed in the contract, that the buyer, or any other person having an insurable interest in the goods, shall be entitled to claim directly from the insurer and provide the buyer with the insurance policy or other evidence of insurance cover.

The insurance shall be contracted with underwriters or an insurance company of good repute and, failing express agreement to the contrary, be in accordance with minimum cover of the Institute Cargo Clauses (Institute of London Underwriters) or any similar set of clauses. The duration of insurance cover shall be in accordance with B.5. and B.4. When required by the buyer, the seller shall provide at the buyer's expense war, strikes, riots and civil commotion risk insurances if procurable. The minimum insurance shall cover the price provided in the contract plus ten per cent (i.e. 110 %) and shall be provided in the currency of the contract.

Comments

The only difference between the CPT and the CIP term is that the latter requires the seller to also obtain and pay for cargo insurance. This is particularly important for the buyer, since under CIP the risk of loss of or damage to the goods will pass from the seller to the buyer when the goods have been delivered to the carrier at the place of dispatch (See CPT A5).

In addition, it is vital for the buyer to be given the right to claim against the insurer independently of the seller. For this purpose it may be necessary to provide the buyer with the insurance policy under which the insurer makes his undertaking directly to the buyer.

Seller need only provide "minimum cover"

It is important to note that the seller only has to provide for so-called "minimum cover". Such limited cover is only suitable for bulk cargoes, which normally do not suffer loss or damage in transit unless something happens to the means of conveyance as well as to the cargo (strandings, collisions, fire, etc). The buyer and seller are therefore advised to agree that the seller should provide a more suitable insurance cover. The buyer should then specify the extended cover he prefers.

The insurance cover according to the so-called Institute Cargo Clauses is available in categories A, B and C. The C category provides the minimum cover, and the cover is extended progressively in categories B and A. However, even the most extended cover in A does not provide for what is misleadingly called "all-risk insurance". Furthermore, there are other important exceptions which category A insurance does not cover, e.g. cases when the loss of the goods has been caused by insolvency or fraud, or when financial loss has been incurred by delay in delivery.

Duration of insurance cover

The duration of the insurance cover must coincide with the carriage and must protect the buyer from the moment he has to bear the risk of loss of or damage to the goods (i.e. from the moment the goods have been delivered to the carrier at the place of dispatch). It must extend until the goods arrive at the agreed place of destination.

Some risks require additional cover

Some particular risks require additional insurance, and if the buyer requests it, the seller must arrange this additional cover at the buyer's expense - e.g. insurance against the risks of war, strikes, riots and civil commotions - if this cover can possibly be arranged.

Amount of the insurance cover

The amount of the insurance should correspond to the price provided in the contract plus 10 per cent. The additional 10 per cent is intended to cover the average profit which buyers of goods expect from the sale. The insurance should be provided in the same currency as stipulated in the contract for the price of the goods. Consequently, if the price of the goods is to be paid in convertible currency, the seller may not provide insurance in other than convertible currency.

(See also the comments to CPT A3a)

CARRIAGE AND INSURANCE PAID TO
(... named place of destination)

B THE BUYER MUST

B1 to B9
(See the comments to CPT B1 to B9)

B10 Other obligations

Pay all costs and charges incurred in obtaining the documents or equivalent electronic messages mentioned in A.10. and reimburse those incurred by the seller in rendering his assistance in accordance therewith.

Provide the seller, upon request, with the necessary information for procuring insurance.

Comments

It is vital for the buyer to understand that the seller only has to take out minimum insurance cover. This cover in most cases is insufficient when manufactured goods are involved. In the contract of sale, therefore, the buyer should require the seller to take out additional cover, usually according to the Institute Clauses A or a corresponding cover. If, however, the contract does not deal with this matter at all, the seller's obligation is limited as stipulated in A 3, and the buyer has to arrange and pay for any additional insurance cover required.

In most cases the seller will know how to arrange the insurance from the contract of sale (from the invoice value of the goods, their destination, etc.). But if this is not the case, the buyer has to provide the seller, upon the latter's request, with any additional necessary information.

(See also the comments to CPT B10)

DELIVERED AT FRONTIER
(... named place)

A SELLER'S PRIMARY DUTIES

- Deliver the goods cleared for export at the named frontier (or the named place at that frontier) (**A2, A4**)
- Provide documents to enable the buyer to take delivery at the frontier (e.g. document of transport or warehouse warrant) and assist the buyer to obtain any through transport document (**A8**)

DIFFERENCE FROM *CPT*

When the parties merely wish to clarify that the seller should arrange and pay for the transpor the CPT term should be used. However, if the seller is to bear

DOCUMENTS

Required documents

- Commercial invoice (**A1**)
- Customary document of transport, warehouse warrant, dock warrant or delivery order (**A8**)
- Export licence (**A2**)

NOTE:
All documents may be replaced by EDI messages

SELLER

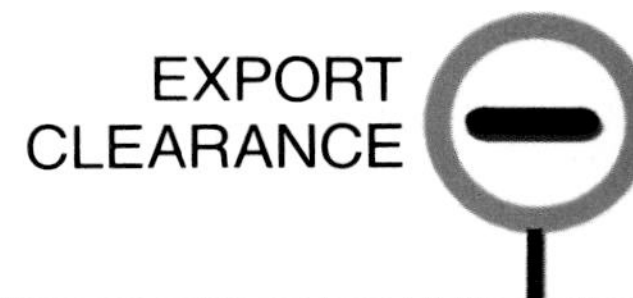

Goods

PRE-CARRIAGE

Seller's risk

Seller's costs

livered at Frontier" means that the seller fulfils his gation to deliver when the goods have been made lable, cleared for export, at the named point and place he frontier, but before the customs border of the ining country. The term "frontier" may be used for any tier including that of the country of export. Therefore, it is of vital importance that the frontier in question be defined precisely by always naming the point and place in the term. The term is primarily intended to be used when goods are to be carried by rail or road, but it may be used for any mode of transport.

only the costs but the risks of of or damage to the goods as then the DAF term ıld be used.

B BUYER'S PRIMARY DUTIES

- Take delivery of the goods at the named frontier (or the named place at that frontier) (**B4**)
- Pay for on-carriage (**B6**)
- Provide import clearance (import licence, pay import duties, taxes and fees, if required) (**B2**)

onal documents

rough document of transport **B**)

her documents needed for nsit of the goods through other country or for import arance (**A10**)

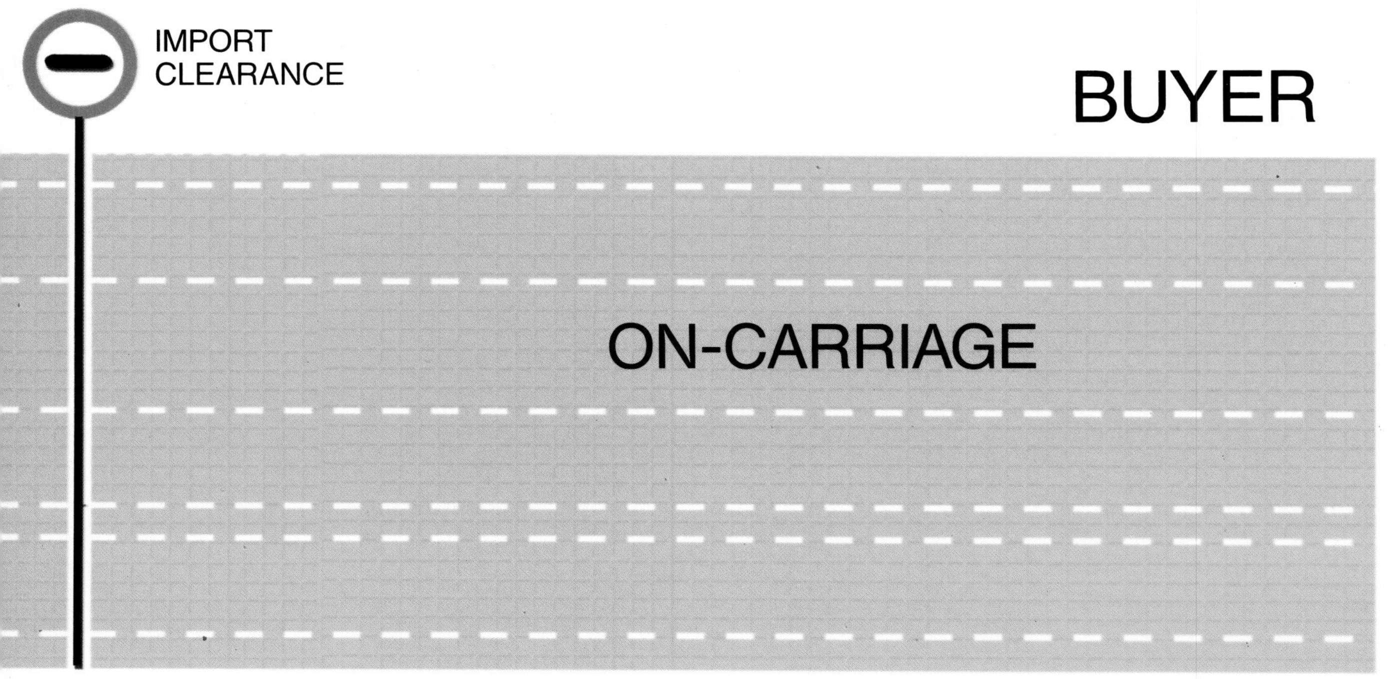

DELIVERED AT FRONTIER
(... named place)

A THE SELLER MUST

A1 Provision of goods in conformity with the contract

Provide the goods and the commercial invoice, or its equivalent electronic message, in conformity with the contract of sale and any other evidence of conformity which may be required by the contract.

Comments

The seller must provide the goods in conformity with the contract. It is also usual practice that the seller, in order to be paid, has to invoice the buyer. In addition, the seller must submit any other evidence stipulated in the contract itself that the goods conform with that contract.

This text only serves as a reminder of the seller's main obligation under the contract of sale.

A2 Licences, authorisations and formalities

Obtain at his own risk and expense any export licence or other official authorisation or other document necessary for placing the goods at the buyer's disposal. Carry out all customs formalities for the exportation of the goods to the named place of delivery at the frontier and, where necessary, for their prior transit through another country.

Comments

The seller has to clear the goods for export and assume any risk or expense which this involves. Consequently, if there is an export prohibition or if there are particular taxes on the export of the goods - and if there are other government-imposed requirements which may render the export of the goods more expensive than contemplated - all of these risks and costs must be borne by the seller. However, contracts of sale usually contain particular provisions which the seller may invoke to protect himself in the event of these contingencies. Under the 1980 Convention on International Sale of Goods (CISG) and corresponding provisions in various national Sale of Goods Acts, unforeseen or reasonably unforeseeable export prohibitions may relieve the seller from his obligations under the contract of sale.

A2 stipulates that the seller has to do whatever may be necessary with respect to prior transit formalities. This is the case even when the goods are to be carried through several countries before they reach the point named after DAF in the contract of sale. DAF is frequently used in these circumstances, usually with the goods being carried by rail. Non-compliance with the above requirements would prevent the seller from reaching the agreed place of delivery.

A3 Contract of carriage and insurance

a) Contract of carriage
Contract at his own expense for the carriage of the goods by a usual route and in a customary manner to the named point at the place of delivery at the frontier (including, if necessary, for their transit through another country).

If a point at the named place of delivery at the frontier is not agreed or is not determined by practice, the seller may select the point at the named place of delivery which best suits his purpose.

b) Contract of insurance
No obligation.

Comments

Under all D-terms the seller must ensure that the goods actually arrive at destination. It follows from this that the seller must arrange and pay for any carriage of the goods. Though it may seem that the seller should have the right to contract for carriage as he deems fit - since any inadequate measures in this regard would automatically be at his own peril - it is nevertheless stipulated in the D-terms, as in the C-terms, that the seller should contract for carriage "by a usual route and in a customary manner".

Under the D-terms, the seller's choice of transport is only of importance to the buyer insofar as it affects the buyer's obligation to receive the goods from the carrier. If the seller chooses an unusual mode of transport which makes it more difficult or expensive for the buyer to receive the goods from the carrier, any additional costs or risks caused by the seller's choice of transport will be for the seller's account.

Normally, the point mentioned after the D-term will indicate where the goods should be delivered at destination. But if there are several alternatives available, and the contract of sale or commercial practice does not indicate which alternative the seller must choose, he "may select the point at the named place of delivery which best suits his purpose".

A4 Delivery

Place the goods at the disposal of the buyer at the named place of delivery at the frontier on the date or within the period stipulated.

Comments

Under all D-terms the seller must "place the goods at the disposal of the buyer" at destination. The precise point for the delivery of the goods depends upon the D-term chosen. According to DAF A4 the goods should be placed at the disposal of the buyer "at the named place of delivery at the frontier".

If in the contract of sale only the frontier of the country concerned is named and not the place at that frontier where the delivery should take place (e.g. the contract may say, for example, "DAF Italian border") the seller can then select the place at the border which best suits his purpose.

DAF may be used irrespective of the intended mode of transport, though it is more frequently used for rail carriage. The rail carriage usually continues past the border without any discharge of the goods from the railway wagon and re-loading on another one. Consequently, there will be no real "placing of the goods at the disposal of the buyer". Instead, the seller, on the buyer's request, will provide the buyer with a through railway consignment note to the place of final destination in the country of importation (See the comments to A8).

A5 Transfer of risks

Subject to the provisions of B.5., bear all risks of loss of or damage to the goods until such time as they have been delivered in accordance with A.4.

Comments

All Incoterms are based on the same principle that the risk of loss of or damage to the goods is transferred from the seller to the buyer when the seller has fulfilled his delivery obligation according to A4. A5 of FOB, CFR and CIF further specifies that the risk is transferred when the goods "have passed the ship's rail at the named port of shipment".

All Incoterms, in conformity with the general principle of CISG, connect the transfer of the risk with the delivery of the goods and not with other circumstances, such as the passing of ownership or the time of the conclusion of the contract. Neither Incoterms nor CISG deal with transfer of title to the goods or other property rights with respect to the goods.

The passing of risk of loss of or damage to the goods concerns the risk of fortuitous events (accidents) and does not include loss or damage caused by the seller or the buyer, e.g. inadequate packing or marking of the goods. Therefore, even if damage occurs subsequent to the transfer of the risk, the seller may still be responsible if the damage could be attributed to the fact that the goods were not delivered in conformity with the contract (See A1 and the comments to A9).

A5 of all Incoterms starts with the phrase "subject to the provisions of B5". This means that there are exceptions to the main rule concerning the passing of risk under the circumstances mentioned in B5, which may result in a premature passing of the risk because of the buyer's failure to fulfil his obligations properly (See the comments to B5).

A6 Division of costs

Subject to the provisions of B. 6.

- pay all costs of the goods until they have been delivered in accordance with A.4. as well as, in addition to costs resulting from A.3.a), the expenses of discharge operations (including lighterage and handling charges), if it is necessary or customary for the goods to be discharged on their arrival at the named place of delivery at the frontier, in order to place them at the buyer's disposal;
- pay the costs of customs formalities necessary for exportation as well as all duties, taxes or other official charges payable upon exportation and, where necessary, for their transit through another country prior to delivery in accordance with A. 4.

Comments

As is the case with the transfer of the risk of loss of or damage to the goods, all Incoterms follow the same rule, that the division of costs occurs at the delivery point. All costs occurring before the seller has fulfilled his obligation to deliver according to A4 are for his account, while further costs are for the account of the buyer (See the comments to B6). This rule is made subject to the provisions of B6, which indicates that the buyer may have to bear additional costs incurred by his failure to give appropriate notice to the seller.

Since under D-terms the seller does not fulfil his obligation until the goods have actually arrived at destination and been placed at the disposal of the buyer, the seller has to do everything required to achieve this. A3 in all D-terms still stipulates that the seller must contract for carriage; and A6 of all D-terms stipulates that he must pay the costs resulting from A3 for the carriage of the goods "and, where necessary, for their transit through another country prior to delivery in accordance with A4". Needless to say, any transit costs incurred subsequent to delivery willl have to be paid by the buyer.

A7 Notice to the buyer

Give the buyer sufficient notice of the dispatch of the goods to the named place at the frontier as well as any other notice required in order to allow the buyer to take measures which are normally necessary to enable him to take the goods.

Comments

The seller must give the buyer sufficient notice as to when the goods are available at the agreed or chosen delivery point, so that the buyer can make preparations in time to take delivery according to B4. There is no stipulation in Incoterms spelling out the consequences of the seller's failure to give such notice. But it follows from Incoterms that the seller's failure constitutes a breach of contract. This means that the seller could be held responsible for the breach according to the law applicable to the contract of sale.

A8 Proof of delivery, transport document or equivalent electronic message

Provide the buyer at the seller's expense with the usual document or other evidence of the delivery of the goods at the named place at the frontier.

Provide the buyer at the latter's request, risk and expense, with a through document of transport normally obtained in the country of dispatch covering on usual terms the transport of the goods from the point of dispatch in that country to the place of final destination in the country of importation named by the buyer.

Where the seller and the buyer have agreed to communicate electronically, the document referred to in the preceding paragraph may be replaced by an equivalent electronic data interchange (EDI) message.

Comments

When the goods have actually been delivered physically at the frontier, the seller, at his own expense, has to provide the buyer "with the usual document or other evidence of delivery". However, as noted in the comments to DAF A4, goods carried by rail will frequently remain on the railway wagon and continue to the final destination. If the parties intend this to be the case, the seller - at the buyer's request, risk and expense - must assist the buyer to obtain the usual "through document of transport". These documents can be replaced by EDI messages when the parties have agreed to communicate electronically.

A9 Checking - packaging - marking

Pay the costs of those checking operations (such as checking quality, measuring, weighing, counting) which are necessary for the purpose of delivering the goods in accordance with A.4.

Provide at his own expense packaging (unless it is usual for the particular trade to deliver the goods of the contract description unpacked) which is required for the delivery of the goods at the frontier and for the subsequent transport to the extent that the circumstances (e.g. modalities, destination) are made known to the seller before the contract of sale is concluded. Packaging is to be marked appropriately.

Comments

It is important that the buyer ensure that the seller has duly fulfilled his obligation with respect to the condition of the goods, particularly if the buyer is called upon to pay for the goods before he has received and checked them. However, the seller has no duty to arrange and pay for the inspection of the goods before shipment, unless this is specifically agreed in the contract of sale.

A10 Other obligations

Render the buyer at the latter's request, risk and expense, every assistance in obtaining any documents or equivalent electronic messages (other than those mentioned in A.8.) issued or transmitted in the country of dispatch and/or origin which the buyer may require for the importation of the goods and, where necessary, for their transit through another country.

Provide the buyer, upon request, with the necessary information for procuring insurance.

Comments

The seller has the obligation to carry out all customs formalities for the exportation of the goods and for their prior transit. But he has no obligation after the goods have reached the frontier to bear any costs and risks for their transit through another country or for import clearance. However, he has the duty to render the buyer assistance in obtaining the documents (e.g. a certificate of origin, a health certificate, a clean report of findings, an import licence) or equivalent electronic messages which may be required for import clearance of the goods.

The buyer, in turn, must reimburse the seller for any expenses which the seller might have incurred in connection with this assistance. Moreover, if something goes wrong, the buyer will have to assume the risk.

The seller may also be requested to provide the buyer with any information relating to the goods which the buyer might require for insurance purposes, if this information is not provided in the description of the goods in the contract of sale.

DELIVERED AT FRONTIER
(... named place)

B THE BUYER MUST

B1 Payment of the price

Pay the price as provided in the contract of sale.

Comments

The buyer must pay the price agreed in the contract of sale. B1 constitutes a reminder of this main obligation, which corresponds with the seller's obligation to provide the goods in conformity with the contract of sale, as stipulated in A1.

B2 Licences, authorisations and formalities

Obtain at his own risk and expense any import licence or other official authorisation and carry out all customs formalities at the named point of delivery at the frontier or elsewhere for the importation of the goods and, where necessary, for their subsequent transport.

Comments

The buyer must take care of the import clearance and bear any costs and risks in connection with it. Therefore, an import prohibition will not relieve the buyer of his obligation to pay for the goods, unless there is a particular "relief clause" in the contract of sale which he invokes to obtain this relief. Such clauses may provide for the extension of time or the right to avoid the contract under the applicable law (See the comments to A2).

B3 Contract of carriage

No obligation.

Comments

Although B3 merely stipulates "No obligation" for the buyer, on-carriage from the place of delivery is necessary in most cases, and it is the buyer's responsibility to do whatever is required for this purpose. But the seller is not concerned with the further carriage of the goods and the buyer has no obligation to the seller in this respect. The words "No obligation" mean that whatever the buyer does is in his own interest and is not covered by the contract of sale.

B4 Taking delivery

Take delivery of the goods as soon as they have been placed at his disposal in accordance with A.4.

Comments

As in all D-terms, B4 has wording stating that the buyer shall take delivery as soon as the goods have been placed at his disposal in accordance with A4. The seller, according to A4 in the D-terms, shall place the goods at the buyer's disposal "on the date or within the period stipulated". If the goods are placed at the buyer's disposal earlier than agreed, the buyer is not obliged to take delivery before the agreed time, though it may normally be in his own interest to do so. If the goods are placed at the buyer's disposal too late, the buyer may hold the seller responsible for breach of contract according to the applicable law. He may also recover damages from the seller or, in the event of a fundamental breach, cancel the contract.

B5 Transfer of risks

Bear all risks of loss of or damage to the goods from the time they have been placed at his disposal in accordance with A.4.

Should he fail to give notice in accordance with B. 7., bear all risks of loss of or damage to the goods from the agreed date or the expiry date of the period stipulated for delivery provided, however, that the goods have been duly appropriated to the contract, that is to say, clearly set aside or otherwise identified as the contract goods.

Comments

According to the main rule, while the seller under A5 bears the risk of loss of or damage to the goods until the delivery point, the buyer has to bear the risk thereafter. The delivery point is different under the different terms. In EXW and all D-terms the goods are simply placed "at the disposal of the buyer" at the relevant point, while under the F- and C-terms the delivery point is related to the handing over of the goods to the carrier in the country of dispatch or shipment (See the comments to A4 of these terms). In the terms used for goods intended to be carried by sea, reference is made to delivery alongside the named vessel (FAS A4) or delivery onboard the vessel (FOB, CFR, CIF).

Consequences of buyer's failure to give notice

While the seller under EXW and all D-terms can transfer the risk by his own act of placing the goods at the buyer's disposal, he may be prevented from doing so by the buyer's failure to give notice according to B7. This can occur when it is the buyer's responsibility to determine (1) the time within a stipulated period when the goods are to be made available or (2) the place of delivery (See the comments to B7). The failure to perform these tasks results in a premature passing of the risk: It is not acceptable that the buyer should be able to delay the delivery and passing of the risk longer than contemplated when the contract of sale was made. Therefore, his failure to notify according to B7 will cause the risk to pass "from the agreed date or the expiry date of any period fixed for taking delivery".

Appropriation and the passing of risk

The risk, however, cannot pass until the goods "have been appropriated to the contract". If the goods are unascertained - i.e. goods of a certain kind which the seller will deliver to various buyers - appropriation only occurs when the goods are "clearly set aside as the contract goods".

This appropriation will normally be made when the seller has handed over the goods for carriage and the consignment has been marked as intended for the buyer - unless the cargo is carried in bulk and intended to be appropriated between different buyers only upon the arrival of the goods at destination.

B6 Division of costs

Pay all costs relating to the goods from the time they have been placed at his disposal in accordance with A.4.

Should he fail to take delivery of the goods when they have been placed at his disposal in accordance with A.4., or to give notice in accordance with B. 7., bear all additional costs incurred thereby provided, however, that the goods have been appropriated to the contract, that is to say, clearly set aside or otherwise identified as the contract goods.

Pay all duties, taxes and other official charges as well as the costs of carrying out customs formalities payable upon importation of the goods and, where necessary, for their subsequent transport.

Comments

If, as stipulated in A4, the goods are placed at the disposal of the buyer at the named place of delivery at the frontier, the buyer, under DAF B6 and under all other D-terms, would have to pay all costs from the time the goods have been made available to him in this manner. The seller has to pay all costs of discharge required in order to place the goods at the disposal of the buyer. But if the goods are intended to be re-loaded upon an on-carrying vehicle, the parties are advised to stipulate specifically who should perform the unloading and re-loading operations, e.g. by adding the words "loaded upon on-carrying vehicle" after the Incoterm.

When DAF is used for railway traffic, the goods will usually remain on the same railway wagon, and the point mentioned in the contract will then primarily serve as a point for dividing the railway freight between the parties (i.e. as a tariff point). The seller has to bear all costs and risks until that point has been reached.

Under all D-terms the buyer has to take delivery of the goods at the agreed point and time. The same principle governs even if there is no delivery in the physical sense, e.g. if the goods remain on the same vehicle when it passes the agreed delivery point. If the buyer fails to take delivery or to take the required measures for on-carriage, he will have to bear any additional costs incurred thereby.

Appropriation required if goods arrive in bulk

At the delivery stage, the seller will normally have identified the goods as the contract goods (through so-called "appropriation"). But if he has not done so - e.g. if the goods arrive at destination in bulk for later appropriation by delivery orders or otherwise - the buyer does not have to bear any additional costs relating to the goods until they have been duly appropriated.

Subject to the goods having been appropriated, the buyer then has to pay any additional costs incurred as a result of his failure to notify the seller of the time or place of taking delivery, according to B7, e.g. additional storage and insurance costs.

Buyer's duties in clearing goods for import

As noted in the comments to B2, the buyer has the duty to clear the goods for import; B6 declares that he also has to pay the costs arising in that connection ("duties, taxes and other official charges as well as the costs of carrying out customs formalities"). The buyer also has to pay any duties, taxes and other charges arising with regard to the transit of the goods through another country, after they have been delivered by the seller in accordance with A4.

B7 Notice to the seller

Whenever he is entitled to determine the time within a stipulated period and/or the place of taking delivery, give the seller sufficient notice thereof.

Comments

As discussed in the comments to B5 and B6, the failure of the buyer to notify the seller of the time and place of taking delivery - when the buyer in the contract of sale has been given the option to determine these matters - may cause the risk of the loss of or damage to the goods to pass before the goods have been delivered according to A4. In addition, it can make the buyer liable to pay any additional costs incurred by the seller as a result of the buyer's failure.

B8 Proof of delivery, transport document or equivalent electronic message

Accept the transport document and/or other evidence of delivery in accordance with A.8.

Comments

The buyer has to accept the document if it conforms with the contract and with the requirements of A8 (See the comments to A8). If the buyer rejects the document (e.g. by instructions to a bank not to pay the seller under a documentary credit), he commits a breach of contract, which would give the seller remedies available for such a breach under the contract of sale.

These remedies could include, for example, a right to cancel the contract or to claim damages for breach. However, the buyer is not obliged to accept a document which does not provide adequate proof of delivery, e.g. one which has notations on it showing that the goods are defective or that they have been provided in less than the agreed quantity. In these cases, the document is termed "unclean".

B9 Inspection of goods

Pay, unless otherwise agreed, the costs of pre-shipment inspection except when mandated by the authorities of the country of exportation.

Comments

As noted in the comments to A9, the buyer has to pay for any costs of checking the goods, unless the contract determines that these costs should be wholly or partly borne by the seller. In some cases, the contract may provide that the costs should be borne by the seller if the inspection reveals that the goods do not conform with the contract.

In some countries, where import licences or permission to obtain foreign currency for the payment of the price may be required, the authorities may demand an inspection of the goods before shipment, to ensure that the goods are in conformity with the contract. (This is usually called pre-shipment inspection, PSI.) If this is the case, the inspection is normally arranged by instructions from the authorities to an inspection company, which they appoint. The costs following from this inspection have to be paid by the authorities. Any reimbursement to the authorities for the inspection costs, however, must be made by the buyer, unless otherwise specifically agreed between the buyer and the seller.

B10 Other obligations

Pay all costs and charges incurred in obtaining the documents or equivalent electronic messages mentioned in A. 10. and reimburse those incurred by the seller in rendering his assistance in accordance therewith.

If necessary, provide the seller at his request and the buyer's risk and expense with exchange control authorisation, permits, other documents or certified copies thereof, or with the address of the final destination of the goods in the country of importation for the purpose of obtaining the through document of transport or any other document contemplated in A.8.

Comments

As discussed in the comments to A10, the seller has to render the buyer assistance in obtaining the documents or electronic messages which may be required for the transit and importation of the goods. However, this assistance is rendered at the buyer's risk and expense. Therefore, B10 stipulates that the buyer must pay all costs and charges incurred in obtaining these documents or electronic messages. He will also have to reimburse the seller for the seller's costs in rendering his assistance in these matters.

According to A8 the seller may have to assist the buyer to obtain a through document of transport. This process may also involve other measures, such as obtaining "control authorisation, permits, other documents or certified copies thereof". The buyer must also, at his risk and expense, provide the seller with these documents, etc. when the seller requests that he do so.

DELIVERED EX SHIP
(... named port of destination)

A SELLER'S PRIMARY DUTIES

- Deliver the goods on board the ship at the port of destination (**A4**)
- Provide documents to enable buyer to take delivery from the ship (e.g bill of lading or delivery order) (**A8**)

DIFFERENCE FROM *CFR* AND *CPT*

As with CFR and CPT, the selle has to pay for the costs of carriage. However, for DES, he also has to assume the risk of

DOCUMENTS

Required documents

- Commercial invoice (**A1**)
- Bill of lading or delivery order (**A8**)

NOTE:
All documents may be replaced by EDI messages

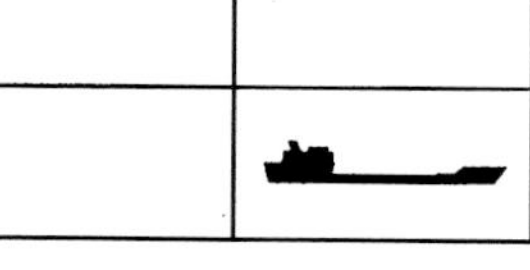

EXPORT CLEARANCE

SELLER

Goods

PRE-CARRIAGE

MAIN C

Seller's risk

Seller's costs

Delivered Ex Ship" means that the seller fulfils his obligation to deliver when the goods have been made available to the buyer on board the ship uncleared for import at the named port of destination. The seller has to bear all the costs and risks involved in bringing the goods to the named port of destination.
This term can only be used for sea or inland waterway transport.

B BUYER'S PRIMARY DUTIES

- Take delivery of the goods from the ship at the port of destination (**B4**)
- Pay unloading costs (**B6**)
- Provide import clearance (import licence, pay import duties, taxes and fees, if required) (**B2**)

oss of or damage to the goods as well as of any cost increases to the point of delivery.

ptional documents

Other documents needed for transit of the goods through another country or for import clearance (**A10**)

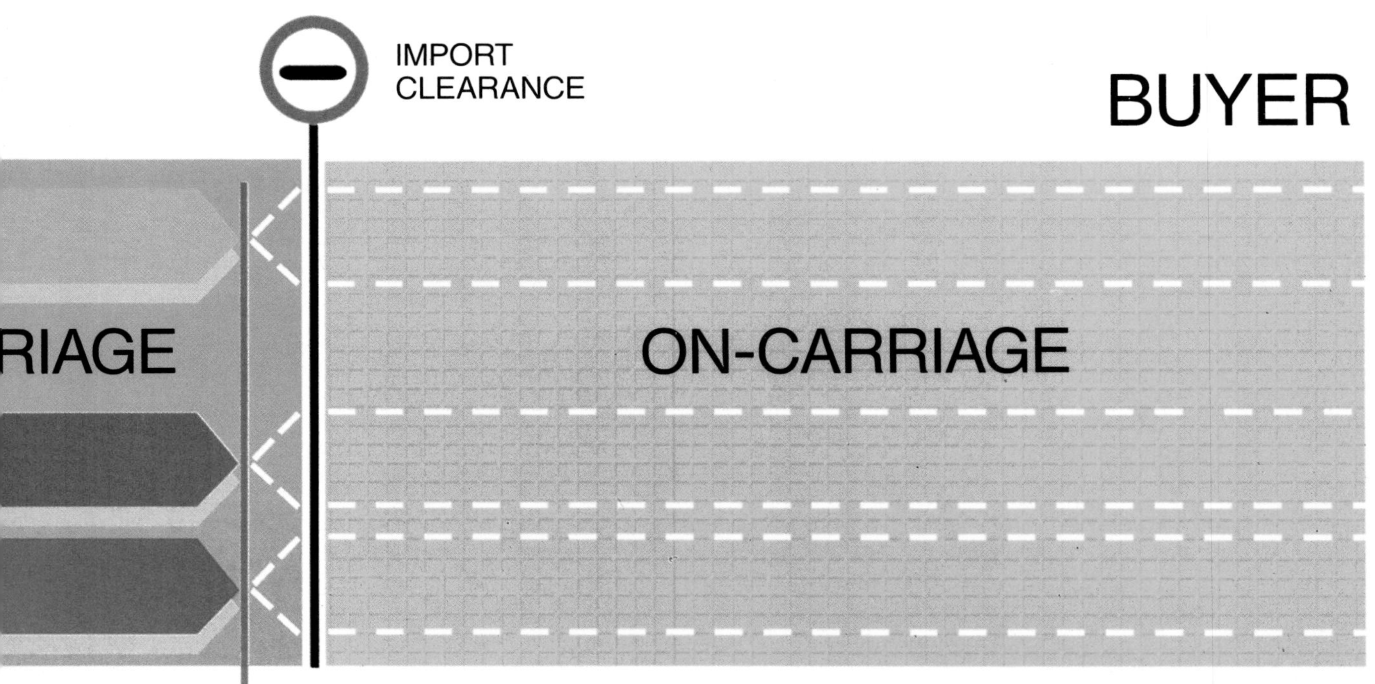

DELIVERED EX SHIP

(... named port of destination)

A THE SELLER MUST

A1 Provision of goods in conformity with the contract

Provide the goods and the commercial invoice, or its equivalent electronic message, in conformity with the contract of sale and any other evidence of conformity which may be required by the contract.

Comments

The seller must provide the goods in conformity with the contract. It is also usual practice that the seller, in order to be paid, has to invoice the buyer. In addition, the seller must submit any other evidence stipulated in the contract itself that the goods conform with that contract.

This text only serves as a reminder of the seller's main obligation under the contract of sale.

A2 Licences, authorisations and formalities

Obtain at his own risk and expense any export licence or other official authorisation and carry out all customs formalities necessary for the exportation of the goods and, where necessary, for their transit through another country.

Comments

The seller has to clear the goods for export and assume any risk or expense which this involves. Consequently, if there is an export prohibition or if there are particular taxes on the export of the goods - and if there are other government-imposed requirements which may render the export of the goods more expensive than contemplated - all of these risks and costs must be borne by the seller. However, contracts of sale usually contain particular provisions which the seller may invoke to protect himself in the event of these contingencies. Under the 1980 Convention on International Sale of Goods (CISG) and corresponding provisions in various national Sale of Goods Acts, unforeseen or reasonably unforeseeable export prohibitions would relieve the seller from his obligations under the contract of sale.

A3 Contract of carriage and insurance

a) Contract of carriage

Contract at his own expense for the carriage of the goods by a usual route and in a customary manner to the named port of destination. If a point is not agreed or is not determined by practice, the seller may select the point at the named port of destination which best suits his purpose.

b) Contract of insurance

No obligation.

Comments

Under all D-terms the seller must ensure that the goods actually arrive at destination. It follows from this that the seller must arrange and pay for any carriage of the goods. Though it may seem that the seller should have the right to contract for carriage as he deems fit - since any inadequate measures in this regard would automatically be at his own peril - it is nevertheless stipulated in the D-terms, as in the C-terms, that the seller should contract for carriage "by a usual route and in a customary manner".

Under the D-terms, the seller's choice of transport is only of importance to the buyer insofar as it affects the buyer's obligation to receive the goods from the carrier. If the seller chooses an unusual transport which makes it more difficult or expensive for the buyer to receive the goods from the carrier, any additional costs or risks caused by the seller's choice of transport will be for the seller's account.

Normally, the point mentioned after the D-term will indicate where the goods should be delivered at destination. But if there are several alternatives available, and the contract of sale or commercial practice does not indicate which alternative the seller must choose, he "may select the point at the named port of destination which best suits his purpose".

A4 Delivery

Place the goods at the disposal of the buyer on board the vessel at the usual unloading point in the named port of destination uncleared for import on the date or within the period stipulated, in such a way as to enable them to be removed from the vessel by unloading equipment appropriate to the nature of the goods.

Comments

Under all D-terms the seller must "place the goods at the disposal of the buyer" at destination. The precise point for the delivery of the goods depends upon the D-term chosen. According to DES A4 the goods should be made available to the buyer "on board the vessel at the usual unloading point in the named port of destination uncleared for import".

A5 Transfer of risks

Subject to the provisions of B.5., bear all risks of loss of or damage to the goods until such time as they have been delivered in accordance with A.4.

Comments

All Incoterms are based on the same principle that the risk of loss of or damage to the goods is transferred from the seller to the buyer when the seller has fulfilled his delivery obligation according to A4. A5 of FOB, CFR and CIF further specifies that the risk is transferred when the goods "have passed the ship's rail at the named port of shipment".

All Incoterms, in conformity with the general principle of CISG, connect the transfer of the risk with the delivery of the goods and not with other circumstances, such as the passing of ownership or the time of the conclusion of the contract. Neither Incoterms nor CISG deal with transfer of title to the goods or other property rights with respect to the goods.

The passing of risk of loss of or damage to the goods concerns the risk of fortuitous events (accidents) and does not include loss or damage caused by the seller or the buyer, e.g. inadequate packing or marking of the goods. Therefore, even if damage occurs subsequent to the transfer of the risk, the seller may still be responsible if the damage could be attributed to the fact that the goods were not delivered in conformity with the contract (See A1 and the comments to A9).

A5 of all Incoterms starts with the phrase "subject to the provisions of B5". This means that there are exceptions to the main rule concerning the passing of risk under the circumstances mentioned in B5, which may result in a premature passing of the risk because of the buyer's failure properly to fulfil his obligations (See the comments to B5).

A6 Division of costs

Subject to the provisions of B.6.

- in addition to costs resulting from A.3.a), pay all costs relating to the goods until such time as they have been delivered in accordance with A.4.;
- pay the costs of customs formalities necessary for exportation as well as all duties, taxes or other official charges payable upon exportation and, where necessary, for their transit through another country prior to delivery in accordance with A.4.

Comments

As is the case with the transfer of the risk for loss of or damage to the goods, all Incoterms follow the same rule, that the division of costs occurs at the delivery point. All costs occurring before the seller has fulfilled his obligation to deliver according to A4 are for his account, while further costs are for the account of the buyer (See the comments to B6). This rule is made subject to the provisions of B6, which indicates that the buyer may have to bear additional costs incurred by his failure to give appropriate notice to the seller.

Since, under D-terms, the seller does not fulfil his obligation until the goods have actually arrived at destination and been placed at the disposal of the buyer, the seller has to do everything required to achieve this. Nevertheless, A3 in all D-terms still stipulates that the seller must contract for carriage; and A6 of all D-terms stipulates that he must pay the costs resulting from A3 for the carriage of the goods "and, where necessary, for their transit through another country prior to delivery in accordance with A4". Needless to say, any transit costs incurred subsequent to delivery will have to be paid by the buyer.

A7 Notice to the buyer

Give the buyer sufficient notice of the estimated time of arrival of the named vessel in accordance with A.4., as well as any other notice required in order to allow the buyer to take measures which are normally necessary to enable him to take the goods.

Comments

The seller must give the buyer sufficient notice as to the estimated time of arrival of the vessel (ETA) and other essential notices, so that the buyer can make preparations in time to take delivery according to B4. There is no stipulation in Incoterms spelling out the consequences of the seller's failure to give such notice. But it follows from Incoterms that the seller's failure constitutes a breach of contract. This means that the seller could be held responsible for the breach according to the law applicable to the contract of sale.

A8 Proof of delivery, transport document or equivalent electronic message

Provide the buyer at the seller's expense with the delivery order and/or the usual transport document (for example, a negotiable bill of lading, a non-negotiable sea waybill, an inland waterway document or a multimodal transport document) to enable the buyer to take delivery of the goods.

Where the seller and the buyer have agreed to communicate electronically, the document referred to in the preceding paragraph may be replaced by an equivalent electronic data interchange (EDI) message.

Comments

In most cases the buyer will require a document in order to be able to obtain the goods from the carrier. Traditionally, the relevant document is a negotiable bill of lading, and this is still the predominant document when DES is used for carriage of bulk commodities. However, bills of lading are often replaced by delivery orders splitting up the total bill of lading quantity into smaller lots for several buyers.

Documents can be replaced by EDI messages when the parties have agreed to communicate electronically.

A9 Checking - packaging - marking

Pay the costs of those checking operations (such as checking quality, measuring, weighing, counting) which are necessary for the purpose of delivering the goods in accordance with A.4.

Provide at his own expense packaging (unless it is usual for the particular trade to deliver the goods of the contract description unpacked) which is required for the delivery of the goods. Packaging is to be marked appropriately.

Comments

It is important that the buyer ensure that the seller has duly fulfilled his obligation with respect to the condition of the goods, particularly if the buyer is called upon to pay for the goods before he has received and checked them. However, the seller has no duty to arrange and pay for the inspection of the goods unless this is specifically agreed in the contract of sale.

A10 Other obligations

Render the buyer at the latter's request, risk and expense, every assistance in obtaining any documents or equivalent electronic messages (other than those mentioned in A.8.) issued or transmitted in the country of dispatch an/or of origin which the buyer may require for the importation of the goods.

Provide the buyer, upon request, with the necessary information for procuring insurance.

Comments

The seller has the obligation to clear the goods for export. But he has no obligation to bear any costs and risks for import clearance of the goods at destination. However, he has the duty to render the buyer assistance in obtaining the documents (e.g. a certificate of origin, a health certificate, a clean report of findings, an import licence) or equivalent electronic messages which may be required for this purpose. The buyer, in turn, must reimburse the seller for any expenses which the seller might have incurred in connection with this assistance. Moreover, if something goes wrong, the buyer will have to assume the risk.

The seller may also be requested to provide the buyer with any information relating to the goods which the buyer might require for insurance purposes, if this information is not provided in the description of the goods in the contract of sale.

DELIVERED EX SHIP

(... named port of destination)

B THE BUYER MUST

B1 Payment of the price

Pay the price as provided in the contract of sale.

Comments

The buyer must pay the price agreed in the contract of sale. B1 constitutes a reminder of this main obligation, which corresponds with the seller's obligation to provide the goods in conformity with the contract of sale, as stipulated in A1.

B2 Licences' authorisations and formalities

Obtain at his own risk and expense any import licence or other official authorisation and carry out all customs formalities necessary for the importation of the goods.

Comments

The buyer must take care of the import clearance and bear any costs and risks in connection with it. Therefore, an import prohibition will not relieve the buyer of his obligation to pay for the goods, unless there is a particular "relief clause" in the contract of sale which he invokes to obtain this relief. Such clauses may provide for the extension of time or the right to avoid the contract under the applicable law (See the comments to A2).

B3 Contract of carriage

No obligation.

Comments

Although B3 merely stipulates "No obligation" for the buyer, on-carriage from the port of destination is necessary in most cases, and it is the buyer's responsibility to do whatever is required for this purpose. But the seller is not concerned with the further carriage of the goods and the buyer has no obligation to the seller in this respect. The words "No obligation" mean that whatever the buyer does is in his own interest and is not covered by the contract of sale.

B4 Taking delivery

Take delivery of the goods as soon as they have been placed at his disposal in accordance with A.4.

Comments

As in all D-terms, B4 has wording stating that the buyer shall take delivery as soon as the goods have been placed at his disposal in accordance with A4. (The same wording is also used in EXW B4, but under EXW the placing of the goods at the buyer's disposal usually occurs at the seller's own premises.) The seller, according to A4 in the D-terms, shall place the goods at the buyer's disposal "on the date or within the period stipulated".

If the goods are placed at the buyer's disposal earlier than agreed, the buyer is not obliged to take delivery before the agreed time, though it may normally be in his own interest to do so. If the goods are placed at the buyer's disposal too late, the buyer may hold the seller responsible for breach of contract according to the applicable law. He may also recover damages from the seller or, in the event of a fundamental breach, cancel the contract.

B5 Transfer of risks

Bear all risks of loss of or damage to the goods from the time they have been placed at his disposal in accordance with A.4.

Should he fail to give notice in accordance with B.7., bear all risks of loss of or damage to the goods from the agreed date or the expiry date of the period stipulated for delivery provided, however, that the goods have been duly appropriated to the contract, that is to say, clearly set aside or otherwise identified as the contract goods.

Comments

According to the main rule, while the seller under A5 bears the risk of loss of or damage to the goods until the delivery point, the buyer has to bear the risk thereafter. The delivery point is different under the different terms. In EXW and all D-terms the goods are simply placed "at the disposal of the buyer" at the relevant point, while under the F- and C-terms the delivery point is related to the handing over of the goods to the carrier in the country of dispatch or shipment (See the comments to A4 of these terms). In the terms used for goods intended to be carried by sea, reference is made to delivery alongside the named vessel (FAS A4) or delivery onboard the vessel (FOB, CFR, CIF).

B6 Division of costs

Pay all costs relating to the goods including unloading from the time they have been placed at his disposal in accordance with A.4.

Should he fail to take delivery of the goods when they have been placed at his disposal in accordance with A.4., or to give notice in accordance with B.7., bear all additional costs incurred thereby provided, however, that the goods have been appropriated to the contract, that is to say, clearly set aside or otherwise identified as the contract goods.

Pay all duties, taxes and other official charges as well as the costs of carrying out customs formalities payable upon importation of the goods.

Comments

Since the goods according to A4 are made available to the buyer "on board the vessel at the usual unloading point in the named port of destination", the buyer has to pay all costs of discharge.

If the buyer fails to take delivery of the goods as agreed - e.g. within the stipulated time during which the vessel is available for discharge free of charge (the so-called laytime) - the buyer must pay any additional costs incurred thereby. In particular, he must pay demurrage to the shipowner when the laytime is exceeded. The buyer also has to pay any additional costs which may arise because of his failure to notify the seller of the time or place of delivery according to B7. The obligation of the buyer to pay these additional costs is always subject to the identification of the goods as the contract goods ("appropriation").

B7 Notice to the seller

Whenever he is entitled to determine the time within a stipulated period and/or the place of taking delivery, give the seller sufficient notice thereof.

Comments

As discussed in the comments to B5 and B6, the failure of the buyer to notify the seller of the time and place of taking delivery - when the buyer in the contract of sale has been given the option to determine these matters - may cause the risk of the loss of or damage to the goods to pass before the goods have been delivered according to A4. In addition, it can make the buyer liable to pay any additional costs incurred by the seller as a result of the buyer's failure.

B8 Proof of delivery, transport document or equivalent electronic message

Accept the delivery order or transport document in accordance with A.8.

Comments

The buyer has to accept the document if it conforms with the contract and with the requirements of A8 (See the comments to A8). If the buyer rejects the document (e.g. by instructions to a bank not to pay the seller under a documentary credit), he commits a breach of contract, which would give the seller remedies available for such a breach under the contract of sale.

These remedies could include, for example, a right to cancel the contract or to claim damages for breach. However, the buyer is not obliged to accept a document which does not provide adequate proof of delivery, e.g. one which has notations on it showing that the goods are defective or that they have been provided in less than the agreed quantity. In these cases, the document is termed "unclean".

B9 Inspection of goods

Pay, unless otherwise agreed, the costs of pre-shipment inspection except when mandated by the authorities of the country of exportation.

Comments

As noted in the comments to A9, the buyer has to pay for any costs of checking the goods, unless the contract determines that these costs should be wholly or partly borne by the seller. In some cases, the contract may provide that the costs should be borne by the seller if the inspection reveals that the goods do not conform with the contract.

In some countries, where import licences or permission to obtain foreign currency for the payment of the price may be required, the authorities may demand an inspection of the goods before shipment, to ensure that the goods are in conformity with the contract. (This is usually called pre-shipment inspection, PSI.) If this is the case, the inspection is normally arranged by instructions from the authorities to an inspection company, which they appoint. The costs following from this inspection have to be paid by the authorities. Any reimbursement to the authorities for the inspection costs, however, must be made by the buyer, unless otherwise specifically agreed between the buyer and the seller.

B10 Other obligations

Pay all costs and charges incurred in obtaining the documents or equivalent electronic messages mentioned in A.10. and reimburse those incurred by the seller in rendering his assistance in accordance therewith.

Comments

As discussed in the comments to A10, the seller has to render the buyer assistance in obtaining the documents or electronic messages which may be required for the transit and importation of the goods. However, this assistance is rendered at the buyer's risk and expense. Therefore, B10 stipulates that the buyer must pay all costs and charges incurred in obtaining these documents or electronic messages. He will also have to reimburse the seller for the seller's costs in rendering his assistance in these matters.

DELIVERED EX QUAY (DUTY PAID)

(... named port of destination)

A SELLER'S PRIMARY DUTIES

- Deliver the goods on the quay at the port of destination (**A4**)
- Provide documents to enable buyer to take delivery from the quay (e.g. delivery order or bill of lading) (**A8**)
- Pay unloading costs (**A6**)
- Provide import clearance (import licence, pay import duties, taxes and fees, if required) (**A2**)

DIFFERENCE FROM *DES*

As in the term DES, under DEQ the points of division of costs ar risks coincide, but they have no been moved one step further - from the ship onto the quay. The seller not only has to contract fo the carriage and pay the freight

DOCUMENTS

Required documents

- Commercial invoice (**A1**)
- Delivery order or bill of lading (**A8**)
- Import licence (**A2**)

NOTE:
All documents may be replaced by EDI messages

SELLER

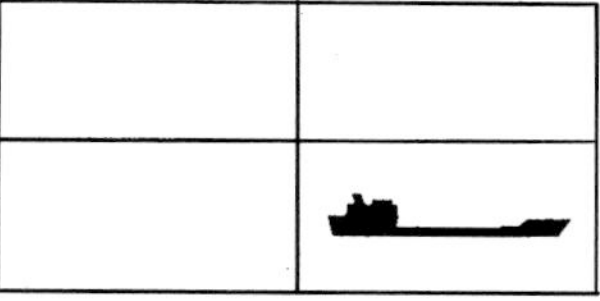

Goods

PRE-CARRIAGE

MAIN C

Seller's risk

Seller's costs

livered Ex Quay (duty paid)" means that the seller fulfils obligation to deliver when he has made the goods ilable to the buyer on the quay (wharf) at the named t of destination, cleared for importation. The seller has ear all risks and costs including duties, taxes and other rges of delivering the goods thereto.
s term should not be used if the seller is unable directly ndirectly to obtain the import licence.
ne parties wish the buyer to clear the goods for importation and pay the duty the words "duty unpaid" should be used instead of "duty paid".
If the parties wish to exclude from the seller's obligations some of the costs payable upon importation of the goods (such as value added tax (VAT)), this should be made clear by adding words to this effect: "Delivered ex quay, VAT unpaid (... named port of destination)".
This term can only be used for sea or inland waterway transport.

also has to bear the additional s and costs to bring the goods ore, that is, pay all costs for ading the goods from the . Further, he has to pass the oms border and clear the ds for import.

B BUYER'S PRIMARY DUTY

- Take delivery of the goods from the quay at the port of destination (**B4**)

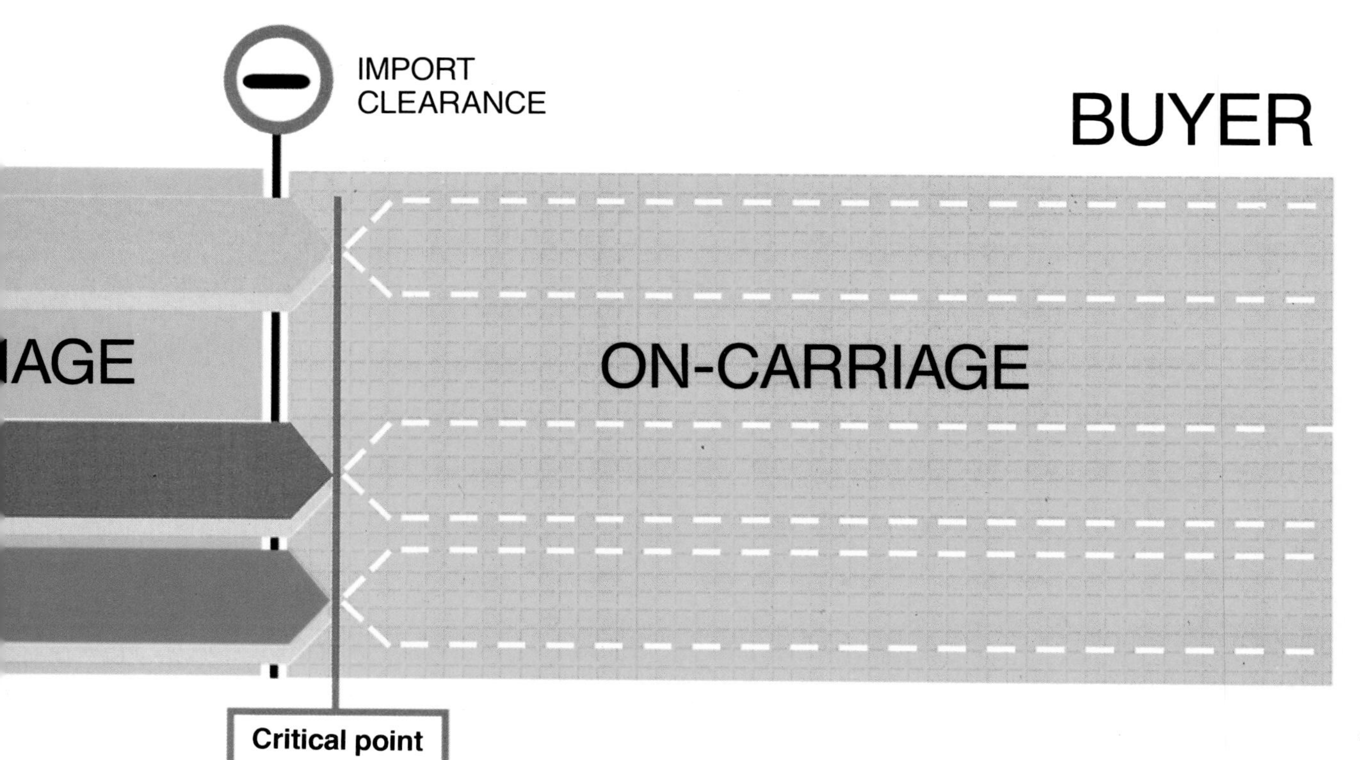

Group D: **Arrival**

DELIVERED EX QUAY (DUTY PAID)

(... named port of destination)

A THE SELLER MUST

A1 Provision of goods in conformity with the contract

Provide the goods and the commercial invoice, or its equivalent electronic message, in conformity with the contract of sale and any other evidence of conformity which may be required by the contract.

Comments

The seller must provide the goods in conformity with the contract. It is also usual practice that the seller, in order to be paid, has to invoice the buyer. In addition, the seller must submit any other evidence stipulated in the contract itself that the goods conform with that contract.

This text only serves as a reminder of the seller's main obligation under the contract of sale.

A2 Licences, authorisations and formalities

Obtain at his own risk and expense any export and import licence or other official authorisation and carry out all customs formalities for the exportation and importation of the goods and, where necessary, for their transit through another country.

Comments

Since the term DEQ is evidence of an arrival contract, the seller has to do whatever may be necessary for the goods to reach the agreed place for delivery. This means the seller is responsible for export as well as import clearance of the goods as well as any transit formalities involved in the transport of the goods through another country before arrival at the agreed destination.

Before agreeing to sell the goods under DEQ, the seller should be sure that the regulations of the buyer's country do not prevent him as a non-resident from applying for any necessary import licence. Normally no such difficulties will be encountered, since the application for licences can be made by freight forwarders (customs brokers) on the seller's behalf.

Advisable to exclude payment of official charges

It may be advisable for the parties to exclude the payment of any official charges intended for the "internal" fiscal system in the country of importation (such as VAT levied upon importation) from the seller's obligation to pay. If this is not done, any right to deduct these expenses or to benefit from particular tax advantages available only to residents could be lost. The charges intended to be excluded should then be identified in conjunction with the DEQ term in the contract of sale, e.g. by using a phrase such as "DEQ VAT unpaid".

Relief from unforeseen or reasonably unforeseeable prohibitions

The seller's obligations under DEQ may become more expensive than contemplated as a result of reasonably unforeseeable circumstances. However, contracts of sale usually contain provisions which the seller may invoke to protect himself in the event of these contingencies. Under the 1980 Convention on International Sale of Goods (CISG) and corresponding provisions in various national Sale of Goods Acts, unforeseen or reasonably unforeseeable prohibitions may relieve the seller from his obligations under the contract of sale.

Seller can avoid requirement to clear goods for import

If the seller wishes to avoid the obligation of clearing the goods for import, he should use DES or add the phrase "not cleared for import" after DEQ.

A3 Contract of carriage and insurance

a) Contract of carriage

Contract at his own expense for the carriage of the goods by a usual route and in a customary manner to the quay at the named port of destination. If a point is not agreed or is not determined by practice, the seller may select the point at the named port of destination which best suits his purpose.

b) Contract of insurance

No obligation.

Comments

Under all D-terms the seller must ensure that the goods actually arrive at destination. It follows from this that the seller must arrange and pay for any carriage of the goods. Though it may seem that the seller should have the right to contract for carriage as he deems fit - since any inadequate measures in this regard would automatically be at his own peril - it is nevertheless stipulated in the D-terms, as in the C-terms, that the seller should contract for carriage "by a usual route and in a customary manner".

Under the D-terms, the seller's choice of transport is only of importance to the buyer insofar as it affects the buyer's obligation to receive the goods from the carrier. If the seller chooses an unusual mode of transport which makes it more difficult or expensive for the buyer to receive the goods from the carrier, any additional costs or risks caused by the seller's choice of transport will be for the seller's account.

Normally, the point mentioned after the D-term will indicate where the goods should be delivered at destination. But if there are several alternatives available, and the contract of sale or commercial practice does not indicate which alternative the seller must choose, he "may select the point at the named port of destination which best suits his purpose".

A4 Delivery

Place the goods at the disposal of the buyer on the quay or wharf at the agreed port of destination and on the date or within the period stipulated.

Comments

Under all D-terms the seller must "place the goods at the disposal of the buyer" at destination. The precise point for the delivery of the goods depends upon the D-term chosen. According to DEQ A4 the goods should be placed at the disposal of the buyer "on the quay or wharf at the agreed port of destination".

A5 Transfer of risks

Subject to the provisions of B.5., bear all risks of loss of or damage to the goods until such time as they have been delivered in accordance with A.4.

Comments

All Incoterms are based on the same principle that the risk of loss of or damage to the goods is transferred from the seller to the buyer when the seller has fulfilled his delivery obligation according to A4. A5 of FOB, CFR and CIF further specifies that the risk is transferred when the goods "have passed the ship's rail at the named port of shipment".

All Incoterms, in conformity with the general principle of CISG, connect the transfer of the risk with the delivery of the goods and not with other circumstances, such as the passing of ownership or the time of the conclusion of the contract. Neither Incoterms nor CISG deal with transfer of title to the goods or other property rights with respect to the goods.

The passing of risk of loss of or damage to the goods concerns the risk of fortuitous events (accidents) and does not include loss or damage caused by the seller or the buyer, e.g. inadequate packing or marking of the goods. Therefore, even if damage occurs subsequent to the transfer of the risk, the seller may still be responsible if the damage could be attributed to the fact that the goods were not delivered in conformity with the contract (See A1 and the comments to A9).

A5 of all Incoterms starts with the phrase "subject to the provisions of B5". This means that there are exceptions to the main rule concerning the passing of risk under the circumstances mentioned in B5, which may result in a premature passing of the risk because of the buyer's failure properly to fulfil his obligations (See the comments to B5).

A6 Division of costs

Subject to the provisions of B.6.

- in addition to costs resulting from A.3.a), pay all costs relating to the goods until such time as they are delivered in accordance with A.4.;
- pay the costs of customs formalities as well as all duties, taxes and other official charges payable upon exportation and importation of the goods, unless otherwise agreed and, where necessary, for their transit through another country prior to delivery in accordance with A.4.

Comments

As is the case with the transfer of the risk of loss of or damage to the goods, all Incoterms follow the same rule, that the division of costs occurs at the delivery point. All costs occurring before the seller has fulfilled his obligation to deliver according to A4 are for his account, while further costs are for the account of the buyer (See the comments to B6). This rule is made subject to the provisions of B6, which indicates that the buyer may have to bear additional costs incurred by his failure to give appropriate notice to the seller.

Since, under D-terms, the seller does not fulfil his obligation until the goods have actually arrived at destination and been placed at the disposal of the buyer, the seller has to do everything required to achieve this. Nevertheless, A3 in all D-terms still stipulates that the seller must contract for carriage; and A6 of all D-terms stipulates that he must pay the costs resulting from A3 for the carriage of the goods and "pay the costs of customs formalities as well as all duties, taxes and other official charges payable upon exportation and importation of the goods, unless otherwise agreed and, where necessary, for their transit through another country prior to delivery in accordance with A.4". Needless to say, any transit costs incurred subsequent to delivery will have to be paid by the buyer.

A7 Notice to the buyer

Give the buyer sufficient notice of the estimated time of arrival of the named vessel in accordance with A.4., as well as any other notice required in order to allow the buyer to take measures which are normally necesssary to enable him to take the goods.

Comments

The seller must give the buyer sufficient notice as to the estimated time of arrival (ETA) of the vessel and other essential notices, so that the buyer can make preparations in time to take delivery according to B4. There is no stipulation in Incoterms spelling out the consequences of the seller's failure to give such notice. But it follows from Incoterms that the seller's failure constitutes a breach of contract. This means that the seller could be held responsible for the breach according to the law applicable to the contract of sale.

A8 Transport document or equivalent electronic message

Provide the buyer at the seller's expense with the delivery order and/or the usual transport document (for example, a negotiable bill of lading, a non-negotiable sea waybill, an inland waterway document or a multimodal transport document) to enable him to take the goods and remove them from the quay.

Where the seller and the buyer have agreed to communicate electronically, the document referred to in the preceding paragraph may be replaced by an equivalent electronic data interchange (EDI) message.

Comments

In most cases the buyer will require a document in order to be able to obtain the goods from the carrier. Traditionally, the relevant document is a negotiable bill of lading, and this is still the predominant document when DEQ is used for carriage of bulk commodities. However, bills of lading are often replaced by delivery orders splitting up the total bill of lading quantity into smaller lots for several buyers.

Documents can be replaced by EDI messages when the parties have agreed to communicate electronically.

A9 Checking - packaging - marking

Pay the costs of those checking operations (such as checking quality, measuring, weighing, counting) which are necessary for the purpose of delivering the goods in accordance with A.4.

Provide at his own expense packaging (unless it is usual for the particular trade to deliver the goods of the contract description unpacked) which is required for the delivery of the goods. Packaging is to be marked appropriately.

Comments

It is important that the buyer ensure that the seller has duly fulfilled his obligation with respect to the condition of the goods, particularly if the buyer is called upon to pay for the goods before he has received and checked them. However, the seller has no duty to arrange and pay for the inspection of the goods unless this is specifically agreed in the contract of sale.

A10 Other obligations

Pay all costs and charges incurred in obtaining the documents or equivalent electronic messages mentioned in B.10. and reimburse those incurred by the buyer in rendering his assistance therewith.

Provide the buyer, upon request, with the necessary information for procuring insurance.

Comments

DEQ requires the seller to clear the goods for import. The seller has to reimburse the buyer for any costs the buyer may incur in rendering any assistance (See B10).

DELIVERED EX QUAY (DUTY PAID)

(... named port of destination)

B THE BUYER MUST

B1 Payment of the price

Pay the price as provided in the contract of sale.

Comments

The buyer must pay the price agreed in the contract of sale. B1 constitutes a reminder of this main obligation, which corresponds with the seller's obligation to provide the goods in conformity with the contract of sale, as stipulated in A1.

B2 Licences, authorisations and formalities

Render the seller at the latter's request, risk and expense, every assistance in obtaining any import licence or other official authorisation necessary for the importation of the goods.

Comments

Since the seller has to make the goods available to the buyer in the country of destination, it is for the seller to do whatever is necessary with respect to the clearance of the goods for export, transit and import.

B3 Contract of carriage

No obligation.

Comments

Although B3 merely stipulates "No obligation" for the buyer, on-carriage from the port of destination is necessary in most cases, and it is the buyer's responsibility to do whatever is required for this purpose. But the seller is not concerned with the further carriage of the goods and the buyer has no obligation to the seller in this respect. The words "No obligation" mean that whatever the buyer does is in his own interest and is not covered by the contract of sale.

B4 Taking delivery

Take delivery of the goods as soon as they have been placed at his disposal in accordance with A.4.

Comments

As in all D-terms, B4 has wording stating that the buyer shall take delivery as soon as the goods have been placed at his disposal in accordance with A4. (The same wording is also used in EXW B4, but under EXW the placing of the goods at the buyer's disposal usually occurs at the seller's own premises.) The seller, according to A4 in the D-terms, shall place the goods at the buyer's disposal "on the date or within the period stipulated".

If the goods are placed at the buyer's disposal earlier than agreed, the buyer is not obliged to take delivery before the agreed time, though it may normally be in his own interest to do so. If the goods are placed at the buyer's disposal too late, the buyer may hold the seller responsible for breach of contract according to the applicable law. He may also recover damages from the seller or, in the event of a fundamental breach, cancel the contract.

B5 Transfer of risks

Bear all risks of loss of or damage to the goods from the time they have been placed at his disposal in accordance with A.4.

Should he fail to give notice in accordance with B.7., bear all risks of loss of or damage to the goods from the agreed date or the expiry date of the period stipulated for delivery provided, however, that the goods have been duly appropriated to the contract, that is to say, clearly set aside or otherwise identified as the contract goods.

Comments

According to the main rule, while the seller under A5 bears the risk of loss of or damage to the goods until the delivery point, the buyer has to bear the risk thereafter. The delivery point is different under the different terms. In EXW and all D-terms the goods are simply placed "at the disposal of the buyer" at the relevant point, while under the F- and C-terms the delivery point is related to the handing over of the goods to the carrier in the country of dispatch or shipment (See the comments to A4 of these terms). In the terms used for goods intended to be carried by sea, reference is made to delivery alongside the named vessel (FAS A4) or delivery onboard the vessel (FOB, CFR, CIF).

Consequences of buyer's failure to give notice

While the seller under EXW and all D-terms can transfer the risk by his own act of placing the goods at the buyer's disposal, he may be prevented from doing so by the buyer's failure to give notice according to B7. This can occur when it is the buyer's responsibility to determine (1) the time within a stipulated period when the goods are to be made available or (2) the place of delivery (See the comments to B7). The failure to perform these tasks results in a premature passing of the risk: It is not acceptable that the buyer should be able to delay the delivery and passing of the risk longer than contemplated when the contract of sale was made. Therefore, his failure to notify according to B7 will cause the risk to pass "from the agreed date or the expiry date of any period fixed for taking delivery".

Appropriation and the passing of risk

The risk, however, cannot pass until the goods "have been appropriated to the contract". If the goods are unascertained - i.e. goods of a certain kind which the seller will deliver to various buyers - appropriation only occurs when the goods are "clearly set aside as the contract goods".

This appropriation will normally be made when the seller has handed over the goods for carriage and the consignment has been marked as intended for the buyer - unless the cargo is carried in bulk and intended to be appropriated between different buyers only upon the arrival of the goods at destination.

B6 Division of costs

Pay all costs relating to the goods from the time they have been placed at his disposal in accordance with A.4.

Should he fail to take delivery of the goods when they have been placed at his disposal in accordance with A.4., or to give notice in accordance with B.7., bear all additional costs incurred thereby provided, however, that the goods have been appropriated to the contract, that is to say, clearly set aside or otherwise identified as the contract goods.

Comments

Since according to A4 the goods are made available to the buyer "on the quay or wharf at the agreed port of destination", the buyer is relieved of the obligation to pay for the costs of discharge. However, once the goods have been placed at his disposal in accordance with A4, the buyer must pay any costs for the storage and further carriage of the goods to their final destination.

If the buyer fails to take delivery or to take such measures as are needed for on-carriage, he will have to bear any additional costs incurred thereby. At this stage, the seller will normally have identified the goods as the contract goods (through the process of "appropriation"). But if he has not done so - e.g. if the goods arrive at destination in bulk for later appropriation by delivery orders or otherwise - the buyer does not have to bear any additional costs relating to the goods until they have been duly appropriated.

Subject to the goods having been appropriated as noted above, the buyer also has to pay any additional costs incurred as a result of his failure to notify the seller according to B7 of the time or place of taking delivery, e.g. additional storage and insurance costs.

Since under DEQ it is the seller's responsibility to clear the goods for import, the buyer does not have to pay any costs in that regard.

B7 Notice to the seller

Whenever he is entitled to determine the time within a stipulated period and/or the place of taking delivery, give the seller sufficient notice thereof.

Comments

As discussed in the comments to B5 and B6, the failure of the buyer to notify the seller of the time and place of taking delivery - when the buyer in the contract of sale has been given the option to determine these matters - may cause the risk of the loss of or damage to the goods to pass before the goods have been delivered according to A4. In addition, it can make the buyer liable to pay any additional costs incurred by the seller as a result of the buyer's failure.

B8 Proof of delivery, transport document or equivalent electronic message

Accept the delivery order or transport document in accordance with A.8.

Comments

The buyer has to accept the document if it conforms with the contract and with the requirements of A8 (See the comments to A8). If the buyer rejects the document (e.g. by instructions to a bank not to pay the seller under a documentary credit), he commits a breach of contract, which would give the seller remedies available for such a breach under the contract of sale.

These remedies could include, for example, a right to cancel the contract or to claim damages for breach. However, the buyer is not obliged to accept a document which does not provide adequate proof of delivery, e.g. one which has notations on it showing that the goods are defective or that they have been provided in less than the agreed quantity. In these cases, the document is termed "unclean".

B9 Inspection of goods

Pay, unless otherwise agreed, the costs of pre-shipment inspection except when mandated by the authorities of the country of exportation.

Comments

As noted in the comments to A9, the buyer has to pay for any costs of checking the goods, unless the contract determines that these costs should be wholly or partly borne by the seller. In some cases, the contract may provide that the costs should be borne by the seller if the inspection reveals that the goods do not conform with the contract.

In some countries, where import licences or permission to obtain foreign currency for the payment of the price may be required, the authorities may demand an inspection of the goods before shipment, to ensure that the goods are in conformity with the contract. (This is usually called pre-shipment inspection, PSI.) If this is the case, the inspection is normally arranged by instructions from the authorities to an inspection company, which they appoint. The costs following from this inspection have to be paid by the authorities. Any reimbursement to the authorities for the inspection costs, however, must be made by the buyer, unless otherwise specifically agreed between the buyer and the seller.

B10 Other obligations

Render the seller, at the latter's request, risk and expense, every assistance in obtaining any documents or equivalent electronic messages issued or transmitted in the country of importation which the seller may require for the purpose of placing the goods at the disposal of the buyer in accordance with these rules.

Comments

Since the seller has the obligation to clear the goods for import, he may require the buyer's assistance to obtain the necessary documents or EDI messages. The buyer must render this assistance when requested by the seller to do so, but the buyer does this at the seller's risk and expense.

DELIVERED DUTY UNPAID

(... named place of destination)

A SELLER'S PRIMARY DUTIES

- Deliver the goods at the named place of destination (**A4**)
- Provide the documents to enable the buyer to take delivery at the named place. (e.g. delivery order, warehouse warrant or document of transport) (**A8**)

DIFFERENCE FROM *DDP*

While under DDP the seller has clear the goods for import and pay the duty, he only has to cle the goods for export under DD

DOCUMENTS

Required documents

- Commercial invoice (**A1**)
- Delivery order, warehouse warrant or document of transport (**A8**)

NOTE:
All documents may be replaced by EDI messages

Goods

PRE-CARRIAGE | MAIN

Seller's risk

Seller's costs

)elivered duty unpaid" means that the seller fulfils his bligation to deliver when the goods have been made vailable at the named place in the country of importa- on. The seller has to bear the costs and risks involved bringing the goods thereto (excluding duties, taxes d other official charges payable upon importation as ell as the costs and risks of carrying out customs for- alities). The buyer has to pay any additional costs and bear any risks caused by his failure to clear the goods r import in time.

If the parties wish the seller to carry out customs formalities and bear the costs and risks resulting therefrom, this has to be made clear by adding words to this effect. If the parties wish to include in the seller's obligations some of the costs payable upon importation of the goods (such as value added tax (VAT)), this should be made clear by adding words to this effect: "Delivered duty unpaid, VAT paid, (... named place of destination)". This term may be used irrespective of the mode of transport.

B BUYER'S PRIMARY DUTIES

- Take delivery of the goods at the named place of destination (**B4**)
- Provide import clearance (import licence, pay import duties, taxes and fees, if required) (**B2**)

ptional documents

Other documents needed for transit of the goods through another country or for import clearance (**A10**)

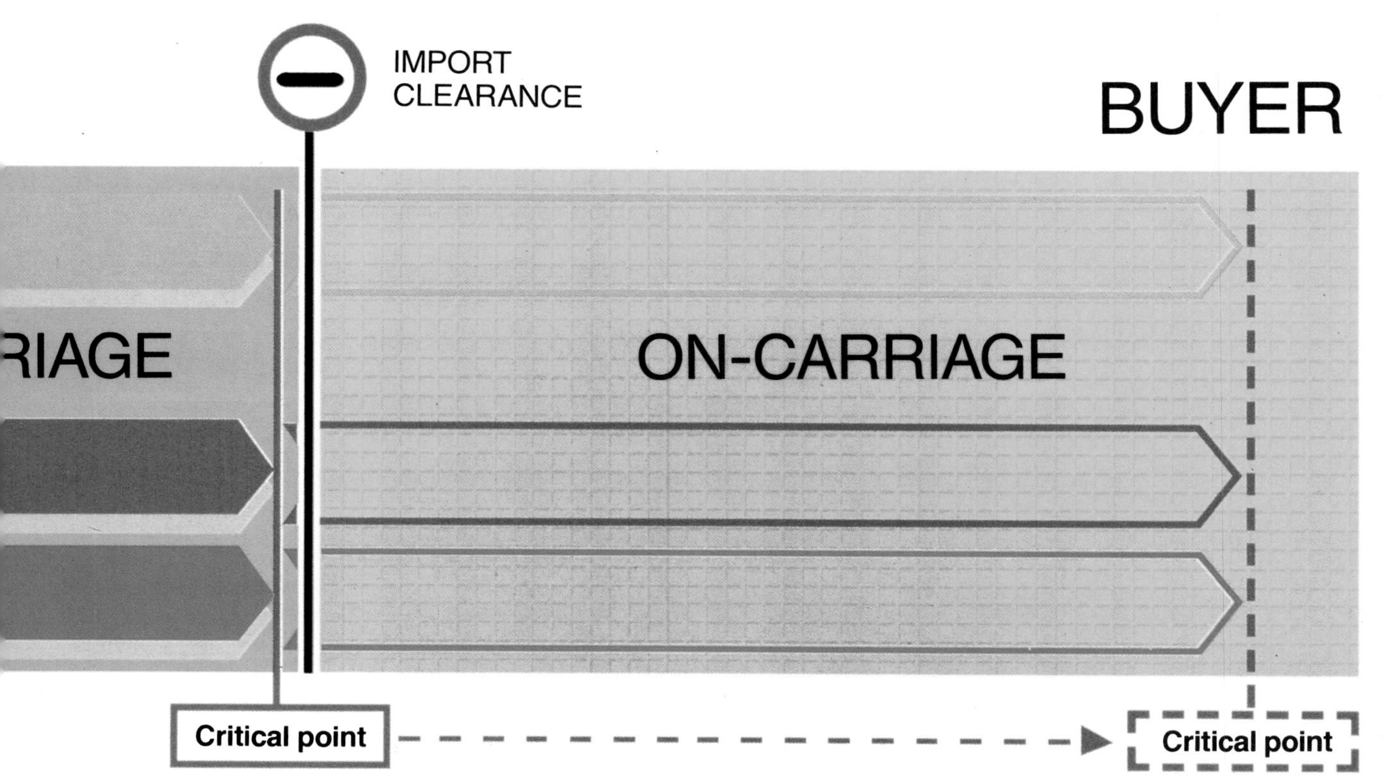

Group D: **Arrival**

DELIVERED DUTY UNPAID

(... named place of destination)

A THE SELLER MUST

A1 Provision of the goods in conformity with the contract

Provide the goods and the commercial invoice, or its equivalent electronic message, in conformity with the contract of sale and any other evidence of conformity which may be required by the contract.

Comments

The seller must provide the goods in conformity with the contract. It is also usual practice that the seller, in order to be paid, has to invoice the buyer. In addition, the seller must submit any other evidence stipulated in the contract itself that the goods conform with that contract.

This text only serves as a reminder of the seller's main obligation under the contract of sale.

A2 Licences, authorisations and formalities

Obtain at his own risk and expense any export licence and other official authorisation and carry out all customs formalities for the exportation of the goods and, where necessary, for their transit through another country.

Comments

The seller has to clear the goods for export and assume any risk or expense which this involves. Consequently, if there is an export prohibition or if there are particular taxes on the export of the goods - and if there are other government-imposed requirements which may render the export of the goods more expensive than contemplated - all of these risks and costs must be borne by the seller. However, contracts of sale usually contain particular provisions which the seller may invoke to protect himself in the event of these contingencies. Under the 1980 Convention on International Sale of Goods (CISG) and corresponding provisions in various national Sale of Goods Acts, unforeseen or reasonably unforeseeable export prohibitions may relieve the seller from his obligations under the contract of sale.

A3 Contract of carriage and insurance

a) Contract of carriage
Contract on usual terms at his own expense for the carriage of the goods by a usual route and in the customary manner to the agreed point at the named place of destination. If a point is not agreed or is not determined by practice, the seller may select the point at the named place of destination which best suits his purpose.

b) Contract of insurance
No obligation.

Comments

Under all D-terms the seller must ensure that the goods actually arrive at destination. It follows from this that the seller must arrange and pay for any carriage of the goods. Though it may seem that the seller should have the right to contract for carriage as he deems fit - since any inadequate measures in this regard would automatically be at his own peril - it is nevertheless stipulated in the D-terms, as in the C-terms, that the seller should contract for carriage "by a usual route and in a customary manner".

Under the D-terms, the seller's choice of transport is only of importance to the buyer insofar as it affects the buyer's obligation to receive the goods from the carrier. If the seller chooses an unusual transport which makes it more difficult or expensive for the buyer to receive the goods from the carrier, any additional costs or risks caused by the seller's choice of transport will be for the seller's account.

Normally, the point mentioned after the D-term will indicate where the goods should be delivered at destination. But if there are several alternatives available, and the contract of sale or commercial practice does not indicate which alternative the seller must choose, he "may select the point at the named place of destination which best suits his purpose".

A4 Delivery

Place the goods at the disposal of the buyer in accordance with A.3. on the date or within the period stipulated.

Comments

Under DDU the seller must "place the goods at the disposal of the buyer" at the named place of destination. The precise point for the delivery of the goods depends upon the D-term chosen.

A5 Transfer of risks

Subject to the provisions of B.5., bear all risks of loss of or damage to the goods until such time as they have been delivered in accordance with A.4.

Comments

All Incoterms are based on the same principle that the risk of loss of or damage to the goods is transferred from the seller to the buyer when the seller has fulfilled his delivery obligation according to A4. A5 of FOB, CFR and CIF further specifies that the risk is transferred when the goods "have passed the ship's rail at the named port of shipment".

All Incoterms, in conformity with the general principle of CISG, connect the transfer of the risk with the delivery of the goods and not with other circumstances, such as the passing of ownership or the time of the conclusion of the contract. Neither Incoterms nor CISG deal with transfer of title to the goods or other property rights with respect to the goods.

The passing of risk of loss of or damage to the goods concerns the risk of fortuitous events (accidents) and does not include loss or damage caused by the seller or the buyer, e.g. inadequate packing or marking of the goods. Therefore, even if damage occurs subsequent to the transfer of the risk, the seller may still be responsible if the damage could be attributed to the fact that the goods were not delivered in conformity with the contract (See A1 and the comments to A9).

A5 of all Incoterms starts with the phrase "subject to the provisions of B5". This means that there are exceptions to the main rule concerning the passing of risk under the circumstances mentioned in B5, which may result in a premature passing of the risk because of the buyer's failure properly to fulfil his obligations (See the comments to B5).

A6 Division of costs

Subject to the provisions of B.6.

- in addition to costs resulting from A.3.a), pay all costs relating to the goods until such time as they have been delivered in accordance with A.4.;
- pay the costs of customs formalities necessary for exportation as well as all duties, taxes and other official charges payable upon exportation and, where necessary, for their transit through another country prior to delivery in accordance with A.4.

Comments

As is the case with the transfer of the risk for loss of or damage to the goods, all Incoterms follow the same rule, that the division of costs occurs at the delivery point. All costs occurring before the seller has fulfilled his obligation to deliver according to A4 are for his account, while further costs are for the account of the buyer (See the comments to B6). This rule is made subject to the provisions of B6, which indicates that the buyer may have to bear additional costs incurred by his failure to give appropriate notice to the seller.

Since, under D-terms, the seller does not fulfil his obligation until the goods have actually arrived at destination and been placed at the disposal of the buyer, the seller has to do everything required to achieve this. Nevertheless, A3 in all D-terms still stipulates that the seller must contract for carriage; and A6 of all D-terms stipulates that he must pay the costs resulting from A3 for the carriage of the goods "and, when necessary, for their transit through another country prior to delivery in accordance with A4". Needless to say, any transit costs incurred subsequent to delivery willl have to be paid by the buyer.

A7 Notice to the buyer

Give the buyer sufficient notice of the dispatch of the goods as well as any other notice required in order to allow the buyer to take measures which are normally necessary to enable him to take the goods.

Comments

The seller must give the buyer sufficient notice as to when the goods have been dispatched and when they will be available at the agreed or chosen delivery point, so that the buyer can make preparations in time to take delivery according to B4. There is no stipulation in Incoterms spelling out the consequences of the seller's failure to give such notice. But it follows from Incoterms that the seller's failure constitutes a breach of contract. This means that the seller could be held responsible for the breach according to the law applicable to the contract of sale.

A8 Proof of delivery, transport document or equivalent electronic message

Provide at his own expense the delivery order and/or the usual transport document (for example a negotiable bill of lading, a non-negotiable sea waybill, an inland waterway document, an air waybill, a railway consignment note, a road consignment note, or a multimodal transport document) which the buyer may require to take delivery of the goods.

Where the seller and the buyer have agreed to communicate electronically, the document referred to in the preceding paragraph may be replaced by an equivalent electronic data interchange (EDI) message.

Comments

In most cases the buyer will require a document in order to be able to obtain the goods from the carrier. Traditionally, the relevant document for carriage by sea is a negotiable bill of lading, and this is still the predominant document when DDU is used for carriage of bulk commodities. However, bills of lading are often replaced by delivery orders splitting up the total bill of lading quantity into smaller lots for several buyers.

Documents can be replaced by EDI messages when the parties have agreed to communicate electronically.

A9 Checking - packaging - marking

Pay the costs of those checking operations (such as checking quality, measuring, weighing, counting) which are necessary for the purpose of delivering the goods in accordance with A.4.

Provide at his own expense packaging (unless it is usual for the particular trade to deliver the goods of the contract description unpacked) which is required for the delivery of the goods. Packaging is to be marked appropriately.

Comments

It is important that the buyer ensure that the seller has duly fulfilled his obligation with respect to the condition of the goods, particularly if the buyer is called upon to pay for the goods before he has received and checked them. However, the seller has no duty to arrange and pay for the inspection of the goods before dispatch unless this is specifically agreed in the contract of sale.

A10 Other obligations

Render the buyer at the latter's request, risk and expense, every assistance in obtaining any documents or equivalent electronic messages other than those mentioned in A.8. issued or transmitted in the country of dispatch and/or of origin which the buyer may require for the importation of the goods.

Provide the buyer, upon request, with the necessary information for procuring insurance.

Comments

As noted in A2, the seller has the obligation to clear the goods for export. But he has no obligation after dispatch to bear any costs and risks with respect to import clearance of the goods at destination. However, he has the duty to render the buyer assistance in obtaining any documents (e.g. a certificate of origin, a health certificate, a clean report of findings, an import licence) or equivalent electronic messages which the seller may require for these purposes. The buyer, on the other hand, must reimburse the seller for any expenses which the seller might have incurred in connection with this assistance. Moreover, if something goes wrong, the buyer, not the seller will have to assume the risk.

Group D: ***Arrival***

DELIVERED DUTY UNPAID

(... named place of destination)

B THE BUYER MUST

B1 Payment of the price

Pay the price as provided in the contract of sale.

Comments

The buyer must pay the price agreed in the contract of sale. B1 constitutes a reminder of this main obligation, which corresponds with the seller's obligation to provide the goods in conformity with the contract of sale, as stipulated in A1.

B2 Licences, authorisations and formalities

Obtain at his own risk and expense any import licence or other official authorisation and carry out all customs formalities necessary for the importation of the goods.

Comments

The buyer must take care of the import clearance and bear any costs and risks in connection with it. Therefore, an import prohibition will not relieve the buyer of his obligation to pay for the goods, unless there is a particular "relief clause" in the contract of sale which he invokes to obtain this relief. Such clauses may provide for the extension of time or the right to avoid the contract under the applicable law (See the comments to A2).

B3 Contract of carriage

No obligation.

Comments

Although B3 merely stipulates "No obligation" for the buyer, on-carriage from the place of destination may be necessary in some cases, and it is the buyer's responsibility to do whatever is required for this purpose. But the seller is not concerned with the further carriage of the goods and the buyer has no obligation to the seller in this respect. The words "No obligation" mean that whatever the buyer does is in his own interest and is not covered by the contract of sale.

B4 Taking delivery

Take delivery of the goods as soon as they have been placed at his disposal in accordance with A.4.

Comments

As in all D-terms, B4 has wording stating that the buyer shall take delivery as soon as the goods have been placed at his disposal in accordance with A4. (The same wording is also used in EXW B4, but under EXW the placing of the goods at the buyer's disposal usually occurs at the seller's own premises.) The seller, according to A4 in the D-terms, shall place the goods at the buyer's disposal "on the date or within the period stipulated".
disposal earlier than agreed, the buyer is not obliged to take delivery before the agreed time, though it may normally be in his own interest to do so. If the goods are placed at the buyer's disposal too late, the buyer may hold the seller responsible for breach of contract according to the applicable law. He may also recover damages from the seller or, in the event of a fundamental breach, cancel the contract.

B5 Transfer of risks

Bear all risks of loss of or damage to the goods from the time they have been placed at his disposal in accordance with A.4.

Should he fail to fulfil his obligations in accordance with B.2., bear all additional risks of loss of or damage to the goods incurred thereby and should he fail to give notice in accordance with B.7., bear all risks of loss of or damage to the goods from the agreed date or the expiry date of the period stipulated for delivery provided, however, that the goods have been duly appropriated to the contract, that is to say, clearly set aside or otherwise identified as the contract goods.

Comments

According to the main rule, while the seller under A5 bears the risk of loss of or damage to the goods until the delivery point, the buyer has to bear the risk thereafter. The delivery point is different under the different terms. In EXW and all D-terms the goods are simply placed "at the disposal of the buyer" at the relevant point, while under the F- and C-terms the delivery point is related to the handing over of the goods to the carrier in the country of dispatch or shipment (See the comments to A4 of these terms). In the terms used for goods intended to be carried by sea, reference is made to delivery alongside the named vessel (FAS A4) or delivery onboard the vessel (FOB, CFR, CIF).

Consequences of buyer's failure to give notice

While the seller under EXW and all D-terms can transfer the risk by his own act of placing the goods at the buyer's disposal, he may be prevented from doing so by the buyer's failure to give notice according to B7. This can occur when it is the buyer's responsibility to determine (1) the time within a stipulated period when the goods are to be made available or (2) the place of delivery (See the comments to B7). The failure to perform these tasks results in a premature passing of the risk: It is not acceptable that the buyer should be able to delay the delivery and the passing of the risk longer than contemplated when the contract of sale was made. Therefore, his failure to notify according to B7 will cause the risk to pass "from the agreed date or the expiry date of the period stipulated for taking delivery".

Appropriation and the passing of risk

The risk, however, cannot pass until the goods "have been appropriated to the contract". If the goods are unascertained - i.e. goods of a certain kind which the seller will deliver to various buyers - appropriation only occurs when the goods are "clearly set aside as the contract goods".

This appropriation will normally be made when the seller has handed over the goods for carriage and the consignment has been marked as intended for the buyer - unless the cargo is carried in bulk and intended to be appropriated between different buyers only upon the arrival of the goods at destination.

Buyer's obligation to clear goods for import

Under DDU the buyer has the obligation to clear the goods for import (B2). If he fails to do so, the seller may be prevented from reaching the agreed delivery point. Any "additional risks of loss of or damage to the goods incurred thereby" must then be borne by the buyer. Therefore, the risk may pass even before the goods have reached the agreed delivery point, for example when the goods are detained at a customs station because of the buyer's failure to fulfil his obligation to clear the goods for import.

B6 Division of costs

Pay all costs relating to the goods from the time they have been placed at his disposal at the named point of destination in accordance with A.4.

Should he fail to fulfil his obligations in accordance with B.2., or to take delivery of the goods when they have been placed at his disposal in accordance with A.4., or to give notice in accordance with B. 7., bear all additional costs incurred thereby provided, however, that the goods have been duly appropriated to the contract, that is to say, clearly set aside or otherwise identified as the contract goods.

Pay all duties, taxes and other official charges as well as the costs of carrying out customs formalities payable upon importation of the goods.

Comments

While in DAF, DES and DEQ, the place of delivery is inherent in the term itself - the named frontier, the ship and the quay respectively - under DDU the parties have to specify the place themselves. Moreover, the buyer must pay any further costs subsequent to the delivery of the goods to that place.

The buyer must pay any additional costs which may arise because of his failure to take delivery as agreed or to notify the seller of the time and place of delivery according to B7. In DDU the failure of the buyer to clear the goods for import according to B2 may prevent the seller from reaching the agreed delivery point or it may give rise to additional costs. If so, the buyer has to bear the consequences of these events and pay any additional costs incurred thereby. The buyer's obligation to pay additional costs in these circumstances is subject to the identification of the goods as the contract goods ("appropriation").

As noted in the comments to B2, the buyer has the duty to clear the goods for import; B6 declares that he also has to pay the costs arising in that connection ("duties, taxes and other official charges as well as the costs of carrying out customs formalities"). The buyer also has to pay any duties, taxes and other charges arising with regard to the transit of the goods through another country, after they have been delivered by the seller in accordance with A4.

B7 Notice to the seller

Whenever he is entitled to determine the time within a stipulated period and/or the place of taking delivery, give the seller sufficient notice thereof.

Comments

As discussed in the comments to B5 and B6, the failure of the buyer to notify the seller of the time and place of taking delivery - when the buyer in the contract of sale has been given the option to determine these matters - may cause the risk of the loss of or damage to the goods to pass before the goods have been delivered according to A4. In addition, it can make the buyer liable to pay any additional costs incurred by the seller as a result of the buyer's failure.

B8 Proof of delivery, transport document or equivalent electronic message

Accept the appropriate delivery order or transport document in accordance with A.8.

Comments

The buyer has to accept the document if it conforms with the contract and with the requirements of A8 (See the comments to A8). If the buyer rejects the document (e.g. by instructions to a bank not to pay the seller under a documentary credit), he commits a breach of contract, which would give the seller remedies available for such a breach under the contract of sale.

These remedies could include, for example, a right to cancel the contract or to claim damages for breach. However, the buyer is not obliged to accept a document which does not provide adequate proof of delivery, e.g. one which has notations on it showing that the goods are defective or that they have been provided in less than the agreed quantity. In these cases, the document is termed "unclean".

B9 Inspection of goods

Pay, unless otherwise agreed, the costs of pre-shipment inspection except when mandated by the authorities of the country of exportation.

Comments

As noted in the comments to A9, the buyer has to pay for any costs of checking the goods, unless the contract determines that these costs should be wholly or partly borne by the seller. In some cases, the contract may provide that the costs should be borne by the seller if the inspection reveals that the goods do not conform with the contract.

In some countries, where import licences or permission to obtain foreign currency for the payment of the price may be required, the authorities may demand an inspection of the goods before shipment, to ensure that the goods are in conformity with the contract. (This is usually called pre-shipment inspection, PSI.) If this is the case, the inspection is normally arranged by instructions from the authorities to an inspection company, which they appoint. The costs following from this inspection have to be paid by the authorities. Any reimbursement to the authorities for the inspection costs, however, must be made by the buyer, unless otherwise specifically agreed between the buyer and the seller.

B10 Other obligations

Pay all costs and charges incurred in obtaining the documents or equivalent electronic messages mentioned in A.10. and reimburse those incurred by the seller in rendering his assistance in accordance therewith.

Comments

As discussed in the comments to A10, the seller has to render the buyer assistance in obtaining the documents or electronic messages which may be required for the transit and importation of the goods. However, this assistance is rendered at the buyer's risk and expense. Therefore, B10 stipulates that the buyer must pay all costs and charges incurred in obtaining these documents or electronic messages. He will also have to reimburse the seller for the seller's costs in rendering his assistance in these matters.

Group D : Arrival

DELIVERED DUTY PAID
(... named place of destination)

A SELLER'S PRIMARY DUTIES

- Deliver the goods at the named place of destination (**A4**)
- Provide import clearance (import licence, pay import duties, taxes and fees, if required) (**A2**)
- Provide documents to enable the buyer to take delivery at the named place (e.g. delivery order, warehouse warrant or document of transport) (**A8**)

DIFFERENCE FROM *DDU*

While under the term DDU the seller does not have to clear the goods for import and pay the duty, he has to do so under DDP

DOCUMENTS

Required documents

- Commercial invoice (**A1**)
- Delivery order, warehouse warrant or document of transport (**A8**)
- Import licence (**A2**)

NOTE:
All documents may be replaced by EDI messages

SELLER

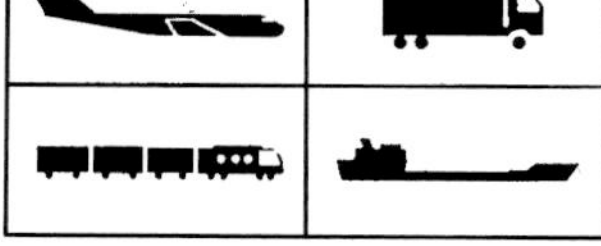

Goods

PRE-CARRIAGE

MAIN C

Seller's risk

Seller's costs

elivered duty paid" means that the seller fulfils his igation to deliver when the goods have been made ilable at the named place in the country of importation. e seller has to bear the risks and costs, including duties, es and other charges of delivering the goods thereto, ared for importation. Whilst the EXW term represents the nimum obligation for the seller, DDP represents the ximum obligation.

s term should not be used if the seller is unable directly ndirectly to obtain the import licence.

If the parties wish the buyer to clear the goods for importation and to pay the duty, the term DDU should be used.

If the parties wish to exclude from the seller's obligations some of the costs payable upon importation of the goods (such as value added tax (VAT)), this should be made clear by adding words to this effect: "Delivered duty paid, VAT unpaid (... named place of destination)".

This term may be used irrespective of the mode of transport.

B BUYER'S PRIMARY DUTY

- Take delivery of the goods at the named place of destination (**B4**)

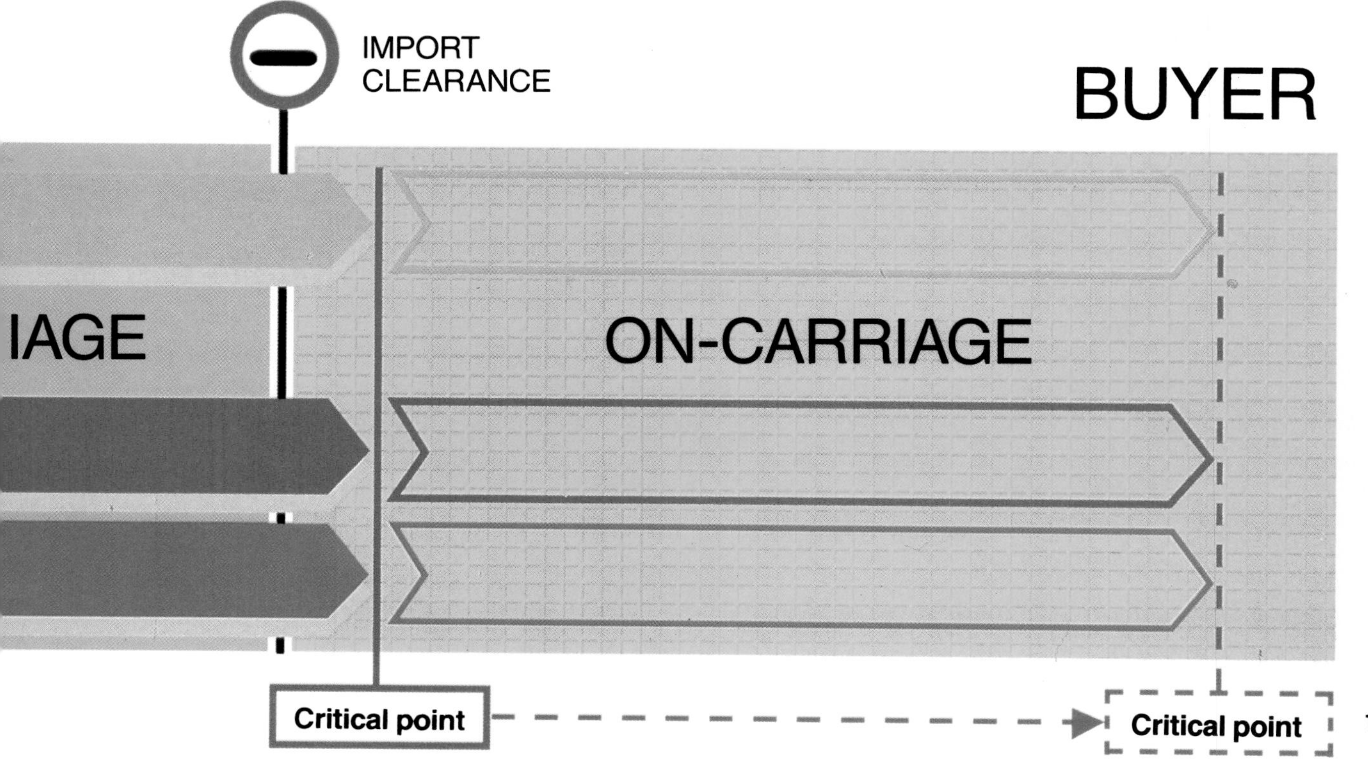

Group D: **Arrival**

DELIVERED DUTY PAID

(... named place of destination)

A THE SELLER MUST

A1 Provision of the goods in conformity with the contract

Provide the goods and the commercial invoice, or its equivalent electronic message, in conformity with the contract of sale and any other evidence of conformity which may be required by the contract.

Comments

The seller must provide the goods in conformity with the contract. It is also usual practice that the seller, in order to be paid, has to invoice the buyer. In addition, the seller must submit any other evidence stipulated in the contract itself that the goods conform with that contract.

This text only serves as a reminder of the seller's main obligation under the contract of sale.

Relief from unforeseen or reasonably unforeseeable prohibitions

The seller's obligations under DDP may become more expensive than contemplated as a result of reasonably unforeseeable circumstances. However, contracts of sale usually contain provisions which the seller may invoke to protect himself in the event of these contingencies. Under the 1980 Convention on International Sale of Goods (CISG) and corresponding provisions in various national Sale of Goods Acts, unforeseen or reasonably unforeseeable export prohibitions may relieve the seller from his obligations under the contract of sale.

If the seller wishes to avoid the obligation of clearing the goods for import, he should use DDU or add the phrase "not cleared for import" after DDP.

A2 Licences, authorisations and formalities

Obtain at his own risk and expense any export and import licence and other official authorisation and carry out all customs formalities for the exportation and importation of the goods and, where necessary, for their transit through another country.

Comments

Since the term DDP is evidence of an arrival contract, the seller has to do whatever may be necessary for the goods to reach the agreed place for delivery. This means the seller is responsible for export as well as import clearance of the goods as well as any transit of the goods through third countries.

Before agreeing to sell the goods under DDP, the seller should be sure that the regulations of the buyer's country do not prevent him as a non-resident from applying for any necessary import licence. Normally no such difficulties will be encountered, since the application for licences can be made by freight forwarders (customs brokers) on the seller's behalf.

Advisable to exclude payment of official charges

It may be advisable for the parties to exclude the payment of any official charges intended for the "internal" fiscal system in the country of importation (such as VAT levied upon importation) from the seller's obligation to pay. If this is not done, any right to deduct these expenses or to benefit from particular tax advantages available only to residents could be lost. The charges intended to be excluded should then be identified in conjunction with the DEQ term in the contract of sale, e.g. by using a phrase such as "DDP VAT unpaid".

A3 Contract of carriage and insurance

a) Contract of carriage

Contract at his own expense for the carriage of the goods by a usual route and in a customary manner to the agreed point at the named place of destination. If a point is not agreed or is not determined by practice, the seller may select the point at the named place of destination which best suits his purpose.

b) Contract of insurance

No obligation.

Comments

Under DDP the seller must ensure that the goods actually arrive at destination. It follows from this that the seller must arrange and pay for any carriage of the goods. Though it may seem that the seller should have the right to contract for carriage as he deems fit - since any inadequate measures in this regard would automatically be at his own peril - it is nevertheless stipulated in the D-terms, as in the C-terms, that the seller should contract for carriage "by a usual route and in a customary manner".

Under the D-terms, the seller's choice of transport is only of importance to the buyer insofar as it affects the buyer's obligation to receive the goods from the carrier. If the seller chooses an unusual transport which makes it more difficult or expensive for the buyer to receive the goods from the carrier, any additional costs or risks caused by the seller's choice of transport will be for the seller's account.

Normally, the point mentioned after the D-term will indicate where the goods should be delivered at destination. But if there are several alternatives available, and the contract of sale or commercial practice does not indicate which alternative the seller must choose, he "may select the point at the named place of destination which best suits his purpose".

A4 Delivery

Place the goods at the disposal of the buyer in accordance with A.3. on the date or within the period stipulated.

Comments

Under DDP the seller must "place the goods at the disposal of the buyer" at destination. The precise point for the delivery of the goods depends upon the D-term chosen.

A5 Transfer of risks

Subject to the provisions of B.5., bear all risks of loss of or damage to the goods until such time as they have been delivered in accordance with A.4.

Comments

All Incoterms are based on the same principle that the risk of loss of or damage to the goods is transferred from the seller to the buyer when the seller has fulfilled his delivery obligation according to A4. A5 of FOB, CFR and CIF further specifies that the risk is transferred when the goods "have passed the ship's rail at the named port of shipment".

All Incoterms, in conformity with the general principle of CISG, connect the transfer of the risk with the delivery of the goods and not with other circumstances, such as the passing of ownership or the time of the conclusion of the contract. Neither Incoterms nor CISG deal with transfer of title to the goods or other property rights with respect to the goods.

The passing of risk of loss of or damage to the goods concerns the risk of fortuitous events (accidents) and does not include loss or damage caused by the seller or the buyer, e.g. inadequate packing or marking of the goods. Therefore, even if damage occurs subsequent to the transfer of the risk, the seller may still be responsible if the damage could be attributed to the fact that the goods were not delivered in conformity with the contract (See A1 and the comments to A9).

A5 of all Incoterms starts with the phrase "subject to the provisions of B5". This means that there are exceptions to the main rule concerning the passing of risk under the circumstances mentioned in B5, which may result in a premature passing of the risk because of the buyer's failure properly to fulfil his obligations (See the comments to B5).

A6 Division of costs

Subject to the provisions of B.6.

- in addition to costs resulting from A.3.a), pay all costs relating to the goods until such time as they have been delivered in accordance with A.4.;
- pay the costs of customs formalities as well as all duties, taxes and other official charges payable upon exportation and importation of the goods, unless otherwise agreed and, where necessary, their transit through another country prior to delivery in accordance with A.4.

Comments

As is the case with the transfer of the risk of loss of or damage to the goods, all Incoterms follow the same rule, that the division of costs occurs at the delivery point. All costs occurring before the seller has fulfilled his obligation to deliver according to A4 are for his account, while further costs are for the account of the buyer (See the comments to B6). This rule is made subject to the provisions of B6, which indicates that the buyer may have to bear additional costs incurred by his failure to give appropriate notice to the seller.

Since, under D-terms, the seller does not fulfil his obligation until the goods have actually arrived at destination and been placed at the disposal of the buyer, the seller has to do everything required to achieve this. Nevertheless, A3 in all D-terms still stipulates that the seller must contract for carriage; and A6 of all D-terms stipulates that he must pay the costs resulting from A3 for the carriage of the goods "and, where necessary, for their transit through another country prior to delivery in accordance with A4". Needless to say, any transit costs incurred subsequent to delivery will have to be paid by the buyer.

A7 Notice to the buyer

Give the buyer sufficient notice of the dispatch of the goods as well as any other notice required in order to allow the buyer to take measures which are normally necessary to enable him to take the goods.

Comments

The seller must give the buyer sufficient notice as to when the goods have been dispatched and when they will be available at the agreed or chosen delivery point, so that the buyer can make preparations in time to take delivery according to B4. There is no stipulation in Incoterms spelling out the consequences of the seller's failure to give such notice. But it follows from Incoterms that the seller's failure constitutes a breach of contract. This means that the seller could be held responsible for the breach according to the law applicable to the contract of sale.

A8 Proof of delivery, transport document or equivalent electronic message

Provide the buyer at the seller's expense with the delivery order and/or the usual transport document (for example, a negotiable bill of lading, a non-negotiable sea waybill, an inland waterway document, an air waybill, a railway consignment note, a road consignment note, or a multimodal transport document) which the buyer may require to take the goods.

Where the seller and the buyer have agreed to communicate electronically, the document referred to in the preceding paragraph may be replaced by an equivalent electronic data interchange (EDI) message.

Comments

In most cases the buyer will require a document in order to be able to obtain the goods from the carrier.

Traditionally, the relevant document for carriage by sea is a negotiable bill of lading, and this is still the predominant document when DDP is used for carriage of bulk commodities. However, bills of lading are often replaced by delivery orders splitting up the total bill of lading quantity into smaller lots for several buyers.

Documents can be replaced by EDI messages when the parties have agreed to communicate electronically.

A9 Checking - packaging - marking

Pay the costs of those checking operations (such as checking quality, measuring, weighing, counting) which are necessary for the purpose of delivering the goods in accordance with A.4.

Provide at his own expense packaging (unless it is usual for the particular trade to deliver the goods of the contract description unpacked) which is required for the delivery of the goods. Packaging is to be marked appropriately.

Comments

It is important that the buyer ensure that the seller has duly fulfilled his obligation with respect to the condition of the goods, particularly if the buyer is called upon to pay for the goods before he has received and checked them. However, the seller has no duty to arrange and pay for the inspection of the goods before dispatch unless this is specifically agreed in the contract of sale.

A10 Other obligations

Pay all costs and charges incurred in obtaining the documents or equivalent electronic messages mentioned in B. 10. and reimburse those incurred by the buyer in rendering his assistance therewith.

Provide the buyer, upon request, with the necessary information for procuring insurance.

Comments

DDP requires the seller to clear the goods for import, but if the seller so requests the buyer must assist in obtaining any documents (e.g. a certificate of origin, a health certificate, a clean report of findings, an import licence) or equivalent electronic messages which the seller may require for these purposes. The seller, however, has to reimburse the buyer for any costs the buyer may incur in rendering this assistance.

DELIVERED DUTY PAID

(... named place of destination)

B THE BUYER MUST

B1 Payment of the price

Pay the price as provided in the contract of sale.

Comments

The buyer must pay the price agreed in the contract of sale. B1 constitutes a reminder of this main obligation, which corresponds with the seller's obligation to provide the goods in conformity with the contract of sale, as stipulated in A1.

B2 Licences, authorisations and formalities

Render the seller at the latter's request, risk and expense every assistance in obtaining any import licence and other official authorisation necessary for the importation of the goods.

Comments

Since the seller has to make the goods available to the buyer in the country of destination, it is for the seller to do whatever is necessary with respect to the clearance of the goods for export, transit and import.

B3 Contract of carriage

No obligation.

Comments

Although B3 merely stipulates "No obligation" for the buyer, on-carriage from the place of destination may be necessary in some cases, and it is the buyer's responsibility to do whatever is required for this purpose. But the seller is not concerned with the further carriage of the goods and the buyer has no obligation to the seller in this respect. The words "No obligation" mean that whatever the buyer does is in his own interest and is not covered by the contract of sale.

B4 Taking delivery

Take delivery of the goods as soon as they have been placed at his disposal in accordance with A.4.

Comments

As in all D-terms, B4 has wording stating that the buyer shall take delivery as soon as the goods have been placed at his disposal in accordance with A4. (The same wording is also used in EXW B4, but EXW B3 specifies that the placing of the goods at the buyer's disposal occurs at the seller's own premises.) The seller, according to A4 in the D-terms, shall place the goods at the buyer's disposal "on the date or within the period stipulated".

If the goods are placed at the buyer's disposal earlier than agreed, the buyer is not obliged to take delivery before the agreed time, though it may normally be in his own interest to do so. If the goods are placed at the buyer's disposal too late, the buyer may hold the seller responsible for breach of contract according to the applicable law. He may also recover damages from the seller or, in the event of a fundamental breach, cancel the contract.

B5 Transfer of risks

Bear all risks of loss of or damage to the goods from the time they have been placed at his disposal in accordance with A.4.

Should he fail to give notice in accordance with B.7., bear all risks of loss of or damage to the goods from the agreed date or the expiry date of the period stipulated for delivery provided, however, that the goods have been duly appropriated to the contract, that is to say, clearly set aside or otherwise identified as the contract goods.

Comments

According to the main rule, while the seller under A5 bears the risk of loss of or damage to the goods until the delivery point, the buyer has to bear the risk thereafter. The delivery point is different under the different terms. In EXW and all D-terms the goods are simply placed "at the disposal of the buyer" at the relevant point, while under the F- and C-terms the delivery point is related to the handing over of the goods to the carrier in the country of dispatch or shipment (See the comments to A4 of these terms). In the terms used for goods intended to be carried by sea, reference is made to delivery alongside the named vessel (FAS A4) or delivery onboard the vessel (FOB, CFR, CIF).

Consequences of buyer's failure to give notice

While the seller under EXW and all D-terms can transfer the risk by his own act of placing the goods at the buyer's disposal, he may be prevented from doing so by the buyer's failure to give notice according to B7. This can occur when it is the buyer's responsibility to determine (1) the time within a stipulated period when the goods are to be made available or (2) the place of delivery (See the comments to B7). The failure to perform these tasks results in a premature passing of the risk: It is not acceptable that the buyer should be able to delay the delivery and the passing of the risk longer than contemplated when the contract of sale was made. Therefore, his failure to notify according to B7 will cause the risk to pass "from the agreed date or the expiry date of any period fixed for taking delivery".

Appropriation and the passing of risk

The risk, however, cannot pass until the goods "have been appropriated to the contract". If the goods are unascertained - i.e. goods of a certain kind which the seller will deliver to various buyers - appropriation only occurs when the goods are "clearly set aside as the contract goods".

This appropriation will normally be made when the seller has handed over the goods for carriage and the consignment has been marked as intended for the buyer - unless the cargo is carried in bulk and intended to be appropriated between different buyers only upon the arrival of the goods at destination.

B6 Division of costs

Pay all costs relating to the goods from the time they have been placed at his disposal in accordance with A.4.

Should he fail to take delivery of the goods when they have been placed at his disposal in accordance with A.4., or to give notice in accordance with B.7., bear all additional costs incurred thereby provided, however, that the goods have been appropriated to the contract, that is to say, clearly set aside or otherwise identified as the contract goods.

Comments

While in DAF, DES and DEQ, the place of delivery is inherent in the term itself - the named frontier, ship and quay respectively - under DDP the parties have to specify the place themselves. Moreover, the buyer must pay any further costs subsequent to the delivery of the goods to that place.

In DDP, it may not always be clear which of the parties must unload the goods from the arriving vehicle and pay for this unloading process. Nor will it necessarily be clear, if further transport is required, who should reload the goods onto an on-carrying vehicle and pay for the reloading. If these responsibilities are unclear, the parties are advised to specify who is responsible by adding phrases to DDP - for example, "loaded upon arriving vehicle", "unloaded from arriving vehicle", or "reloaded upon on-carrying vehicle".

The buyer must pay any additional costs which may arise if he fails to take delivery as agreed or if he fails to notify the seller of the time and place of delivery according to B7. The buyer's obligation to pay additional costs in these cases is subject to the identification of the goods as the contract goods ("appropriation").

Since under DDP the seller has to clear the goods for import, the buyer does not have to pay any costs in that regard.

B7 Notice to the seller

Whenever he is entitled to determine the time within a stipulated period and/or the place of taking delivery, give the seller sufficient notice thereof.

Comments

As discussed in the comments to B5 and B6, the failure of the buyer to notify the seller of the time and place of taking delivery - when the buyer in the contract of sale has been given the option to determine these matters - may cause the risk of the loss of or damage to the goods to pass before the goods have been delivered according to A4. In addition, it can make the buyer liable to pay any additional costs incurred by the seller as a result of the buyer's failure.

B8 Proof of delivery, transport document or equivalent electronic message

Accept the appropriate delivery order or transport document in accordance with A.8.

Comments

The buyer has to accept the document if it conforms with the contract and with the requirements of A8 (See the comments to A8). If the buyer rejects the document (e.g. by instructions to a bank not to pay the seller under a documentary credit), he commits a breach of contract, which would give the seller remedies available for such a breach under the contract of sale.

These remedies could include, for example, a right to cancel the contract or to claim damages for breach. However, the buyer is not obliged to accept a document which does not provide adequate proof of delivery, e.g. one which has notations on it showing that the goods are defective or that they have been provided in less than the agreed quantity. In these cases, the document is termed "unclean".

B9 Inspection of goods

Pay, unless otherwise agreed, the costs of pre-shipment inspection except when mandated by the authorities of the country of exportation.

Comments

As noted in the comments to A9, the buyer has to pay for any costs of checking the goods, unless the contract determines that these costs should be wholly or partly borne by the seller. In some cases, the contract may provide that the costs should be borne by the seller if the inspection reveals that the goods do not conform with the contract.

In some countries, where import licences or permission to obtain foreign currency for the payment of the price may be required, the authorities may demand an inspection of the goods before shipment, to ensure that the goods are in conformity with the contract. (This is usually called pre-shipment inspection, PSI.) If this is the case, the inspection is normally arranged by instructions from the authorities to an inspection company, which they appoint. The costs following from this inspection have to be paid by the authorities. Any reimbursement to the authorities for the inspection costs, however, must be made by the buyer, unless otherwise specifically agreed between the buyer and the seller.

B10 Other obligations

Render the seller, at his request, risk and expense, every assistance in obtaining any documents or equivalent electronic messages issued or transmitted in the country of importation which the seller may require for the purpose of placing the goods at the disposal of the buyer in accordance with these rules.

Comments

Since the seller has the obligation to clear the goods for import, he may require the buyer's assistance to obtain the necessary documents or EDI messages. The buyer must render this assistance when requested by the seller to do so, but this is done at the seller's risk and expense.

ANNEXES

CMI UNIFORM RULES FOR SEA WAYBILLS

CMI RULES FOR ELECTRONIC BILLS OF LADING

COMBITERMS

ICC SERVING WORLD BUSINESS

SOME ICC PUBLICATIONS

CMI UNIFORM RULES FOR SEA WAYBILLS*

1. Scope of Application

(i) These Rules shall be called the «CMI Uniforms Rules for Sea Waybills».

(ii) They shall apply when adopted by a contract of carriage which is not covered by a bill of lading or similar document of title, whether the contract be in writing or not.

2. Definitions

In these Rules:

«Contract of carriage» shall mean any contract of carriage subject to these Rules which is to be performed wholly or partly by sea.

«Goods» shall mean any goods carried or received for carriage under a contract of carriage.

«Carrier» and «Shipper» shall mean the parties named in or identifiable as such from the contract of carriage.

«Consignee» shall mean the party named in or identifiable as such from the contract of carriage, or any person substituted as consignee in accordance with rule 6(i).

«Right of Control» shall mean the rights and obligations referred to in rule 6.

3. Agency

(i) The shipper on entering into the contract of carriage does so not only on his own behalf but also as agent for and on behalf of the consignee, and warrants to the carrier that he has authority so to do.

(ii) This rule shall apply if, and only if, it be necessary by the law applicable to the contract of carriage so as to enable the consignee to sue and be sued thereon. The consignee shall be under no greater liability than he would have been had the contract of carriage been covered by a bill of lading or similar document of title.

4. Rights and Responsibilities

(i) The contract of carriage shall be subject to any International Convention or National Law which is, or if the contract of carriage had been covered by a bill of lading or similar document of title would have been, compulsorily applicable thereto. Such convention or law shall apply notwithstanding anything inconsistent therewith in the contract of carriage.

(ii) Subject always to subrule (i), the contract of carriage is governed by:

(a) these Rules;

(b) unless otherwise agreed by the parties, the carrier's standard terms and conditions for the trade, if any, including any terms and conditions relating to the non-sea part of the carriage;

(c) any other terms and conditions agreed by the parties.

(iii) In the event of any inconsistency between the terms and conditions mentioned under subrule (ii)(b) or (c) and these Rules, these Rules shall prevail.

5. Description of the Goods

(i) The shipper warrants the accuracy of the particulars furnished by him relating to the goods, and shall indemnifiy the carrier against any loss, damage or expense resulting from any inaccuracy.

(ii) In the absence of reservation by the carrier, any statement in a sea waybill or similar document as to the quantity or condition of the goods shall

(a) as between the carrier and the shipper be prima facie evidence of receipt of the goods as so stated;

(b) as between the carrier and the consignee be conclusive evidence of receipt of the goods as so stated, and proof to the contrary shall not be permitted, provided always that the consignee has acted in good faith.

6. Right of Control

(i) Unless the shipper has exercised his option under subrule (ii) below, he shall be the only party entitled to give the carrier instructions in relation to the contract of carriage. Unless prohibited by the applicable law, he shall be entitled to change the name of the consignee at any time up to the consignee claiming delivery of the goods after their arrival at destination, provided he gives the carrier reasonable notice in writing, or by some other means acceptable to the carrier, thereby undertaking to indemnify the carrier against any additional expense caused thereby.

(ii) The shipper shall have the option, to be exercised not later than the receipt of the goods by the carrier, to transfer the right of control to the consignee. The exercise of this option must be noted on the sea waybill or similar document, if any. Where the option has been exercised the consignee shall have such rights as are referred to in subrule (i) above and the shipper shall cease to have such rights.

7. Delivery

(i) The carrier shall deliver the goods to the consignee upon production of proper identification.

(ii) The carrier shall be under no liability for wrong delivery if he can prove that he has exercised reasonable care to ascertain that the party claiming to be the consignee is in fact that party.

8. Validity

In the event of anything contained in these Rules or any such provisions as are incorporated into the contract of carriage by virtue of rule 4, being inconsistent with the provisions of any International Convention or National Law compulsorily applicable to the contract of carriage, such Rules and provisions shall to that extent but no further be null and void.

* Publication by kind permission of the Comité Maritime International

CMI RULES FOR ELECTRONIC BILLS OF LADING*

1. Scope of Application

These rules shall apply whenever the parties so agree.

2. Definitions

a. «Contract of Carriage» means any agreement to carry goods wholly or partly by sea.

b. «EDI» means Electronic Data Interchange, i.e. the interchange of trade data effected by teletransmission.

c. «UN/EDIFACT» means the United Nations Rules for Electronic Data Interchange for Administration, Commerce and Transport.

d. «Transmission» means one or more messages electronically sent together as one unit of dispatch which includes heading and terminating data.

e. «Confirmation» means a Transmission which advises that the content of a Transmission appears to be complete and correct, without prejudice to any subsequent consideration or action that the content may warrant.

f. «Private Key» means any technically appropriate form, such as a combination of numbers and/or letters, which the parties may agree for securing the authenticity and integrity of a Transmission.

g. «Holder» means the party who is entitled to the rights described in Article 7(a) by virtue of its possession of a valid Private Key.

h. «Electronic Monitoring System» means the device by which a computer system can be examined for the transactions that it recorded, such as a Trade Data Log or an Audit Trail.

i. «Electronic Storage» means any temporary, intermediate or permanent storage of electronic data including the primary and the back-up storage of such data.

3. Rules of procedure

a. When not in conflict with these Rules, the Uniform Rules of Conduct for Interchange of Trade Data by Teletransmission, 1987 (UNCID) shall govern the conduct between the parties.

b. The EDI under these Rules should conform with the relevant UN/EDIFACT standards. However, the parties may use any other method of trade data interchange acceptable to all of the users.

c. Unless otherwise agreed, the document format for the Contract of Carriage shall conform to the UN Layout Key or compatible national standard for bills of lading.

d. Unless otherwise agreed, a recipient of a Transmission is not authorised to act on a Transmission unless he has sent a Confirmation.

e. In the event of a dispute arising between the parties as to the data actually transmitted, an Electronic Monitoring System may be used to verify the data received. Data concerning other transactions not related to the data in dispute are to be considered as trade secrets and thus not available for examination. If such data are unavoidably revealed as part of the examination of the Electronic Monitoring System, they must be treated as confidential and not released to any outside party or used for any other purpose.

f. Any transfer of rights to the goods shall be considered to be private information, and shall not be released to any outside party not connected to the transport or clearance of the goods.

4. Form and content of the receipt message

a. The carrier, upon receiving the goods from the shipper, shall give notice of the receipt of the goods to the shipper by a message at the electronic address specified by the shipper.

b. This receipt message shall include:
   - (i) the name of the shipper;
   - (ii) the description of the goods, with any representations and reservations, in the same tenor as would be required if a paper bill of lading were issued;
   - (iii) the date and place of the receipt of the goods;
   - (iv) a reference to the carrier's terms and conditions of carriage; and
   - (v) the Private Key to be used in subsequent Transmissions.

   The shipper must confirm this receipt message to the carrier, upon which Confirmation the shipper shall be the Holder.

c. Upon demand of the Holder, the receipt message shall be updated with the date and place of shipment as soon as the goods have been loaded on board.

d. The information contained in (ii), (iii) and (iv) of paragraph (b) above including the date and place of shipment if updated in accordance with paragraph (c) of this Rule, shall have the same force and effect as if the receipt message were contained in a paper bill of lading.

5. Terms and conditions of the Contract of Carriage

a. It is agreed and understood that whenever the carrier makes a reference to its terms and conditions of carriage, these terms and conditions shall form part of the Contract of Carriage.

b. Such terms and conditions must be readily available to the parties to the Contract of Carriage.

c. In the event of any conflict or inconsistency between such terms and conditions and these Rules, these Rules shall prevail.

6. Applicable law

The Contract of Carriage shall be subject to any international convention or national law which would have been compulsorily applicable if a paper bill of lading had been issued.

7. Right of Control and Transfer

a. The Holder is the only party who may, as against the carrier:
   - (1) claim delivery of the goods;
   - (2) nominate the consignee or substitute a nominated consignee for any other party, including itself;
   - (3) transfer the Right of Control and Transfer to another party;
   - (4) instruct the carrier on any other subject concerning the goods, in accordance with the terms and conditions of the Contract of Carriage, as if he were the holder of a paper bill of lading.

b. A transfer of the Right of Control and Transfer shall be effected: (i) by notification of the current Holder to the carrier of its intention to transfer its Right of Control and Transfer to a proposed new Holder, and (ii) confirmation by the carrier of such notification message, whereupon (iii) the carrier shall transmit the information as referred to in article 4 (except for the Private Key) to the proposed new Holder, whereafter (iv) the proposed new Holder shall advise the carrier of its acceptance of the Right of Control and Transfer, whereupon (v) the carrier shall cancel the current Private Key and issue a new Private Key to the new Holder.

c. If the proposed new Holder advises the carrier that it does not accept the Right of Control and Transfer or fails to advise the carrier of such acceptance within a reasonable time, the proposed transfer of the Righ of Control and Transfer shall not take place. The carrier shall notify the current Holder accordingly and the current Private Key shall retain its validity.

d. The transfer of the Right of Control and Transfer in the manner described above shall have the same effects as the transfer of such rights under a paper bill of lading.

8. The Private Key

a. The Private Key is unique to each successive Holder. It is not transferable by the Holder. The carrier and the Holder shall each maintain the security of the Private Key.

b. The carrier shall only be obliged to send a Confirmation of an electronic message to the last Holder to whom it issued a Private Key, when such Holder secures the Transmission containing such electronic message by the use of the Private Key.

c. The Private Key must be separate and distinct from any means used to identify the Contract of Carriage, and any security password or identification used to access the computer network.

9. Delivery

a. The carrier shall notify the Holder of the place and date of intended delivery of the goods. Upon such notification the Holder has a duty to nominate a consignee and to give adequate delivery instructions to the carrier with verification by the Private Key. In the absence of such nomination, the Holder will be deemed to be the consignee.

b. The carrier shall deliver the goods to the consignee upon production of proper identification in accordance with the delivery instructions specified in paragraph (a) above; such delivery shall automatically cancel the Private Key.

c. The carrier shall be under no liability for misdelivery if it can prove that it exercised reasonable care to ascertain that the party who claimed to be the consignee was in fact that party.

10. Option to receive a paper document

a. The Holder has the option at any time prior to delivery of the goods to demand from the carrier a paper bill of lading. Such document shall be made available at a location to be determined by the Holder, provided that no carrier shall be obliged to make such document available at a place where it has no facilities and in such instance the carrier shall only be obliged to make the document available at the facility nearest to the location determined by the Holder. The carrier shall not be responsible for delays in delivering the goods resulting from the Holder exercising the above option.

b. The carrier has the option at any time prior to delivery of the goods to issue to the Holder a paper bill of lading unless the exercise of such option could result in undue delay or disrupts the delivery of the goods.

c. A bill of lading issued under Rules 10 (a) or (b) shall include: the information set out in the receipt message referred to in Rule 4 (except for the Private Key); and (ii) a statement to the effect that the bill of lading has been issued upon termination of the procedures for EDI under the CMI Rules for Electronic Bills of Lading. The aforementioned bill of lading shall be issued at the option of the Holder either to the order of the Holder whose name for this purpose shall then be inserted in the bill of lading or «to bearer».

d. The issuance of a paper bill of lading under Rule 10 (a) or (b) shall cancel the Private Key and terminate the procedures for EDI under these Rules. Termination of these procedures by the Holder or the carrier will not relieve any of the parties to the Contract of Carriage of their rights, obligations or liabilities while performing under the present Rules nor of their rights, obligations or liabilities under the Contract of Carriage.

e. The Holder may demand at any time the issuance of a print-out of the receipt message referred to in Rule 4 (except for the Private Key) marked as «non-negotiable copy». The issuance of such a print-out shall not cancel the Private Key nor terminate the procedures for EDI.

11. Electronic data is equivalent to writing

The carrier and the shipper and all subsequent parties utilizing these procedures agree that any national or local law, custom or practice requiring the Contract of Carriage to be evidenced in writing and signed, is satisfied by the transmitted and confirmed electronic data residing on computer data storage media displayable in human language on a video screen or as printed out by a computer. In agreeing to adopt these Rules, the parties shall be taken to have agreed not to raise the defence that this contract is not in writing.

* Publication by kind permission of the Comité Maritime International

COMBITERMS 1990

Cost distribution between seller and buyer according to Incoterms 1990 in summary—**sea transport only**

Trade terms[1]

- **003** FAS Free Alongside Ship (named port of shipment)
- **004** FOB Free On Board (named port of shipment)
- **008** CFR Cost and Freight (named port of destination)
- **009** CIF Cost, Insurance and Freight (named port of destination)
- **016** DES Delivered Ex Ship (named port of destination)
- **017** DEQ Delivered Ex Quay (named port of destination), duty unpaid
- **020** DEQ Delivered Ex Quay (named port of destination), duty paid, exclusive of (named tax)

	Cost headings	020	017	016	009	008	004	003
100	Loading at seller's premises	S	S	S	S	S	S	S
150	Domestic precarriage/Local cartage	S	S	S	S	S	S	S
200	Contract of carriage and dispatch	S	S	S	S	S	S	B
250	Trade documentation in country of exportation	S	S	S	S	S	S	B
300	Customs clearance in country of exportation	S	S	S	S	S	S	B
350	Export charges	S	S	S	S	S	S	B
400	Loading at carrier's terminal[2]	S	S	S	S	S	B	B
450	Transportation equipment and accessories	S	S	S	S	S	B	B
500	Transport (Cargo) insurance				S			
550	International main carriage	S	S	S	S	S	B	B
600	Unloading at terminal[2]	S	S	B	S	S	B	B
650	Trade documentation in country of transit/importation	S	B	B	B	B	B	B
700	Customs clearance in country of importation	S	B	B	B	B	B	B
750	Import charges	S[3]	B	B	B	B	B	B
800	Local cartage/Domestic on-carriage	B	B	B	B	B	B	B
850	Unloading at buyer's premises	B	B	B	B	B	B	B
900	Other costs	**Cost distribution according to party agreement not regulated in Incoterms.**						

S = **Seller pays** B = **Buyer pays**

At certain cost headings there may be divergences to be observed from the cost distribution stated above. See remarks in Combiterms 1990 under the detailed description of each trade term.

Remarks

1) The terms FOB, CFR or CIF should be used only when the distribution of costs and/or risks between seller and buyer has been fixed at such time as the goods have passed the ship's rail in the named port of shipment. In other cases one of the corresponding terms FCA, CPT or CIP is more appropriate to use (see back page).
2) "Terminal" stands for quay/wharf/port warehouse.
3) Costs, which are stated in the trade term to be excluded, are to be paid by the buyer.

□ Brolins Offset 256388

COMBITERMS 1990

Cost distribution between seller and buyer according to Incoterms 1990 in summary—**all modes of transport**

Trade terms (main terms and certain common sub-variants)

001	EXW	Ex Works
002	FCA	Free Carrier seller's premises
005	FCA	Free Carrier (named terminal[1])
006	CPT	Carriage Paid To (named frontier point in country of dispatch)
007	CIP	Carriage and Insurance Paid to (named frontier point in country of dispatch)
010	CPT	Carriage Paid To (named frontier point in country of destination)
011	CIP	Carriage and Ins. Paid to (named frontier point in country of dest.)
012	CPT	Carriage Paid To (named terminal[2])
013	CIP	Carriage and Insurance Paid to (named terminal[2])
014	CPT	Carriage Paid To buyer's premises
015	CIP	Carriage and Insurance Paid to buyer's premises
018	DAF	Delivered At Frontier (named terminal[2])
019	DDU	Delivered (named terminal[2]) Duty Unpaid
021	DDP	Delivered (named terminal[2]) Duty Paid, exclusive of (named tax)
022	DDU	Delivered buyer's premises Duty Unpaid
023	DDP	Delivered buyer's premises Duty Paid, exclusive of (named tax)

Cost headings	023	022	021	019	018	015	014	013	012	011	010	007	006	005	002	001
100 Loading at seller's premises	S	S	S	S	S	S	S	S	S	S	S	S	S	S	S	B
150 Domestic precarriage/Local cartage	S	S	S	S	S	S	S	S	S	S	S	S	S	S	B	B
200 Contract of carriage and dispatch	S	S	S	S	S	S	S	S	S	S	S	S	S	S	S	B
250 Trade documentation in country of exportation	S	S	S	S	S	S	S	S	S	S	S	S	S	S	S	B
300 Customs clearance in country of exportation	S	S	S	S	S	S	S	S	S	S	S	S	S	S	S	B
350 Export charges	S	S	S	S	S	S	S	S	S	S	S	S	S	S	S	B
400 Loading at carrier's terminal[1]	S	S	S	S	S	S	S	S	S	S	S	S	S	B	B	B
450 Transportation equipment and accessories	S	S	S	S	S	S	S	S	S	S	S	S	S	B	B	B
500 Transport (Cargo) insurance						S		S		S		S				
550 International main carriage	S	S	S	S	S	S	S	S	S	S/B[3]	S/B[3]	S/B[3]	S/B[3]	B	B	B
600 Unloading at terminal[2]	S	S	S	S	S	S	S	S	S	B	B	B	B	B	B	B
650 Trade documentation in country of transit/importation	S	B	S	B	B	B	B	B	B	B	B	B	B	B	B	B
700 Customs clearance in country of importation	S	B	S	B	B	B	B	B	B	B	B	B	B	B	B	B
750 Import charges	S[4]	B	S[4]	B	B	B	B	B	B	B	B	B	B	B	B	B
800 Local cartage/Domestic on-carriage	S	S	B	B	B	S	S	B	B	B	B	B	B	B	B	B
850 Unloading at buyer's premises	B	B	B	B	B	B	B	B	B	B	B	B	B	B	B	B

900 Other costs — **Cost distribution according to party agreement not regulated in Incoterms.**

S = **Seller pays** B = **Buyer pays**

At certain cost headings there may be divergences to be observed from the cost distribution stated above. See remarks in Combiterms 1990 under the detailed description of each trade term.

Remarks

1) "Terminal" is equal to cargo terminal, railway station, quay/wharf/port warehouse and airport. Here it normally means a terminal at an inland or frontier location in the country of exportation.

2) "Terminal" is equal to cargo terminal, railway station, quay/wharf/port warehouse and airport. Here it normally means a terminal with customs facilities (e.g. customs warehouse) in the country of importation.

3) The point stated after "Carriage... Paid To..." determines how to distribute the cost. The seller pays the cost to the named frontier point. The buyer pays the cost from the named frontier point.

4) Costs, which are stated in the trade term to be excluded, are to be paid by the buyer.

ICC

SERVING WORLD BUSINESS

The ICC is a non-governmental organisation serving world business.

ICC members in 110 countries comprise tens of thousands of companies and business organisations. ICC National Committees or Councils in 59 countries co-ordinate activities at the national level.

The ICC:

- represents the world business community at national and international levels;
- promotes world trade and investment based on free and fair competition;
- harmonizes trade practices and formulates terminology and guidelines for importers and exporters;
- provides a growing range of practical services to business.

The ICC also produces a wide range of publications published by ICC Publishing S.A., and holds vocational seminars and business conferences in cities throughout the world.

Some ICC services:

International Commercial Practices Commission
The Incoterms series was prepared by the ICC Commission on International Commercial Practices.

This Commission currently has the following principal objectives:
- to standardize existing commercial usage and prepare international definitions for new trade terms introduced as a result of advancing technology;
- to prepare model clauses for use by, for example, traders facing problems with the drafting of contracts during a period of unstable trading conditions (e.g. hardship clauses, force majeure clauses);
- to put forward the business community's solutions to problems created by divergencies between national law;
- to represent the business community to intergovernmental agencies concerned with the unification of business law, in particular the United Nations Commission on International Trade Law (UNCITRAL).

The ICC International Court of Arbitration
Founded in 1923, it is the world's leading international arbitration institution. Each year some 300 new cases are submitted to it, involving every sector of international economic activity and parties from every major economic and political system. The ICC Arbitration Rules provide for supervised arbitration in order to best ensure the smooth conduct of the case and the validity of arbitral awards rendered. The arbitrations may take place in any country and in any language.

The ICC International Maritime Bureau (London)
International commercial fraud, often committed on the high seas, is one of the growth crimes of the 1990s. Intelligence gathered and transmitted by the IMB has helped national police forces make major arrests. Launched in 1981, the IMB is internationally recognized for its competence.

The ICC Centre for Maritime Cooperation (London)
Founded in 1985, stimulates and facilitates international business cooperation in all aspects of the shipping industry. The CMC encourages an open-market approach to maritime development, fosters maritime joint ventures, cooperates with other governmental and non-governmental bodies in the maritime sector, and helps develop maritime skills through on-the-job training schemes.

The ICC Counterfeiting Intelligence Bureau (London)
It serves as a focal point for industries and all other affected interests to combat the growing global plague of trademark piracy. The CIB gathers intelligence on the activities of counterfeiters, investigates the sources and distribution of counterfeit goods worldwide and provides law enforcement agencies with the evidence needed to make arrests and seize bogus goods.

The ICC International Bureau of Chambers of Commerce (Paris)
The ICC International Bureau of Chambers of Commerce (IBCC) is the only world forum of Chambers of Commerce. It acts as spokesman for Chambers around the world interfacing with the private sector, and international, national and governmental bodies. The IBCC administers the ATA Carnet system, a trade-facilitation measure designed by the ICC and the Customs Cooperation Council (CCC) for the temporary duty-free admission into countries of commercial samples, scientific and educational equipment, and goods for exhibition (the value of goods covered by ATA Carnets exceeds $10 billion per year).

The ICC Institute of International Business Law and Practice
The ICC Institute of International Business Law and Practice, established in 1979 and based in Paris, is chaired by Professor Pierre Lalive from the University of Geneva. Its Council is made up of some 40 eminent lawyers and legal practitioners from all parts of the world. The ICC Institute's main objectives are to foster wider knowledge and the development of the law and practices of international business, through close cooperation with practitioners and scholars and through training and research.

The ICC International Environmental Bureau (Geneva) is an international clearing-house of environmental information on industrial and commercial activity. Founded in 1986, it promotes improved environmental quality by making available to other companies and interested parties examples of practical pollution control and abatement expertise from its member companies and other business organizations.

For more detailed information on the activities above, and to receive the programme of ICC seminars, please contact ICC Headquarters in Paris or the National Committee in your country.

HOW TO BECOME A MEMBER OF THE ICC

There are two possible ways of becoming a member of the International Chamber of Commerce: either through direct membership or through affiliation to an ICC National Committee or Group.

In a country without a National Committee, a Chamber of Commerce or a trade association can adhere individually as an Organization Member; companies, firms and businessmen can adhere as Associate Members.

If you need more information, please feel free to contact the National Committee in your country or the International Headquarters of the ICC.

SOME ICC PUBLICATIONS

E: English **F:** French **D:** German **S:** Spanish **A:** Arabic **I:** Italian **EF:** bilingual English-French **ED:** bilingual English-German **EDF:** trilingual English-German-French

BANKING AND FINANCE

Uniform Rules for Collections

This publication assists banks in their collection operations by codifying the main rules to be applied. An indispensable aid in everyday banking operations.

E-F-ED 19 pp - 10.5 x 21 cm N° 322

Uniform Rules for Contract Guarantees

This booklet presents rules designed to regulate contract guarantees, as well as an introduction explaining their use. The rules invest these guarantees with a moral content and strive to achieve a fair balance between the legitimate interests of the parties involved.

E-F-D 31 pp - 10.5 x 21 cm N° 325

Uniform Customs and Practice for Documentary Credits (1983 Revision)

The ICC Uniform Customs and Practice for Documentary Credits (UCP) are the universal set of rules governing letters of credit in about 200 countries world-wide. An indispensable working aid for all bankers and many executives in transport forwarding, insurance and other related sectors, concerned with international trade operations. Implemented since October 1983.

E-F-S-A-ED 40 pp - 10.5 x 21 cm N° 400

ICC BEST-SELLER

Guide to Documentary Credit Operations

Some guidance may prove helpful for those who have not had much practice with documentary credits. This guide will assist the reader regarding the problems and needs of the commercial parties. The colourfully and clearly illustrated flow charts will help the reader understand the practicalities and priorities in such a commercial transaction.

E-F 52 pp - 21 x 29.7 cm ISBN 92-842-1021-6 N° 415

Standard Documentary Credit Forms

Standard Documentary Credit Forms is designed for bankers, attorneys, importers/exporters and everyone with documentary credit transactions around the world.

E 80 pp - 21 x 29.7 cm ISBN 92-842-1026-7 N° 416

Available as a separate publication for bank customers:

Standard Forms and Guidance Notes for Credit Applicants

Specially designed to assist applicants in the issuance of documentary credits.

E 24 pp - 21 x 29.7 cm ISBN 92-842-1027-5 N° 416/A

Managing Exchange Rate Risks

Large fluctuations in exchange rates have considerably complicated financial and strategic decisions. This publication describes the different types of risk and explains how to cope with them.

E-F 31 pp - 10.5 x 21 cm N° 422

Interbank Fund Transfers and Compensation

This guide ties together the main themes of the transfer process into a coherent whole. It joins a series of ICC guides on banking and business practice which have become classics in their fields.

E-F 40 pp - 10 x 21 cm ISBN 92.842.0102.0 N° 457

Bills of Exchange - A guide to legislation in European countries

Bills of exchange and promissory notes, long important as methods of payments, will have a growing role in the context of the dynamic Europe of 1992. Despite the Geneva harmonization of 1930, many differences still exist in Europe because of slightly different texts or rules of national jurisprudence. Written by Dr. Jur. Uwe Jahn, the present publication reviews those differences under several headings. The resulting text is the most comprehensive comparison of bills of exchange law now available.

E 82 pp - 14 x 21 cm ISBN 92-842-1097-6 N° 476

ICC BEST-SELLER

Case Studies on Documentary Credits (Vol. I)

More than 150 questions from bankers and users concerning the day-to-day use of the ICC's Uniform Customs and Practice for Documentary Credits (UCP) are herein answered by a panel of ICC experts. The questions cover a wide range of issues - from charter party bills of lading to the validity of orders sent by telefax. They consider all aspects of documentary credit activity, from the pre-issuance stage to the expiration of the credit.

E 144 pp - 21 x 29.7 cm ISBN 92-842-1079-8 N° 459

New Case Studies on Documentary Credits (Vol.II)

E *Available 1991* ISBN 92-842-1110.7 N° 489

SERIES

Opinions of the ICC Banking Commission (1987-1988)

An essential supplement to the ICC's Uniform Customs and Practice for Documentary Credits (UCP N° 400), *Opinions* gives the ICC Banking Commission's expert views on practical questions regarding the UCP submitted from all over the world by banks, lawyers and other commercial parties. This edition of the Commission's Opinions is the fourth in a highly successful series dating back to 1975. Highly recommended for all parties involved in documentary credit transactions. *To be used in conjunction with Opinions 1984-1986 (n° 434).*

E 85 pp - 18 x 24 cm ISBN 92-842-1091-7 N° 469

Opinions of the ICC Banking Commission (1989-1990)

E *Available end 1991* N° 494

SOME ICC PUBLICATIONS

INTERNATIONAL ARBITRATION

ICC Arbitration (2nd edition)

(by Craig, Park and Paulsson) A co-publication with Oceana. This revision of the classic text by Craig, Park and Paulsson details the history and workings of one of the world's foremost arbitration institutions, the ICC International Court of Arbitration. Since its founding in 1923, the Court has handled more than 7,000 cases involving commercial agreements by parties all over the world. Hailed by critics as a lucid review of the Court's activities, *ICC Arbitration* is a major reference work for lawyers, legal specialists and all who have an interest in the arbitral process.

E about 700 pp - 18 x 26 cm ISBN 92-842-1080-1 N° 414/2

Collection of ICC Arbitral Awards (1974-1985)

A co-publication with Kluwer

This text contains a selection of cases decided by ICC arbitrators over the 11-year period prior to 1985. It reproduces case notes in English and French, with extracts of awards in their original language. Clearly indexed so that questions dealing with the cases can be easily found, the *Collection* is a helpful reference for anyone who wants to be informed about the ICC arbitration procedure and the awards made applying the laws of a number of different nations.

EF about 650 pp - 16 x 24 cm ISBN 92-842-0081-4 N° 433

ICC Rules of Conciliation and Arbitration

Thousands of business contracts refer to the ICC Rules of Conciliation and Arbitration. These rules can avoid costly legal conflicts which may arise in international contracts. This edition contains the ICC Conciliation Rules and amended Arbitration Rules in force after January 1, 1988.

E-F-S-D-A 44 pp - 10.5 x 21 cm ISBN 92-842-1058-5 N° 447 *(free of charge)*

Bulletin of the ICC International Court of Arbitration

The ICC International Court of Arbitration is now publishing its own Bulletin twice a year. Intended for all those who are involved in ICC Arbitration and in international commercial dispute resolution, most of the first-hand information it contains, such as extracts of ICC Awards, current ICC arbitration practice, reports from the Commission on International Arbitration, articles by leading authorities, etc..., cannot be found anywhere else. Also includes general information on international commercial arbitration (new legislation, multilateral and bilateral treaties, conferences and seminars) and a special supplement once a year.

E-F *(subscription)*

Inter-American Commercial Arbitration

A co-publication with Oceana

This publication brings together the texts of all major treaties and conventions on the subject and an analysis of arbitration practices in 33 American countries. A unique work combining the experience of the American Arbitration Association and the ICC International Court of Arbitration, it is destined to become the standard text on arbitration in the Americas.

E ISBN 92-842-1109-3 N° 465

The Arbitral Process and the Independence of Arbitrators

Experts from diverse cultural and legal backgrounds and representatives of international institutions (the American Arbitration Association, the ICC International Court of Arbitration, the International Centre for the Settlement of Investment Disputes) share their experience in examining the independence and impartiality required of arbitrators in an increasingly international context. An unprecedented publication on this topic.

E-F ISBN 92-842-0093.8 N° 472

DOSSIERS OF THE ICC INSTITUTE OF INTERNATIONAL BUSINESS LAW AND PRACTICE

This series, published by ICC Publishing for the ICC Institute of International Business Law and Practice, reflects the Institute's main objectives: to foster wider knowledge and development of the laws and practices of international business through close cooperation between practitioners and scholars. The ICC Institute, based in Paris, is chaired by Prof. Pierre Lalive of the University of Geneva.

Formation of Contracts and Precontractual Liability

To negotiate an international contract requires sound information and knowledge of the legal consequences of a proposal or promise made during negotiations by one of the partners. The legal rules and case laws differ tremendously among countries. This publication will call the attention of readers to such differences and help them avoid misunderstandings during negotiations of contracts with foreign partners.

E 360 pp - 21 x 29.7 cm ISBN N° 92-842-0107-1 N° 440/9

Other dossiers

Taking of Evidence in International Arbitral Proceedings

EF 250 pp - 21 x 29.7 cm ISBN 92-842-0086-5 N° 440/8

International Contracts for Sale of Information Services

E 202 pp - 21 x 29.7 cm ISBN 92-842-1071-2 N° 440/5

International Trade Usages

E 78 pp - 21 x 29.7 cm ISBN 92-842-1053-4 N° 440/4

Exchange Rate Risks in International Contracts

E 433 pp - 21 x 29.7 cm ISBN 92-842-1041-0 N° 440/3

For more information on the list of other Dossiers available, please contact ICC Publishing.

INTERNATIONAL TRANSACTIONS AND CONTRACTS

ICC BEST-SELLER

Key Words in International Trade (3rd edition)

The ICC's best-selling *Key Words* has been issued in a new, expanded edition containing more than 1,800 business words and expressions, translated into English, German, Spanish, French and Italian. Many of the new terms are taken from the rapidly changing fields of computing, data processing and telecommunications and are translated here for the first time. As in previous editions, separate alphabetical indexes are included for all languages.

EFDSI 416 pp - 13.5 x 24 cm ISBN 92-842-0072-5 N° 417/2
EFDSA 416 pp - 13.5 x 24 cm ISBN 92-842-0073-3 N° 417/A

Guide to Drafting International Distributorship Agreements

The Guide provides parties drafting and negotiating international distributorship agreements with information on the difficulties that arise in business practice. It considers the manufacturers' and distributors' obligations, compensation on termination of the agreement, and questions of exclusivity. Written in simple, non-technical language, it sheds new light on a practice of growing commercial importance.

E-F 42 pp - 14 x 21 cm ISBN 92-842-1076-3 N° 441

Uniform Rules of Conduct for Interchange of Trade Data by Teletransmission (UNCID)

The Rules provide a foundation on which parties using electronic language in a trading transaction can build a communication agreement - a contract with legally binding effect.

E-F 23 pp - 10.5 x 21 cm ISBN 92-842-1057-7 N° 452

The ICC World Directory of Chambers of Commerce - 2nd edition

This 1990-91 edition lists approximately 10,000 Chambers of Commerce world-wide and can be a very useful tool for traders, economic libraries, international companiès and individual entrepreneurs. It gives vital information to businessmen about chamber activities world-wide *(Updated regularly).*

E-F 551 pages - 16 x 24.5 cm ISBN 92-842-0103-9 N° 471

Clean Transport Documents

New and updated edition of the ICC's *The Problem of Clean Bills of Lading* (n° 283) reflects the major changes in transportation and methods of payment. It is indispensable to practitioners in international trade.

E-F 20 pp - 10.5 x 21 cm ISBN 92-842-1090-9 N° 473

ICC BEST-SELLER

Incoterms 1990

Incoterms - the ICC definitions of trade terms such as FOB and CIF - have become part of the everyday language of trade. They have long been recognized by professional traders as invaluable, cost-saving tools. Now a new edition of Incoterms, the first for ten years, clarifies existing terms and brings the overall list of Incoterms fully into line with the needs of the 1990s. The new Incoterms, which came into force on July 1st 1990, is an event of major importance to bankers, transporters, exporters, lawyers and everyone with an interest in international trade. *To be used in conjunction with the Guide to Incoterms 1990 (N° 461/90).*

EF-ED-ES-EI 215 pp - 13.5 x 24 cm ISBN 92-842-0087-3 N° 460
(other languages available)

Bareboat Charter Registration

A cogent analysis of the practice under which a ship's charterer takes the flag of another nation for a stipulated period of time. It includes a country-by-country run-down of the requirements for bareboat charter registration and an interpretation of the laws and conventions dealing with bareboating.

E 52 pp - 16 x 24 cm ISBN 92-842-1077-1 N° 466

Retention of Title: A practical guide to 19 national legislations

This guide lays out the laws and regulations on retention of title in 19 countries. It also includes a model retention of title clause for each country and a comprehensive bibliography of key books and articles on the subject. Traders, lawyers and practitioners who want to avoid the legal pitfalls of retention will find the guide an invaluable tool for use in the preparation of contracts.

E-F 64 pp - 16 x 24 cm ISBN 92-842-1082-8 N° 467

Guide to Penalty and Liquidated Damages Clauses

Conflicts of law with regard to liquidated damages clauses have caused costly delays and confusion, and the current guide suggests concrete means to avoid them. Traders, bankers, lawyers and others involved in international trade will find in the current guide clarity and precision, in a field long clouded by conflicting rules.

E-F 56 pages - 14 x 21 cm ISBN 92-842-1099-2 N° 478

EAST-WEST

Foreign Investment in the USSR - Key 1990 Legislation

The *Guide to Joint Ventures in the USSR* (N° 456) worked out by the USSR/ICC Task Force and first published in August 1988 was distributed worldwide and reached a large number of businessmen interested or engaged in possible investment in the USSR. Since then, much new legislation have been passed or is under preparation. As a provisional measure, the above Group decided to publish this collection of texts of new laws, decrees and regulations relevant for investing in the USSR.

E ISBN 92-842-1095-X N° 475

ENVIRONMENT

ICC Guide to Effective Environment Auditing

As the 20th century draws to a close, concern for and action to control health, safety and environmental risks to the world's population are rapidly accelerating . Industry leaders are mindful that the responsibility for satisfying a portion of environmental needs rests on them. World political leaders are grappling with enormously complex issues. A response to this awareness has resulted in major voluntary programs as reflected in the *ICC's Environmental Guidelines for World Industry (see N° 435).*

E ISBN 92-842-1115-8 N° 483

ICC Environmental Guidelines for World Industry

E-F-D-S 12 pp - 10 x 21 cm N° 435

Environmental Auditing

E-F 25 pp - 14 x 21 cm ISBN 92-842-1089-5 N° 468

The Greening of Enterprise

E 265 pages - 14 x 21 cm ISBN 92-842-1106-9 N° 487

HOW TO OBTAIN ICC PUBLICATIONS

ICC Publications are available from ICC National Committees or Councils which exist in some 60 countries or from:

ICC PUBLISHING S.A.
38, Cours Albert 1er
75008 - Paris (France)
Tel. 49.53.28.28
Telex: 650770
Telefax (1) 42.25.36.23

ICC PUBLISHING CORPORATION
156 Fifth Avenue, Suite 820
New York, N.Y. 10010
(United States)
Tel. (212) 206-1150
Telex: 661519
Telefax (212) 633 60 25

The new ***Guide to Incoterms*** is the first to appear since the best-selling 1981 edition. Organised with the user in mind, the Guide takes the basic text of Incoterms 1990 and explains how each of the terms is used in practice. It has an expanded introduction placing Incoterms 1990 in the context of previous versions of Incoterms. Subsequent chapters take the user through Incoterms and the contract of sale; the elements of E-, F-, C- and D-terms; an overview of the buyer's and seller's obligations; and a section-by-section analysis of each of the 13 Incoterms.

Crisply written, coherent and easy to follow, the ***Guide to Incoterms*** is the only official Guide to Incoterms 1990, developed under the auspices of the ICC.

ICC PUBLISHING SA
International Chamber of Commerce
The world business organization
38, Cours Albert 1er
75008 Paris

ICC Publication N° 461/90
ISBN 92.842.1088.7